Minotaur, Parrot, and the SS Man

Minotaur, Parrot, and the SS Man: Essays on Jorge de Sena

George Monteiro

Introduction by
Francisco Cota Fagundes

TAGUS PRESS
University of Massachusetts Dartmouth
Dartmouth, MA

Tagus Press is the publishing arm of the
Center for Portuguese Studies and Culture at
the University of Massachusetts Dartmouth.
Center director: Paula Celeste Gomes Noversa

Adamastor Series 14
Tagus Press at UMass Dartmouth
© 2021 George Monteiro
Introduction © 2021 Francisco Cota Fagundes

Executive Editor: Mario Pereira
Series Editors: Viktor Mendes & Ricardo Vasconcelos
Design and composition: Jen Jackowitz
Cover design: Inês Sena

For all inquiries, please contact:
Tagus Press • Center for Portuguese Studies and Culture
UMass Dartmouth • 285 Old Westport Road
North Dartmouth MA 02747-2300
Tel. 508-999-8255 • Fax 508-999-9272
https://www.umassd.edu/portuguese-studies-center/

ISBN: 978-1-933227-97-9
Library of Congress Control Number: 2021943010

CONTENTS

ACKNOWLEDGMENTS

Some of the pieces collected here first appeared in journals—*Eugene O'Neill Review, Hispania, Luso-Brazilian Review, Modern Language Studies, Pessoa Plural, Santa Barbara Portuguese Studies, Traditerm, World Literature Today*—or in books—*The Evidences, Jorge de Sena: O homem que sempre foi, Tudo isto que rodeia Jorge de Sena, "Para emergir nascemos . . .": Estudos e rememoração de Jorge de Sena,* and *Os Descobrimentos portugueses no mundo de língua inglesa 1880–1972.* With revision, they are published here with the consent of the editors of these journals and the publishers of these books.

Minotaur, Parrot, and the SS Man

INTRODUCTION

George Monteiro

In Quest of Jorge de Sena

A notable professor and scholar of nineteenth- and twentieth-century American literature, George Monteiro made contributions to the bibliographies of, among many others, Edgar Allan Poe, Henry James, Edith Wharton, F. Scott Fitzgerald, Robert Frost, and Bob Dylan. He also wrote on American writers who were particularly dear to the writer, scholar, and translator Jorge de Sena: Emily Dickinson, Ernest Hemingway, William Faulkner, and T. S. Eliot. When George Monteiro founded the then Center for Portuguese and Brazilian Studies at Brown University, serving as its director from 1975 to 1980, he also became a celebrated professor and major scholar and translator of Portuguese literature, having made huge contributions to the bibliographies of writers whom Jorge de Sena studied all his life, particularly those of Luís de Camões (*The Presence of Camões*) and Fernando Pessoa (three volumes). Counted among the many Portuguese writers translated by Monteiro we find the likes of Miguel Torga, Fernando Pessoa, Jorge de Sena (*In Crete, with the Minotaur, and Other Poems*), and, among others, José Rodrigues Miguéis, as well as Azorean poets like Pedro da Silveira. As a result of the above, *Minotaur, Parrot, and the SS Man: Essays on Jorge de Sena* is a book wherein the commonality of interests of two scholars and translators (and to some degree creative writers, as we shall see) of both Anglophone and Lusophone literatures intermingles to a degree that is truly singular. For Jorge de Sena studies anywhere, but particularly in the United States, this relationship could not be more advantageous.

The fourteen studies comprising this volume, although they have already been published in reviews and editions of books ranging from at least the 1980s to 2016, are now brought together between the two covers of the same volume and made readily available to scholars who may know some of the pieces but not others. As the reader shall see, given their subject matter and George's view of the Senian corpus, these studies belong together, attaining considerable cohesion with one another despite their wide-ranging generic and thematic scopes. The somewhat intriguing title, *Jorge de Sena: Minotaur, Parrot, and the SS Man* refers, respectively, to essays number 1, "In Quest of the Minotaur"; number 3, "The Green Parrot"; and number 4, "The 'Eichmann' Story." The first of these three essays is, as we shall see later, a quest for one of the characters in Sena's signature exile poem "Em Creta, com o Minotauro" (dated July 5, 1965) and is part of the volume *Peregrinatio Ad Loca Infecta* (1969); the second alludes to the short story "Homenagem ao Papagaio Verde" (dated Assis, June 3, 1961 and Araraquara, June 25, 1962) and is the opening story of *Os Grão-Capitães: uma sequência de contos* (1976); and the third essay points to a short story included in the volume *Novas Andanças do Demónio* (1966), entitled "Defesa e Justificação de Um Ex-Criminoso de Guerra" (dated Assis, May 6, 1961).

Tethered by filaments that tie all of Jorge de Sena's works together in terms of worldview, lived experience, and an extremely wide interest in Western literature, with a very special privileging here of Anglophone literatures, are the remaining eleven pieces covering generic and thematic areas as broad as the author's complex relationship to his mother country, Portugal ("If This Be Treason"); Jorge de Sena's lifelong passion for and labor in Camões's oeuvre ("The

Case for Camões"); the intertextual relation between the views of
Portugal held by poets far and wide—from Camões to Unamuno to
Tomás Ribeiro to Fernando Pessoa—and these authors' echoes, and
in some cases rejoinders, from one to another ("Portugal in 'Figura'");
a Monteiran perspective of the Jorge de Sena correspondence with
Mécia de Sena, José Régio, Vergílio Ferreira, and Eduardo Lourenço
("The Correspondence"); a largely one-sided attempt on the part of
Sena to establish a friendship with his much admired poet Dame
Edith Sitwell, which led to a brief correspondence reproduced in this
volume ("The Sitwell Papers"); a three-part essay ("On American
Writing") divided into three sections: translating Emily Dickinson,
Jorge de Sena's "American poems," that is, poems written in American English and about America or whose setting is America, and,
informing the third section, the almost superhuman feat on the part
of Jorge de Sena in translating his much-admired *Long Day's Journey
into Night* by Eugene O'Neill under incredible pressure and in less
than a month; views of Sena's oeuvre in which George Monteiro
provides his very personal opinion of critical works on Sena that
he particularly values ("Views of Sena's Work"); Sena's perceptions
of English and American cultures and America's overall lukewarm
interest in Jorge de Sena, especially in the publication of translations
of his works by major presses ("An 'Englishman' in America"); a symposium on Fernando Pessoa held at Brown University that elicits a
brilliant lecture by Sena and brings together two giants of Pessoan
studies: João Gaspar Simões and Sena himself ("The First International Symposium on Fernando Pessoa"); and an homage to Mécia
de Sena with whom George Monteiro exchanged correspondence
for decades, concluding with another revealing story involving Jorge
de Sena and the poet Dame Edith Sitwell—in which it is shown
that the Portuguese writer gave much more to the English poet—in
the hope that she might help him promote the poetry of Fernando
Pessoa in England—than he received from her ("Mécia de Sena").

Now that the reader has a horizontal view of the breadth of this
book, I will single out the three titular essays for more in-depth

comments before the reader sets out, guided by George Monteiro, on his or her own quest for Jorge de Sena and some of the writers with whom he interacted: "In Quest of the Minotaur," "The Green Parrot," and "The 'Eichmann' Story." My purpose is *not* to summarize the content of George's texts but to elaborate a context whereby their range, depth, and significance can be more fully brought out and appreciated.

One idea upon which the present book rests is, according to George Monteiro, the consistent presence of "the same mythic Sena" throughout his immense oeuvre, whether it be in *Genesis* (the short stories that recreate the biblical legends of Adam and Eve and Cain and Abel, written, respectively, at ages seventeen and eighteen), many works of fiction that include three thick volumes of short stories and a massive novel, and thousands upon thousands of poems, including one of his most famous ones: "Em Creta, com o Minotauro," whose best translation into English was done by none other than George Monteiro himself. To this, Jorge de Sena's main creative corpus, Monteiro also adds the Senian theater: a tragedy in verse (*O Indesejado: António, Rei*), as well as a number of one-act plays. We must also list Sena's huge corpus of critical and translated works, which include *A Literatura Inglesa* (1963) and the translation with studies of many Anglo-American writers, both poets and fiction writers. Attaining a special place within Sena's critical corpus are the numerous volumes on Camões and on Pessoa, interests that, as stated above, both George and Jorge shared.

By "the same mythic Sena" I take George to be referring to the literary subjectivity that remains consistent throughout the Senian corpus: the deployment of an artistic identity through which we can clearly identify the historical Jorge de Sena. In other words, the Sena that George and I are referring to and have insisted on is the reverse of what Fernando Pessoa accustomed us to as we navigate the shifting waters of the myriad of subjectivities he chose to call heteronyms. And thus the Sena that imagines himself exchanging stories and sipping coffee in Crete with the Minotaur is, despite the fact that he transits from concrete reality (such as the references to his birthplace and to his acquired Brazilian nationality) to *mythland*, somehow still the voice of the same "mythic Sena" or subjectivity we hear speaking to us in poems like "Os Paraísos Artificiais" (*Pedra Filosofal*; 1950) and "Carta aos Meus Filhos sobre 'Os Fuzilamentos de Goya'" (*Metamorfoses*; 1963).

One of the most admired poems in the Senian corpus, "Em Creta, com o Minotauro" could be—some of us crazy Lusophiles sometimes hope—the one poem that might break through the barriers that separate Lusophone letters from the "major" literatures of the Western world. Thus, as I prepared this introduction, especially when I read the paragraph in which George places Sena's "In Crete, with the Minotaur" at the same level as some of the greatest modern poems by the greatest modern poets, I hastened to read a volume, by Theodore Ziolkowski, whose title had attracted my attention a few years ago: *Minos and the Moderns: Cretan Myth in Twentieth-Century Literature* (Oxford and New York: Oxford University Press, 2008). For sure, I told myself, this book will contain at least a reference to Jorge de Sena's poem inspired in part by the most widely known myth of Minoan civilization. If it were necessary, I could now list the huge number of poets, fictionists, and visual artists and even musicians that made the pages of *Minos and the Moderns*. But Jorge de Sena was not one of them. Like the Minotaur himself, as the reader will discover, the author of *Minos and the Moderns*, too, did not know Portuguese!

Withdrawing into our Lusophone world, as is my habit after these generally disappointing quixotic sorties, I began a search in my mind for names that Sena's poem might be echoing or that could themselves represent echoes of Sena's poem. In other words, I started to employ George Monteiro's expression, a quest for possible sources and repercussions of "In Crete, with the Minotaur." As a possible answer for the first question, I hit upon "Regresso à Cúpula da Pena" (*Léah e outras histórias*; 1958) by José Rodrigues Miguéis. In an article much too long and complex to summarize here, I once defended the thesis that the story can be read as a double reentry or return: that of the emigrant or expatriate to his country of origin and that of the patient to life and health. My thesis rests, to some degree, upon the exercise on the part of the Migueisian patient/narrator of guided imagery, in which he imagines himself returning, after twenty years of expatriation, to Portugal in a situation similar to what actually happens in the story: a reencounter with his beloved, the elimination of his rival, and a Hollywood-type ending in the arms of his sweetheart. As an emigrant story, "Regresso à Cúpula da Pena" is maudlin and unconvincing; as a self-therapeutic story it is not only convincing but actually reveals the type of healing experience encouraged by specialists of nonallopathic medicine. (This truth becomes all the more evident for those who know Miguéis's illness narrative *Um Homem Sorri à Morte—com meia cara*, a narrative translated by George Monteiro.) "In Crete, with the Minotaur," too, is a reentry story, a very unique reentry story, but I believe that, given the two writers' radically different attitudes toward their country of origin, both texts would benefit greatly by being considered in relation to each other, taking into account the many similarities and differences between how both writers (and friends!) wrote in exile. Sena knew Miguéis's story and critically commented on it. I look forward to discussing this idea with George.

Regarding forward echoes or repercussions of Sena's story, they are not hard to find. In 1980, the poet George Monteiro related poetically the discussion he sustained, in Crete, with Sena and the Minotaur. The poem-in-six-poems is entitled "The Coffee Exchange," is included in a volume of the same title, and is followed by two poems relating what happened regarding the embalming of the Minotaur, both poems entitled "Post-Scriptum," a title that Jorge de Sena was so fond of that he chose it twice for titles of books of poetry and numerous times for addenda to paratexts. And thus, George Monteiro's quest for the Minotaur—of which the paper included in this volume provides a truly rich account that includes references to other Senian texts—also manifests itself in George's own poetry and reverberates in readers and admirers of both writers—Sena and Monteiro. "The Green Parrot" is a study of one of Jorge de Sena's most justifiably famous short stories, "Homenagem ao Papagaio Verde." The first story of *Os Grão-Capitães: uma sequência de contos* (1976) is capable of standing or making sense independently of the other eight stories (six when the book first appeared). The story is, however, only one unit in the genre *sequence* to which the subtitle attributes it. Much has been written, starting in the 1970s, about integrated short story collections in the Anglophone world. Although the genre has come to be known by many other names, the two that have won out are "cycle" and "sequence." Both have much in common, but they also exhibit a few key differences. Both the cycle and the sequence are based on the concepts of repetition—of settings, themes, image patterns, motifs, and so on. However, the sequence is also largely dependent on the reappearance of characters, approaching a configuration closer to the novel, whereas the cycle, although often attaining a high degree of integration, remains more akin to the heterogenous collection. The reader plays an extremely important role in the processing of cycles and sequences, and hence the importance, in the reading of integrated collections, of reception theory. Famous works of Anglophone literature that have been read as cycles and/or sequences are James Joyce's *Dubliners* (1914), Sherwood Anderson's *Winesburg, Ohio* (1919), and Faulkner's *The Unvanquished* (1938) and *Go Down, Moses* (1942). As far as I know, Jorge de Sena is the first writer of Portuguese-language literature who self-consciously entitled one of his collections of short stories *uma sequência de contos*, although other Portuguese-language works of short fiction have been read as cycles and countless more lend themselves to being viewed as cycles or sequences.

"Homenagem ao Papagaio Verde," bearing the fictitious date 1928, may be read as a parody of the idealized family of Salazar's New State, one that is much discussed in the dictator's *Discursos*, frequently alluded to by his chief of propaganda António Ferro, embodied in the children's attraction Portugal dos Pequenitos, in Coimbra, and perhaps best known to the masses at the time by the 1938 poster *A Lição de Salazar* (https://noseahistoria.wordpress. com/2011/12/12/a-licao-de-salazar/), in which the idealized paternalistic agrarian family—a microcosm of the Salazar-led and propagandistically fashioned national family—was easily decodable. George Monteiro, bringing his own reading to bear on the story, does not cover hermeneutical ground already explored and largely focused on the history of Salazar's New State. Instead, he places the story in a broader intertextual stage: he reads the relationship of the nine-year-old child protagonist and his parrot—the story does indeed have a binary protagonist: child and parrot—against the background of one of Gustave Flaubert's most famous works, one of the three stories comprising *Trois Contes* (1977): "Un cœur simple" or "A Simple Heart," the story of the lonely maid and her beloved pet parrot. George's piece is written such that the similarities, as well as the differences with Sena's story, are not exhaustively drawn out for the reader but instead are brought to the fore so that Sena's text is made much richer and the reader is provided another angle from which to engage both stories. Another intertext that the Anglophone studies specialist George Monteiro is in a unique position to bring in, and thereby enlarge further upon the context of Sena's story, is the novel *The Way of All Flesh* (1903), by Samuel Butler, like "Homenagem" a partly autobiographical work about a dysfunctional family. This time, however, George Monteiro does not draw directly from the intertextual work. He establishes the connection with the Senian and Butlerian texts by quoting a passage from Jorge de Sena's *A Literatura Inglesa*, wherein the Portuguese author himself had suggested the connection. And thus, without denying the viability of more historically focused interpretations, "Homenagem ao Papagaio Verde" attains with George's reading(s) another degree of universality that other more historically focused interpretations had necessarily left out. George Monteiro approaches the analysis of "The 'Eichmann' Story" quite indirectly but effectively.

Sena's story, "Defesa e Justificação de um Ex-Criminoso de Guerra (Das memórias de Herr Werner Stupneim, ex-oficial superior das SS")), a condemnation of German Nazi ideology, never mentions the name of Adolf Eichmann, whose trial in Israel in 1961 lasted 16 weeks at the end of which the Nazi SS Lieutenant Colonel was found guilty and executed. Sena's story, published in *Novas Andanças do Demónio* (1966), written after the publication of an article by Luís Martins appeared in *O Estado de São Paulo* on April 4, 1961, entitled "O Assassino de Milhões," makes it almost inevitable that Jorge de Sena's short story, written in Assis on May 7, 1961, become associated with the Eichmann story being dissected in the Israeli courtroom. Sena retold the Eichmann story, George Monteiro implies, by telling a parallel story inspired by similar crimes and the same heinous ideology. The ethics of Nazi superiority, the alleged oppression of the superior race by the inferior ones, and the evolution of the supreme German race are the focus of Sena's character's narrative. Most shocking of all is Stupneim's recounting of his and his colleagues' atrocities with an absolute sense of amorality. In one of his preambular texts to *Os Grão-Capitães: uma sequência de contos*, "Prefácio (1971)," Jorge de Sena points out what for him was an undeniable truth—unrelated to the Eichmann story, but echoing it—that I believe appropriate to quote here for a broad contextualization of the ideology of Sena's short story and of Monteiro's approach to it:

> Diz-se às vezes que há muito amor do mal no evocá-lo e referi-lo. E que é disso que ele se perpetua. O mal não se perpetua senão no pretender-se que não existe, ou que, excessivo para a nossa delicadeza, há que deixá-lo num discreto limbo. É no silêncio e no calculado esquecimento dos delicados que o mal se apura e afina—tanto assim é, que é tradicional o amor das tiranias pelo silêncio, e que as Inquisições sempre só trouxeram à luz do dia as suas vítimas, para assassiná-las exemplarmente." (3rd ed. [Lisboa: Edições 70, 1983], 20)

In my view, George Monteiro's most current *abordagens* or approaches employed in these fourteen texts fall under the following headings and are applied not necessarily in the order in which they are listed: a genetic approach in which a complex relationship is assumed between Sena's lived experiences and their transmutation into poetry or fiction; an intertextual approach, usually oriented toward intertexts not previously identified by other critics in regard to texts under analysis; a broad historical and bibliographical exploration when appropriate, as in the case of Sena's studies on Camões and the history of the latter's critical and translation history in America; a comparative analysis of translations by two individuals to bring out, and comment on, differences, for example, in the case of the translations of poems of such complexity as those of Emily Dickinson (some examples provided being translations of the same poems by Manuel Bandeira and Jorge de Sena); an open-book approach—as might be expected from a critic of the caliber of George Monteiro— who provides suggestions for rich hermeneutic explorations by opening doors to the reader, rather than pulling down curtains over texts. To no one's surprise, George is a master of close reading, a practice he inherited from New Criticism, which he deploys when it is absolutely necessary, but without ever abusing the privilege.

Finally, one quality that all of these essays possess—and I dare say that all of Monteiro's many volumes of criticism on Portuguese-language literature reveal—is a discourse that is not common to find these days. It is easy to realize that George Monteiro, although always informed, is not one to flash the latest fashionable supernovae in the ever-expanding galaxy of literary theory and methods. Monteiro's volumes of literary criticism have a way of sounding like pleasant narratives. This quality makes it a real pleasure to read George's criticism, for the erudition and theoretical constructs that it brings to bear upon the texts he lays out before the reader never obfuscate or muddle. Instead, they blaze a trail that guides and enlightens.

Francisco Cota Fagundes
Professor Emeritus of Portuguese
University of Massachusetts Amherst

I

In Quest of the Minotaur

Desejo ser um criador de mitos, que é o mistério mais alto que
pode obrar alguém da humanidade.

—Fernando Pessoa, "Aspectos" (1930?)

Jorge de Sena entitled his last public lecture "The Man Who Never
Was."[1] The "man" of his title was Fernando Pessoa, and Sena's thesis,
put plainly, was that there was no Fernando Pessoa per se (or at least
that the man called Fernando Pessoa, who shaved every day and who
answered his and his firms' mail, had no life to speak of). Indeed,
having no flesh-and-bones valet to live his life for him, the poet had
chosen to permit his creations (his so-called heteronyms) to live lives
that he himself could not or would not live. The clear implication, in
short, was that because the biological, physiological, and psychological entity who worked for modest Lisbon wages had chosen to exist
entirely within his creation there would always be little or no point
in searching out the substance and shape of a life that essentially had
not been lived. To read, understand, and discuss Fernando Pessoa,
then (if I follow Sena's argument correctly), is to read, understand,
and discuss a series of imagined creations (no matter who "signs" the

work—Alberto Caeiro, Ricardo Reis, Bernardo Soares, Álvaro de Campos, or Fernando Pessoa as the so-called *ele-mesmo*) that in no possible combination or even in their totality add up to "a man who was." It is not unfair to conclude on this basis, I would add, that one can see Pessoa's career (I avoid using the otherwise obvious term—life) as one of successful flight from the single, individuated self. Less than six months after delivering his lecture on "The Man Who Never Was," the man who was Jorge de Sena died. He was fifty-eight. Unlike Pessoa, whose death in 1935 at the age of forty-seven brought to an end the writings of a series of selves who had by welcome design usurped the possibilities for the forging of a self by their creator, Sena died in full possession of the identity he had so willfully and forcefully hammered out over a lifetime of passion and poetry. Unlike Pessoa, who designed and executed the selves that exculpated him from the onerous and personal quest for the way that might lead to the making of a soul in this vale of a world, Sena died in full possession of a soul the making of which had fully occupied him for nearly all of his close to three score years. Unlike Pessoa, then, for whom we look in vain at last in the published work, among his papers at the Biblioteca Nacional in Lisbon, in the reminiscences and memoirs of his friends and followers, Sena is to be found everywhere—in every piece of his, published or unpublished, in every anecdote told by a friend or student or mere onetime acquaintance, in every reader who has plunged into his vast opus. Unlike Pessoa, whose bubble creations thought their own thoughts in their own ways—always so laying an emotional-passional-intellectual track that leads away from the empty labyrinth of Pessoa's inner being, Sena could not help, no matter what voice and "personality" he assumed (fictional or historical, from Cain to Camões), ending up plunged in the act of forging and refining himself. Unlike Pessoa, whose Álvaro de Campos, in thought and feeling, always spins away from his creator, Sena creates a Camões whose angry, bitter, snarling peroration ineluctably sweeps all into the vortex that was Jorge de Sena. Unlike Sena's Pessoa, who was a man who never was, Jorge de

Sena's Jorge de Sena was a man who was always (and perhaps only) himself. With this notion in mind, I should like now to explore the paths into the maze that beckon the student who would encounter the historical and mythic Jorge de Sena. (I say "mythic," meaning by that sometimes vexed term the self of Jorge de Sena as it is embodied in, as it emerges from, and as he would present it through the millions of words that he wrote and published.) If I am even partly right in seeing that there is, stubbornly, a unity of man and work, then for proof any text (and every text) will do—from the first lyrics fair-copied in his notebooks in his teens to his personal letters in his last years.

Remarkably, on the basis of the published evidence, Sena's mythic life has a shape and direction that are uncommonly consistent. And because, unlike the Irish poet William Butler Yeats, who explained that his late revising of earlier poetry was his way of remaking himself, Sena dated the composition of his poems and other pieces and usually limited revision to polishing (and then apparently not at all extensively), we are safe in looking at texts that reveal their author as he saw and created himself at most of the ages of man. For if "Homenagem ao Papagaio Verde," a story written in 1961–62, tells us a fictionalized version of the story of the boy Jorge de Sena as he was growing up in a Lisbon family of three, and if "Camões dirige-se aos seus contemporâneos," a poem written in 1961, and "Aviso a cardíacos e outras pessoas atacadas de semelhantes males," Sena's last poem (dated March 19, 1978), show us different manifestations of the poet's characteristic rage, his two earliest stories, "Paraíso perdido" and "Caim," both dating from the author's teens, although not published until 1983 (in a slim volume carrying the covering title *Genesis*), demonstrate how nearly intact Sena's mythic life was from his earliest days as a writer.

In her "Breve nota de introdução" to *Genesis*, Mécia de Sena tells us that in the thirteen notebooks kept by Jorge de Sena from 1936 to 1944, we find, side by side, various examples of the writer's poetry and his prose. In fact, at the beginning, in 1936, eight initial poems are followed by an unfinished historical narrative on the twelfth-century figure of Dom Fuas Roupinho, who according to tradition was not only Afonso Henriques's fellow-warrior but Portugal's first admiral of the fleet. It is unfortunate that apparently Sena never got around to finishing his job of fair-copying the whole of a narrative that was probably much longer than the one that has survived, for Dom Fuas was a subject (in the sense of material for his writing as well as a personage conducive to his process of self-forging) that surfaced in his work more than once. Besides being the subject of this early fragment, which begins the story of Dom Fuas straight-forwardly as neutral exposition, the warrior makes an appearance in a poem dated 1972, "Senhora da Nazaré em Luanda," in which Sena writes: "Os azulejos / representam a patada de D. Fuas / à beira do penhasco a que o demónio / pensava que o levava pra o deitar ao mar."[2] And five years later he makes an indirect appearance in Sena's penultimate poem, "Morreu Dom Fuas," a remarkable tribute to the author's cat. Indeed, the historical and mythic Dom Fuas, who is both an admiral—recall that Sena would become, shortly after the writing of his historical narrative on the subject, an ex–naval cadet—and, by magisterial fiat, Sena's own cat (as we shall see in greater detail later), takes on, for the writer, that kind of corporeality native only to a gray eminence.

Written in 1937, when its author was seventeen, and revised a few months later in 1938, "Paraíso perdido" retells, largely by fleshing them out, the chapters in Genesis dealing with the temptation of Adam and Eve, their fall, and their expulsion from the Garden of Eden. About Sena's fictionalized retelling of this primary myth, what one might call Sena's scenario, there are several observations possible. First of all, Sena is already putting into practice the idea that myth must be naturalized, that is to say, that naturalistic details have their modernizing place in the account. But more important is the way he presents the characters in this early morality play. Jehovah, the God of wrath, is seen at the moment of his descent upon Eden: "E como um furacão, cabelos arrepiados na corrida, auréola tombada sobre uma das orelhas, barba desgrenhada, olhos gritando fogo, túnica a esvoaçar, Jeová desceu ao Paraíso."³ Disappointed in his angels, who have become attracted to Adam and Eve's garden (it is no longer *the* Garden), Jehovah attacks them first: "Ó anjos miseráveis que eu criei! Ó vis! A vossa culpa é maior! e calou-se por momentos embebido em cólera. Depois estrondeou de novo: Todos p'ro inferno! Ide p'ra diabos! Desapareçam! Infames! e num arranco de superioridade: Algum se atreve a olhar p'ra mim!?" (23) What is asked rhetorically, however, turns out not to be so rhetorical, for, among the band of angels, "uns olhos verdes se levantaram insolentes" and their owner speaks up: "Eu!" In response, "Tu, Lúcifer! berrou Jeová no auge do furor. Pois ficas Satanás! Ficas chefe do grupo! Vai p'ro inferno!" (23). Although this incident is familiar, having been treated elsewhere by earlier writers (notably Milton in *Paradise Lost*), it does not appear in the Old Testament. So when Sena points out that Lucifer not only has defied the God of wrath but has complied immediately when ordered to Hell by slowly ducking into the ground, he points to an act of obedience resulting, oddly, from an act of defiance. Sena's Lucifer does not say with Milton's Satan that to rule in Hell is far better than to serve in Heaven, but he has enacted a gesture that in itself is enough to endear him to the Jorge de Sena who would entitle his first two collections of stories *Andanças do demónio* (1960) and *Novas andanças do demónio* (1966), the latter containing, significantly, the first appearance of "O físico prodigioso," a novella amalgamating and elaborating two *exemplos* from the *Orto do esposo*, a book dating from the first half of the fifteenth century. Both of those exemplos feature the young physician of the title (called by Sena "aquele meu tão querido") to whom Satan, in sentimental attachment, transmits preternatural powers that will protect him from death.⁴

There is one other thing about "Paraíso perdido" that is of particular importance to those in search of the self that Jorge de Sena so assiduously forged and refined through the decades. Jehovah, picking between Adam and Eve, displays an unmitigated hardness toward Adam and a rather disarmed softness toward Eve. When

Adam somewhat mechanically lifts a bit of the forbidden fruit to his lips, Jehovah screams out at him: "Patife! Diante de mim! Fora! Fora tudo! Esperem no mundo que escolheram a minha condenação! Saiam!" (24). And what is Adams's reaction? "O primeiro homem atemorizado engasgou-se para todo o sempre," writes Sena. But Eve works her wiles. She is "resoluta e medrosa, linda como nunca, o peito arfando, o cabelo desgrenhado docemente pela volúpia, tapando o corpo com um braçado de folhas de parra" (24). And smiling as seductively as she can, she implores: "Não sejas muito severo, meu Senhor!" To which Jehovah, himself surprised that he has not screamed at her, can only say, feeling rather mellowed: "Esta Eva!" (24).

It is intriguing to me that Sena attributed to Eve's wiles Jehovah's conversion from a God of wrath to a God of something approaching charity. It is a successful con job that has as one of its results, as Sena concludes, God's own subsequent vulnerability to human perfidy when later he turns himself into a man to dwell among men. Notice, too, that, as part of her act before Jehovah, Eve covers her nakedness with grape leaves. Here, apparently, is the first recorded instance of Sena's broaching of the themes of human beings' disingenuous use of their shame and their fear of natural nudity. The theme is a constant in Sena's work, surfacing most dramatically in "O físico prodigioso" and the brilliant poems "Sobre a nudez" (1968–69) and "Filmes pornográficos" (the latter dated October 13, 1972, which associates it with the 1972 sequence on Santa Barbara entitled "Sobre esta praia . . . : Oito meditações à beira do Pacífico").

But in "Paraíso perdido" nudity or, rather, the shameful covering up of natural nudity is only a hint. The story's more important theme, one that leads directly to the second (and, as it turned out, final) story in Sena's *Genesis*, is that of God's decision to present himself as one who will show preference for one human being over another. That such favoritism seems to be preordained, possibly capricious, and not to be questioned or contested (at least not successfully so) lies at the heart of "Caim," the story of Cain and Abel standing before the Lord, as Sena reimagined it.

In "Caim," Sena retells and elaborates naturalistically upon the scriptural text in Genesis, retaining the original's emphasis on Cain. It is Cain who plots to gain God's favor by displaying his superior offerings—his bounty of fruits and grains—in competition with Abel's small and meager cattle. Abel agrees to the contest, though he does so reluctantly because he, too, sees that the competition will be unfair to himself, given the poverty of what he has been able to produce. But the imperious Jehovah will have nothing of such openly unprejudiced contesting. Cain's offering is accepted curtly, with seemingly pro forma thanks, but Abel's gift "of the firstlings of his flock" (Genesis 4:4), attended by his apology for its meagerness, is warmly received with a disclaimer: "Não . . . É um belo animal! e sentando-se puxou o carneiro para si. Enquanto falava ia-o afagando e o bicho mais se sentia no céu que na terra.—Vejo, Abel, que és deveras meu amigo . . . e começou com ele a discernir sobre os rebanhos" (32).

Disappointed, Cain allows the fruit he has been carrying to fall to the ground, whereupon the Lord, still caressing the lamb brought to him by Abel, asks him with annoyance: "Que tens?" (32). Cain lays out his complaint, namely that today, as always, his brother's gift has been preferred to his gift, even though his, Cain's gift, is by far the superior of the two. "Nem uma palavra, nem um louvor, nada . . ." laments Cain (32); "Vós sois Deus, vós sois o Senhor . . . Mas não tendes razão . . . Desprezais-me sem motivo . . ." (32). Of course, Jehovah (true to form) sets him straight in no uncertain terms:

> Invejoso imundo! Não posso preferir quem quiser? Tenho de lho pedir? Eu sou quem sou! Tu nem és o que és! O teu coração pesa-te porque está cheio de falsidade e veneno! Os teus olhos choram porque ardem no fogo da tua maldade. Vergas o corpo para o chão porque mãos de demónios se estão já apoderando dele! A tua inveja levou-te ao desrespeito do teu Senhor e da amizade de teu irmão . . . (33)

What is most significant here is that Cain (already accused of Lucifer-like bending toward the devil's world) has made the effort to stand up to Jehovah; and he will do so again after the murder of Abel when the Lord reveals that he knew all along that Cain would kill him. Equally significant in this, moreover, is the author's emphasis upon the searing knowledge that sheer merit cannot make its own way in the eyes of the Lord. This remarkable story deserves extensive quotation, especially for the acerbic exchanges in which the Lord arrogantly reaffirms his right to pick and choose and favor as he wishes, and in which Cain humanistically and blasphemously stands up for himself. I limit myself to quoting only Cain's last speech:

> Hipócrita! Não me compras com as tuas escorregadias palavras de perdão. . . . Vou-me embora, sim! Pode ser que tenha filhos! Pode ser que seja feliz! Que te perdoe, que chame por ti! Mas não há de ser onde tu quiseres! Vou-me embora, mas não pela tua ponte! Não quero nada do que te pertence, não aceito nada do que me ofereces! Vou para onde a minha vontade me levar! Ofereces-me um mundo novo! Tudo quanto quiser conquistarei! Vou com a minha vontade! Ela é mais forte do que tu! (39–40)

It seems appropriate that with "Caim" the eighteen-year-old Jorge de Sena would bring to an end his reworking of Genesis. Not only had he already discovered the humanistic definition of man that he would later credit to Machiavelli—namely that man, not anything supernatural, was responsible for managing and shaping his own affairs—but he had imaginatively discovered in the life of Cain a definition of himself that he would enact and fulfill for the next forty years.[5] Here, in the character and fact of Cain, was Sena the "indesejado" (as well as the "António, rei" whom he called, in his 1951 play of the same title, "O indesejado"), the exiled poet who would traverse countries and continents, and the writer whose work would not so much suffer the fate of direct attack as that of bypass, snub, and shameless neglect. Indeed, so thoroughly was Sena imbued with the Cain mythology he himself had worked out in "Caim" that he not only found it scattered in bits and pieces in the lives of Camões and the "indesejado" but also in his own career, as he records in poems, stories, plays, and even interviews. It is the eighteen-year-old Sena's Cain who is the gray eminence behind the persona that shows forth in the characteristically frank interview Sena granted to *O tempo e o modo* in 1968:

A única razão pela qual parece que eu proclamo a cada instante o meu talento é porque, até muito recentemente, se eu o não fizesse, ninguém o faria. E, se eu sou agudamente sensível a todas as formas de injustiça, haveria de deixar que ela se exercesse impunemente comigo? Poucos escritores portugueses de relativo mérito deverão tão pouco à crítica como eu. De todos os sectores, o silêncio ou o amesquinhamento foram de regra durante quase trinta anos. Onde está a bibliografia a meu respeito durante trinta anos? Com raras e dignas excepções, eu, durante anos, recebi apenas dedicatórias de livros ou cartas particulares, ou devotadamente admiradoras, mas onde estão os equivalentes públicos de tanta admiração dos meus ilustres camaradas? Uma ou outra dentada em prefácio, quando muito. Elogios "à contre-coeur" em histórias litérarias é o mais que eu recebo, quando notórios medíocres são coroados de flores, por serem suficientemente reaccionários, ou suficientemente "dos nossos." Dado que eu não acredito em nenhuma forma de imortalidade, e tenho erudição bastante para saber que cemitérios são as bibliotecas e as histórias literárias; e dado ainda que não me dou a participar de partidarismos que me ofereçam, por substituição, a ilusão da imortalidade, será bem clara a razão de exigir o reconhecimento que me cabe pelo muito e bom que tenho feito. Tenho horror de falsas modéstias, de facto. Mas tenho ainda maior horror da mediocridade que se compraz em recusar-se a reconhecer o que a excede. Não, não sou um dos meus mais seguros admiradores. Se o fosse, seria como a maioria dos membros da vida literária portuguesa, tão satisfeitos de si mesmos que escrevem sempre um livro pior do que o anterior. O problema não está em eu me considerar muito grande—mas sim em os outros serem, na maioria, tão pequenos.[6]

Intentionally exhibited here is a man whose work, Sena insists, has been ignored, neglected, and impugned through the silence of inferiors who do not, will not, or cannot understand that work.

Similar self-portraits are likely to emerge at almost any time in
Sena's work in any genre, from the poem "No país dos sacanas"
(1973) and the story "As ites e o regulamento" (1961), for example,
to the detailed exposition in *O reino da estupidez—II* (1978) of the
circumstances surrounding his attempts in Brazil, when he was in
his forties, to conduct the research into Camões that would lead to
his doctorate from the Universidade de São Paulo—a story that is
lengthy and specific, naming names, places, dates, acts of generosity,
and, above all, acts of perfidy.[7]

In a more discursively revelatory way, this is the same Jorge de
Sena who, in "Em Creta, com o Minotauro" (1965), that magnificent
Cainite (or Ishmaelite) summing-up, concludes:

> Em Creta, com o Minotauro,
> sem versos e sem vida,
> sem pátrias e sem espírito,
> sem nada, nem ninguém,
> que não o dedo sujo,
> hei-de tomar em paz o meu café.[8]

It is the same Jorge de Sena who, commenting on the last line of
this stanza, said, "Isso é o que ele julga."[9] The Jorge de Sena whose
hand was against every man's and whose self was made to withstand
the hand of any man was discovered in Genesis in the guise of Cain
even as he was discovered, in part, in the author of *Os Lusíadas*, and in
numerous other historical and literary rebels. But that mythic Jorge
de Sena, for all of the self-sanctioning he could cull from literature
and history, had its best testimony in profoundly autobiographical
roots. Characteristically, he chose to tell the story of his formative
experiences in a piece of fiction—in an astonishing, marvelous tale!

Written in 1961–62, in the midst of Sena's stay in Brazil (he
became a Brazilian citizen and remained one to his death), this
admittedly autobiographical story, "Homenagem ao Papagaio
Verde," has been successfully read on several levels.[10] Indeed, it lends
itself to sociohistorical readings, psychological analyses, mythic

investigations, and, what is foremost from my point of view at this time, to paradigmatic revelations of the author's conception of self. In this sense, it is entirely legitimate to equate the personages of the story with members of Sena's own immediate family. In fact, Sena encouraged such identification, all the while insisting on the story's status as fiction, by writing: "Na verdade, o 'papagaio verde' foi meu, e não apenas do meu narrador . . ."[11] Identification is thus made; but, through the narrator, there is distancing, too.

"Homenagem ao Papagaio Verde" tells the story of a boy's growing up in a household made up of his mother, two or three maids, some cats, two parrots, and his father, who is largely absent. The latter is a merchant marine officer who, in effect, "visits" his home to stay with his family for short intervals, three months or so apart. The father is tyrannical, imperious, demanding, and abusive. He is, in short, the Jehovah of his family, inspiring fear and trembling when he comes. Here is his typical arrival:

> Depois, era uma expectativa meio nervosa, com muitos "o papá está a chegar" e muitas espreitadelas para a rua, a vermos se ele assomava ao virar a esquina. Até que, com o seu andar balanceado, a estatura corpulenta aparecia atravessando a rua, chapéu de feltro de aba revirada e debruada a seda, bengala com aplicações de prata, charuto havano empinado na boca. (32)

The incidental matter in the narrative—the father's sexual abuse of his wife behind the locked doors of the bedroom, the family dinners that deteriorate into arguments—contributes to a matrix that harbors and feeds the root, stem, and flower of this story: the successful search for a true father. In the course of things, the child's sensitivity and growing awareness of the nature of things in his father's household and, representatively, in the world outside lead him to installing secrets of his own—particularly one large secret—in place of the dirty secrets of the locked boudoir. It is a secret that will be conveyed to him, ultimately, not by another human being—not by the maids (those traditional initiators of children), not by his mother (who will never stand up to his father), and not by his father, who, after all, is (Freudianly, and not so Freudianly) the all-powerful enemy standing in the way of the boy's individuation (he is, of course, the terrible deity to the boy's Cain). The father must be conquered; he must be repudiated psychologically once and for all. One is tempted to anatomize fully the details in which Sena lays out the scene of the boy's victory over his father, but I shall merely quote a few sentences:

Uma vez, minha mãe vestiu-me apressadamente e vestiu-se depressa também, com meu pai, no corredor, de faca da cozinha em punho, e as criadas nas sombras da porta do "quarto escuro" espreitando. Fui informado de que íamos sair para nos deitarmos ao rio, nos afogarmos. À porta, entre gargalhadas do meu pai, eu recusei-me terminantemente a sair, declarando que estava muito frio. E meu pai, brandindo a faca—que era para suicidar-se, ou para matar minha mãe, ou para liquidar-me a mim, conforme as oportunidades daquela "commedia dell'arte"—avançou para minha mãe. Eu dei-lhe um pontapé no baixo-ventre, que o fez, num urro, largar a faca que apanhei. E as criadas e minha mãe tiveram de interpor-se entre ele e mim, até que uma das criadas, abrindo a porta da rua, se esgueirou, comigo pela mão, desarmando-me, e levando-me para a avenida, onde o dia clareava, e os grandes carros de bois, cobertos de hortaliça muito arrumadinha, desciam chiando a caminho do mercado. A criada falava docemente comigo, dizendo-me que o que eu fizera não se fazia, era uma grande maldade, uma grande falta de respeito. Eu, abaixando a boca, mordi-lhe a mão. E ficámos passeando para baixo e para cima, ela surpresa e dolorida atrás de mim, porque me estimava muito, e eu, à frente, dando pontapés aos detritos que havia no passeio, entornando caixotes de lixo, que estavam nas portas, e urinando contra as árvores como faziam os cães. (43–44)

Or shall we say "urinando . . . como faria o Caim"? When the boy enacts this crime against his father ("levantara a mão contra meu pai! fosse o criminoso, o culpado daquilo tudo" [44])—for "the boy" in all this, one can read Cain, but one must also read Jorge de Sena—it has the effect of removing the father from the boy's sphere of formative interests and influences. After this, to the end of the story, it is the boy's relationship with the green parrot that dominates the narrative and most matters. He closes himself into the room containing the piano and plays his music before, and largely for, the parrot. The intimacy between the parrot and the boy grows until the parrot becomes, in a touch of miraculous realism, the very source of knowledge for him:

Foi então que, no meu colo, ele deu em recordar teimosamente, com escândalo de minha mãe que deixou de tratá-lo, o repertório antigo. Murmuradamente dizia de enfiada coisas que eu nunca lhe ouvira, frases, ordens de navegação e manobras, palavrões, palavras em línguas que eu não reconhecia. Como em sonhos, recostado nos meus braços, arrepiando-se às vezes, repetia sem descanso tudo o que decorara na sua longa vida, e o que não decorara, e o que ouvira no convés de navios, em portos de todo o mundo, entre a marinhagem de todas as cores. (46)

In short, it is the green parrot that fires the boy's imagination about life at sea, not his merchant marine officer father.

In the course of events, the green parrot sickens. It turns out to be its final illness. The boy spends more and more time with his failing friend, this "papagaio" who is, spiritually and emotionally, his "papa." In his sickness the green parrot reveals to the boy, with no pathos, the true import of disease and the unfortunate breakdown of living things. "Não era, porém, só a ferida, se era ferida, o que lhe doía," the boy discovers. "Era-lhe igualmente dolorosa a perda do seu garbo, da sua altivez, da elegância majestosa das suas penas brilhantes" (47). It would not be the last time that Sena would perceive the same message showing forth through the illness of an animal.

But at its death the green parrot makes one last revelation. "Voltei a deitá-lo nas almofadas, apertou-me com força o dedo na sua pata," says the boy, "e disse numa voz clara e nítida, dos seus bons tempos de chamar os vendedores que passavam na rua: —Filhos da puta! Eu afaguei-o suavemente, chorando, e senti que a pata esmorecia no meu dedo. Foi a primeira pessoa que eu vi morrer" (48). This—"Filhos da puta!"—is the secret revealed that, coming from his true father, speaks volumes, as we now know, to the Jorge de Sena who was child to the boy who fathered him. It was this secret—knowledge perforce of the way things are in the world—that, one is tempted to say, made the boy into the writer we know he became. For the American poet Walt Whitman, the essential determining secret, also learned from a "singer solitary" (a "he-bird" on Paumanok's shore), was the "delicious word"—"Death, death, death . . ." And for the other American poet, Edgar Allan Poe, the secret, spoken over and over, was "Nevermore." Neither of these secrets could have done for Jorge de Sena. Hearing from the "papagaio verde" what he needed to hear, he heard a message that would not have been lost on Sena's Cain or on the author of the poem "No país dos sacanas."

Their relationship is not exactly like that of the young boy Jorge to his green parrot, but the bond between the already-ill Sena in the last year of his life and Dom Fuas, his regal angora cat, just dead, fits uniquely into the narrative I am trying to construct. On December 18, 1977, Sena wrote what would turn out to be, we are told, the next-to-last of the several hundred poems of his authority. It was an elegy for Dom Fuas. Published posthumously in a volume entitled, fittingly, given the Jorge de Sena I have so far discovered, *40 anos de servidão* (1979), this poem constitutes Sena's final demonstration of his creative need to discover himself in—as he called the green parrot—another person. For the poet, forever changed by the heart attack he had recently suffered, but which, despite his conviction that it would do so (see his very last poem, "Aviso a cardíacos"), would not kill him, this poem can be seen as a catharsis of self-definition. It will be recalled, in this connection, that the Dom Fuas for whom Sena had named his cat and who was the subject of his early historical narrative, a portion of which was copied into the first of the notebooks the young Sena kept from 1936 to 1944, was, at least according to traditional sources, the first admiral of the Portuguese fleet. Moreover, in so nominating his cat, Sena, whose own bitter memory of his aborted career as a naval cadet seems never to have faded or softened, was undoubtedly making a genial joke. Indeed, he acknowledged as much in lines from what I take to be a rejected stanza from the poem: "por troça do Roupinho, um daqueles asnos / que a Portugal fundou . . ."[12] Yet it is also apparent from "Morreu Dom Fuas" that the life achieved by the cat that Sena, perhaps mockingly, named Dom Fuas, puts him in the company of all those whose deaths mattered to Sena, including Adolfo Casais Monteiro, Pablo Neruda, Luís de Camões, and the "papagaio verde." The death, subsequently, of Jorge de Sena turns "Dom Fuas" into a double elegy, the second one being the dark celebration of the death, not of Sena simples, but of Sena's Jorge de Sena, which is quite another matter.[13] The poem is quoted here in its entirety:

Morreu Dom Fuas, gato meu sete anos,
Pomposo, realengo, solene, quase inacessível,
na sua elegância desdenhosa de angorá gigante,
cendrado e branco, de opulento pêlo,
e cauda como pluma de elmo legendário.

Contudo, às suas horas, e quando acontecia
que parava em casa mais que por comer
ou visitar-nos condescendentemente como
a Duquesa de Guermantes recebendo Swann,
tinha instantes de ternura toda abraços,
que logo interrompia retornando
aos seus passos de império, ao seu olhar ducal.

Nunca reconheceu nenhuma outra existência
de gato que não ele nesta casa. Os mais
todos se retiravam para que ele passasse
ou para que ele comesse, eles ficando
ao longe contemplando a majestade
que jamais miou para pedir que fosse.

Andava adoentado, encrenca sobre encrenca,
e via-se no corpo e no opulento pêlo,

como no ar da cabeça quanta humilhação
o sofrimento impunha a tanto orgulho imenso.
Por fim, foi internado americanamente,
no hospital do veterinário. E lá,
por notícia telefónica, sozinho, solitário,
como qualquer humano aqui, sabemos que morreu.

A única diferença, e é melhor assim,
em tão terror ambiente de ser-se o animal que morre
foi não vê-lo mais. Porque ou nós morremos,
como dantes se morria em público,
a família toda, ou toda a corte à volta, ou
é melhor que se não veja no rosto de qualquer
—mesmo ou sobretudo no de um gato que era tão orgulho em
vida—

não só a marca desse morrer sozinho de que se morre sempre
mesmo que o mundo inteiro faça companhia,
mas de outra solidão tecnocrata, higiénica
que nos suprime transformados em
amável voz profissional de secretária solícita.

Dom Fuas, tu morreste. Não direi
que a terra te seja leve, porque é mais que certo
não teres sequer ter tido o privilégio
de dormir para sempre na terra que escavavas
com arte cuidadosa para nela pores
as fezes de existir que tão bem tapavas,
como gato educado e nobre natural.
Nestes anos de tanta morte à minha volta,
também a tua conta. Nenhum mais
terá teu nome como outros tantos gatos
antes de ti foram já Dom Fuas.

2

"If This Be Treason"

Sou de Europa ou de América? De Portugal ou Brasil?

—Jorge de Sena (1970)[1]

A nation which does not produce traitors can hardly be said to be civilized.

—Fernando Pessoa (1914–18)[2]

Esse Pessoa que, no vero pólo oposto daquele grande Camões que ele professava não admirar muito, não deixou a vida pelo mundo em pedaços repartida, como Camões, com boas razões, disse da sua mesma.

—Jorge de Sena (1977)[3]

Citizen of two countries, resident alien in a third, a being who was "international" by inclination and universal by temperament, Jorge de Sena, virtually from the start, found himself spooked by the existence everywhere around him of less capacious, smaller-minded, ungenerous, provincial countrymen. He distinguished himself from these uncultivated or, at best, semicultivated hordes:

Pois que sempre houve, em cultura, dois modos extremos de ser-se
português: o afogar-se satisfeito ou irritado no confinamento literário
da mesquinhez hebdomadária, sempre em angustiosa aflição de que o
lugar ao sol seja roubado por outro na semana seguinte; ou o ampli-
ar-se a todos os tempos e lugares uma visão do mundo, que às vezes
se chega a supor que Portugal teve e perdeu, encolhendo-se dia a dia
num empequenecer perverso. . . . Aos poetas, quanto de poesia se
traduza pode ajudá-los a sentirem-se, no concreto da linguagem, mais
parte de um processo milenário que nunca conheceu fronteiras apesar
da diversidade das línguas, e, portanto, mais integrados nessa coisa
estranha que é a humanidade.[4]

With "poetry" his unquestioned way of being, thinking, and feeling,
Sena took the high road. The vast corpus of work that he produced
insistently crossed linguistic boundaries, ever questioning, in its
protean nature, the putative integrity of received and seemingly
established disciplines. "Uma pátria sem fronteiras seguras nem
independência concreta," as he said in a poem about that other wan-
derer, Chopin.[5]

Yet Sena was also a superpatriot; and superpatriot that he was, he
was, of course, something more and different. And that something
more and different—a universalism, a sort of pan-nationalism—
made him seem, at times, something other than a patriot, possessing
something of the qualities one might imagine Fernando Pessoa to
have attributed to the kind of traitor native to a civilized nation.

Now, Portugal might never have entirely forgiven Sena for having
gone into exile, first in Brazil, then in the United States. The opposi-
tion to Salazar's dictatorial regime might have been willing enough
to avail itself of the exile's outspoken, often acerbic words, uttered
less in anger than sorrow, against political and social conditions in
the Estado Novo. Yet that things were not at all what they seemed
is apparent in the way he was greeted by the first governments that
took office after the 25th of April Revolution in 1974. In the first
years, the newly formed ministries extended precious little recog-
nition to Sena as a national political or governmental resource. He

did not leave the University of California, Santa Barbara—and who could have reasonably expected him to do so?—to re-emigrate to his native land. In subsequent years there were even those, back in Portugal—some of them having themselves been immediate beneficiaries of the revolution—who questioned his sincerity and values when he did not return to the country to teach at a Portuguese university. This was the unequivocal position of one, then young, and now highly successful writer, who should have known better.

It is well known that Sena openly and repeatedly expressed his fears and hopes for Portugal during the dreariest decades of the Estado Novo. Nowhere does he do it more succinctly than in the poem "Quem a tem," from *Fidelidade* (1958). The poem was written on December 9, 1956:

> Não hei-de morrer sem saber
> Qual a cor da liberdade.
>
> Eu não posso senão ser
> Desta terra em que nasci.
> Embora ao mundo pertença
> e sempre a verdade vença,
> qual será ser livre aqui,
> não hei-de morrer sem saber.
>
> Trocaram tudo em maldade,
> É quase um crime viver.
> Mas, embora escondam tudo
> E me queiram cego e mudo,
> Não hei de morrer sem saber
> Qual a cor da liberdade.[6]

Sena makes an important point, apart from the hope and desire to live long enough to see the restoration of liberty and freedom for individuals in his native land, for although he knows himself to be a citizen of the world (something not everyone acknowledges to be true about themselves), he cannot cease belonging to the land of his birth—certainly a basis for determining one's patriotism and treason. Three years after writing this poem Sena found himself in Bahia, to participate in a scholarly conference. He chose to stay in Brazil, and thus began his years of exile.

His first ten years of self-exile he spent in the Americas, dividing them between the northern and southern hemispheres, between Brazil and the United States. That decade was marked at its end by the publication, in September 1969, of *Peregrinatio ad loca infecta*, his eighth or ninth book of poems, depending on how one considers *Poesia—I*. Much of the book was made up of poems that were, as he said in his preface (entitled "Isto não é um prefácio"), the poems of his American "exile":

> [O]s meus "exílios" americanos (do Sul e do Norte), com tudo o que de difícil e de complexo uma tal situação implica, pela confrontação com diversas culturas (ainda que, ironicamente, elas nos sejam familiares) que, para quem não vive nelas em carácter evidentemente provisório, colocam agudamente dolorosos problemas de identidade, e nos levam a meditar diversamente sobre quem somos.[7]

His title, Sena tells us, plays on the title of a fourth-century travel account:

> O título é caricatura de *Peregrinatio ad loca sancta*, espécie de guia e relatório devoto, artístico e prático do peregrino da Terra Santa, que constitui um dos mais preciosos documentos existentes para o estudo do latim vulgar. Terá sido composto por Etéria ou Egéria, ou santa qualquer coisa, freira talvez de Braga, que, em 395 da nossa era, viajou à Palestina, ao Sinai, ao Egipto e a Constantinopla. Como se vê, a mania portuguesa de viajar e relatar as peregrinações feitas é antiga.[8]

The locus of Jorge de Sena's travels is not the Near or Far East but the Americas. And while this latter-day Portuguese peregrine insists that not all of his American experiences over the decade were rosy, and while he acknowledges that some of his visits are to the "'loca infecta' da alma," his principal criticisms are aimed at the world as he finds it—"o nosso mundo de hoje em que brutalmente, insidiosamente, e teimosamente persiste seja em que hemisfério or regime, uma concepção do mundo e da vida como um tirânico vale de lágrimas."[9] Sena divides *Peregrinatio ad loca infecta* into four sections—which he labels "Portugal," "Brasil," "Estados Unidos da América," and "Notas de um regresso à Europa"—followed by a one-poem epilogue. The largest grouping of poems appears in the Brazil section, which is three times as long as the U.S. section. The U.S. section, in turn, runs to slightly more than twice the size of the opening Portugal section. The "return to Europe" section adds up to a unit of five pages. In their aggregate, we have a record of those journeys of expatriation, exile, and repatriation taken by the poet in his post-middle-of-the-journey decade of the 1960s. Heartfelt accusations and painful recriminations mark the poetry of this period, if one is to consider the poetry to be a barely encoded record. The themes of betrayal and treason appear in several poems, sometimes centrally, sometimes peripherally or even parenthetically. Not all of the following examples are employed, to be sure, with the same authorial insistence or with the same pressure. The word "trair," to betray (in one form or another), appears throughout. Here are some examples. In the poem "A Paul Fort" ("E eu, que sou poeta—ó Príncipe— traí-te, / como se com método e com ficha, registando apenas, / no apêndice de uma delas, que morreste"); in "Heptarquia do mundo ocidental" ("E para quê? Se tudo é só traição, / traição que trai ou que nem mesmo trai / na estreita hesitação de só trair"); in "Homenagem à Grécia" ("Os deuses, ladrões, / promíscuos, bestiais, / traiçoeiros"); in "Quem muito viu" ("Quem muito viu, sofreu, passou trabalhos, / mágoas, humilhações, tristes surpresas; / e foi traído"); in "Uma sepultura em Londres" ("um bastião do amor que nunca foi traído"); and in "À memória de Kazantzakis, e a quantos fizeram o filme 'Zorba the Greek'" ("traição à nossa vida amarga").[10]

The notion of betrayal also runs in poems contemporary with those published in *Peregrinatio ad loca infecta* but omitted from that collection (though later collected in *40 anos de servidão* [1979]). Take, for example, "Nada do mundo": "Quanto melhor seria ter servido / alguma ideia, um deus, qualquer senhor, / bem falsos ou mundanos, e traíveis / nesse fingir de crença ou lealdade / com que a miséria humana se imagina / mais rica e nobre do que o nada oculto!"; or, later in the same poem, "E é tudo o que me resta e me resume, / e que de mim cá fica, odiado e inútil / (e mais que inútil—para ser traído)." From *Peregrinatio* Sena had also omitted his long poem "A Portugal," which, studiously avoiding the obvious use of the word "traír" in any form, is unequivocally about the ways a "pátria" can betray a patriot. It begins: "Esta é a ditosa pátria minha amada. Não. / Nem é ditosa, porque o não merece. / Nem minha amada, porque é só madrasta. / Nem pátria minha, porque eu não mereço / a pouca sorte de nascido nela."[11]

But the key text in this consideration of patriotism and treason in *Peregrinatio ad loca infecta* is the penultimate poem in the "Brasil" section—"Em Creta, com o Minotauro," a signature poem for Sena and, in my opinion, one of the strongest twentieth-century poems. Among Portuguese poems I would rank it with Álvaro de Campos's "Tabacaria," and among English-language poems of the same period, I would place it with T. S. Eliot's "The Love Song of J. Alfred Prufrock," with the great difference that Sena's voice in his poem is aggressively stoic and steely ironic, a far cry from Campos's compliant resignation or Prufrock's self-pitying complaint.

"Em Creta, com o Minotauro" begins with a reference to places of birth and residence: "Nascido em Portugal, de pais portugueses, / E pai de brasileiros no Brasil, / Serei talvez norte-americano quando lá estiver."[12] Time and place define the poet's nationality. He is Portuguese because he was born in Portugal and his parents are Portuguese. Then he becomes sort of Brazilian, one infers, because he fathers children who are born in Brazil, who themselves are of course inescapably Brazilian (and not necessarily Portuguese as well) because they were born in Brazil even though their father may or may not be Brazilian. But is he not Brazilian just by being there

and for as long as he is there? After all, he thinks, he just might be a
"norte-americano" when he goes to the United States. How will that
come about? Will it be because (and when) he has children born in
the United States? Will it be because just being there will make him
a "norte-americano"? Does he imply that he will become an American by becoming a naturalized citizen? I entertain the possible ways,
even facetious ways, of reacting to Sena's lines because their implications are varied and serious. The question of one's nationality can be
a slippery thing for some, complicated, confusing, contradictory, and
hard to pin down. In fact, he recognizes this (perhaps boastfully) in
the next three lines: "Coleccionarei nacionalidades como camisas se
despem, / Se usam e se deitam fora, com todo o respeito / Necessário
à roupa que se veste e que prestou serviço."

The trope is brilliant. The comparison of one's nationalities with
useful and serviceable clothing, with one's shirts—shirts that give
good wear but that must sooner or later be discarded—initiates the
poem's principal subtext. In employing the shirt images metaphor-
ically to convey his sense of what nationality means to him (and
should, perhaps, mean to everyone), the poet draws on the common
Portuguese expression "virar a casaca," literally "to turn one's coat,"
figuratively to change one's tune, to do an about-face on some matter.
Hence, in short, to become a turncoat. The sudden and unexpected
changing of one's nationality is like the sudden changing of one's
"shirt." "Virar a casaca" is, on some public level, an act of treachery.
When that act is worked on the national level, it becomes an act of
treason. To shed one's nationality for another nationality may well
border on treason. Hence Sena's use of the image of turning in one's
shirt for another shirt, in certain contexts and situations, inevitably
calls up suggestions of treachery. It is probably unnecessary to recall
that the political use of shirts would be especially meaningful to
anyone knowing that the 1920s and 1930s saw the advent of fascist
parties and factions as well as government organizations that chose
to designate their membership by the color of their shirts—brown,
black, and green—green, of course, being the color appropriated

by the Brazilian Integralistas. Much like Camões, who left his life scattered in pieces throughout the worlds of Asia and Africa, Sena will leave behind his shirts—his nationalities—in Portugal, Brazil, and Wisconsin. And a last word on the connection between "turning one's coat" and betrayal. While the Portuguese words *trajo* and *traição* seem not to be related etymologically, they are close enough echoically to constitute a Portuguese version of the English turncoat-treason connection, especially in the verbs *trajar* and *trair*.

To return to the expressed sentiments of the poem—the poet makes it clear that he cannot betray his nationality (or his nationalities, as it were) because, he insists, he is himself his own nationality. And, moreover, it occurs to him, "A pátria / de que escrevo é a língua em que por acaso de gerações / nasci." But he is careful not to present himself as being entirely in accord with these notions. For if the Portuguese language and, by extension, the Portuguese nation are both of them the nation he writes about, it is only because by virtue of coincidence of time and place he was born into that particular language, so to speak, and no other. It is interesting to observe, moreover, that while the poet has left behind his first nation (though he will revisit it), just as he will leave behind his second one, he has not left behind in either place his native language. It has accompanied him wherever he has gone, part and parcel of mind and body, unlike so many nationalities that are like shirts that are purchased, worn, removed, and cast aside. We are now free to infer that apart from whatever citizenship his native language accords him, he cannot be said to belong nominatively or permanently to any nation or to any designated geographical place.

Enter the Minotaur. Someday when the poet will have forgotten everything—the paucity of human kindness and decency extant in this world, the desire to have this world be like the world he would have it be, though he has no belief in the existence of a world beyond this one (a notion expressed here and in the poem "Carta a meus filhos sobre os Fuzilamentos de Goya")—he will grow old. And he will do so not in the company of an erstwhile lover, as is the case, say, with the poet in William Butler Yeats's "Speech after Long Silence," but shamelessly so, in Crete, in the Minotaur's company, under the gaze of equally shameless gods.

The Minotaur also poses problems for the patriot. His "nation" is not even that of the human race, for he is half man and half beast. But even knowing that part of him, at least, comes from human stock (he is the treacherous Ariadne's brother) would not at first help to "place" him. But it does allow the poet to redefine the term "man," for like the Minotaur, he insists, all men are half human, half animal. The Minotaur rapes and devours his victims, as do, in one way or another, all those who are beasts.

Yet the Minotaur does have his qualities. If he is a son of a bitch, a fact that links him to all Greek heroes, he is nevertheless betrayed by his half-sister Ariadne, who, out of love, schemes with Theseus, one of those Greek heroes, to search out the Minotaur and destroy him. It is this betrayal, suffered by the half man, half beast, that makes him kith and kin with the poet. They are exiles both—the Minotaur at the center of his Daedalian labyrinth, away from all human life except for the virgins sent in to satisfy his needs, and the poet set out to wander through strange and foreign lands. They have other things in common. Sunset in Crete will bring nymphs and ephebes out of the shadows swirling into coffee cups to be sweetened in the sugary mix stirred by a finger dirty with its investigations into the origins of life. All this will be swallowed down, one presumes, even as the Minotaur devoured his seemingly ever-renewable portion of virgins sent down to him in darkness.

Like the virgins torn apart by the Minotaur, the poet will have left pieces of himself scattered throughout the so-called new world. Here the poet acknowledges explicitly that he has borrowed the notion from Camões, that fellow human beast whose own patriotism was at the last traduced and dismissed, it is said, by a nation who repaid him for his loyal service by allowing him to die in poverty and misery, even as the nation itself was falling into hands that would betray her.

But an even greater betrayal has befallen Camões, however. No one reads him, for no one reads Portuguese, not the Minotaur or anyone else. Who does not share in this betrayal of poets by not knowing the languages they write in? Even the Minotaur doesn't know Greek, having lived before the time of the Greeks, before the deluge of learned merde, evacuated by those we have enslaved or by us when we ourselves have become the slaves of others, as Sena says in a poem he will not write until he gets to the United States. He and the Minotaur, he decides, will trade complaints about their hurts in Volapük, a language neither of them knows.[13]

In the fourth section of the poem "Em Creta, com o Minotauro," Sena moves up to a more inclusive loop of betrayal and treason. It is by way of nationalities (and the idea of nationalism) that individual human beings are bought and sold into slavery, and the transaction features the extraordinary twist that there are nations so costly that not belonging to them becomes a cause for shame. Hence neither the poet nor the Minotaur will belong to any nation. Instead, they shall share coffee that comes from no nation or place—not from Arabia, not from Brazil, not from Fedecam, not from Angola— but from nowhere at all. Coffee that the poet will watch as it drips from the bull's chin on to the knees of a man who has inherited, not knowing whether from his father or his mother, those whorled horns that are older than Athens and older (who can know?) than Palestine, say, or any other touristic, and immensely patriotic, place.

The fifth and final section of the poem serves as a brief coda. When the poet finally sits down with the Minotaur in Crete, he will bring with him neither poetry nor life. He will be without nationalities or spirit. He will come, unencumbered by anyone or anything (other than his dirty finger), merely to drink coffee, peacefully and quietly.

In the year he published "Em Creta, com o Minotauro," Jorge de Sena set out from Brazil for his third and last "pátria," the United States. If he was not at the verge of "turning" his coat in 1965, he was certainly ready to cast off what had for a while been the useful shirt of Brazilian nationality. Sena did not become a citizen of the United

States when here, as it turned out, though he had become a Brazilian citizen when in Brazil. Nor did he renounce his Brazilian citizenship when he left behind the land of Santa Cruz. He was well aware that some of his Portuguese contemporaries were exercised that he had taken up a new nationality in the first place, and now, he explained, he was retaining his acquired nationality precisely because that very fact would annoy them further. Of course he would really have annoyed virtually everyone back there—Portugal and Brazil—had he become a naturalized citizen of the United States, especially if he had taken that "treacherous" step during the years of the American war in Vietnam.

One of the poetic legacies of the deep convictions that resulted in "Em Creta, com o Minotauro" is the later poem "Noções de linguística."[14] Written in 1970 and published in the volume *Exorcismos* two years later, this poem gives the lie to those received notions about the purity of languages and their unique attributes. In the English spoken around him in Wisconsin and California by his "Portuguese" children, born elsewhere, who are not only Americans now but who have dissolved themselves in a cultural-linguistic "sea" that, in some senses, is not theirs, he sees the death of the language into which he himself was born and in which he conducts his living. The poet's key notion occurs in lines that read: "As línguas, que duram séculos e mesmo sobrevivem / Esquecidas noutras, morrem todos os dias / Na gaguez daqueles que as herdaram."[15]

This is true, argues the poet, even for languages that have lasted for centuries, even those that have survived when they have lain hidden in other tongues. So much for the notion that Portuguese is the extraordinary language of a chosen people. So much for the patriotic shibboleth that has been fashioned out of Fernando Pessoa's exilic words, "minha pátria é a língua portuguesa," words that, to be sure, he attributed not to himself but to the Lisbon-bound semiheteronym Bernardo Soares.[16] Here is evidence pointing to the fact, sadly, that even language itself will enable and foster treachery, for it is the instrument and master of man, the animal that betrays.

Let two final quotations, one from Sena's prose and another from his poetry, bring the matter to a paradoxical conclusion. "Porque ele foi, acima de tudo e dos condicionalismos da vida, um cidadão do mundo em língua portuguesa, que é uma maneira de esse mundo não saber que possui tal cidadão, e de a língua, que o possui, presa aos seus provincianismos, não apreciar a grandeza que por ela se afirma e realiza."[17] Sena might have been describing himself in these very terms, though actually he is eulogizing his fellow-poet Adolfo Casais Monteiro, for it was true for both of them. And yet it was equally true, as he sang out in the poem "Paráfrase de Melina Mercouri," not without irony and some ambiguity: "Nasci português e morrerei português / Ainda que mude de nacionalidade vinte vezes."[18]

3

The Green Parrot

I had a mind to know from . . . Prince *Maurice's* . . . own
mouth . . . of an old *parrot* he had in *Brazil* during his government
there, that spoke and asked and answered common questions like
a reasonable creature. . . . He told me . . . he had so much curiosity
as to send for it . . . ; and when it came first into the room where
the Prince was, with a great many *Dutchmen* about him, it said
presently: *What a company of white men are here?* They asked it what
he thought that man was, pointing to the Prince. It answered, *some
general or other.* When they brought it close to him, he asked it:
D'ou venez-vous? It answered: *De Marinnan.* The Prince: *A qui êtes-
vous?* The parrot: *A un Portugais.* Prince: *Que fais-tu là?* Parrot: *Je
garde les poules.* The prince laughed and said: *Vous gardez les poules?*
The parrot answered: *Oui, moi, & je sais bien faire,* and made the
chuck four or five times that people use to make to chickens when
they call them.

—William Temple (1692)[1]

Why does even a parrot learn swearing before any other form of
speech[?] Because it is more spirited than any other.

—Robert Frost (undated)[2]

1.

In his preface to *Os grão-capitães: Uma sequência de contos* (1971), Jorge de Sena addresses, among other issues, the complex matter of how autobiography is necessarily related to his kind of fiction. "Se a matéria de *Os grão-capitães* é directa ou indirectamente autobiográfica—com que amargura às vezes," he informs the reader, "a estrutura que lhe é dada é inteiramente ficção."³ And it can be no other way for the modern writer, he goes on to insist: "Não creio que, nos tempos de hoje, se possa honestamente fazer ficção de outra coisa, se se quer falar do mundo em que vivemos e da vida que nos foi dado ter, ou a que nos foi dado assistir, nele." After all, he continues, "Um escritor realista é, com a técnica que a sua visão estrutural exige, um escritor capaz de imaginar a realidade." And since that was so, he would explain further, "seria um erro pensar-se, como correntemente se pensa, que a fantasia não é feita da mesma matéria," offering, in example, "O físico prodigioso," his most "fantastic" story, which is yet, "na verdade," according to him, "um dos contos meus em que mais há de mim mesmo e da minha vida."

Sena then goes on to consider other matters, including the generic differences between memorialist writing and fiction, differences that of necessity compel the memorialist to falsify the truth much more than do the writers of stories and novels. The subjects Sena considers are important, his arguments both subtle and incisive as he works his way toward a supple and workable definition of the modern fiction writer's tasks, responsibilities, and opportunities. Undoubtedly, these are matters for prolonged and, I dare say, fruitful discussion. What I would like to do, however, is something much more limited.

Keeping in mind the sentence quoted at the beginning of this paper—"se a matéria de *Os grão-capitães* é directa ou indirectamente autobiográfica . . . , a estrutura que lhe é dada é inteiramente ficção"—I would like to examine the tale "Homenagem ao Papagaio Verde," with which Sena chooses to initiate the sequence of tales he calls *Os grão-capitães*. Before proceeding further, I should clarify that under that "autobiographical experience" I would include not only a person's thoughts, dreams, fantasies, and even hallucinations but the vicarious experiences ineluctably gained from that person's encounters with the arts at any level. In the case of Sena's "Homenagem ao Papagaio Verde"—I would argue— the experience of art most patently reflected (if transformed) involves, not surprisingly, other literary works.

In that same preface, to further his point that his fiction is autobiographical, Sena reveals: "fui eu quem esteve a ponto de morrer em Penafiel; fui eu quem assitiu àquelas cenas portuenses, onde perpassa um 'choro de criança'; eu quem, testemunha omitida, participou do *strip-tease* no 'Bom Pastor'; eu quem ouviu a conversa do quartel e observou os manejos descritos em 'Os irmãos'; eu quem desembarcou na Grã-Canária." In "Homenagem ao Papagaio Verde," however, he acknowledges only one autobiographical detail: "Na verdade, o 'papagaio verde' foi meu, e não apenas do meu narrador."[4]

Note here the distinction made by Sena between "meu" (an autobiographical Jorge de Sena) and a (fictional) "narrator." Putting the parrots aside at this time (both the autobiographical one and the fictional one), let us consider what we know about this narrator. The author chooses to present him anonymously (as he does the family), a decision that tends to generalize and universalize the story. The narrator is an adult (not a child, as I sometimes misremember), offering the reader what is clearly a retrospective, perhaps exploratory, narrative centering on his childhood. None of the story, therefore, except for a handful of direct quotations (including the parrot's words) is rendered in the voices of childhood. The story's verisimilitude lies not in its mimetic recreation of the scenes of childhood but in the substance and quality of an adult male voice choosing, shaping, and arranging what are ostensibly "memorial" materials. It can be assumed that the author presumes the reader will see that the adult's point of view must perforce differ from the child's. Moreover, it is reasonable to think that the narrator's greater experience must have tempered and deepened his understanding of the incidents of childhood. (The same, of course, may be true of the author's looking back through his narrator at his own childhood.) One of the aspects of this greater experience is that one can presume that the author (as well as his narrator) has simply and obviously read more than has the child the narrator depicts and that he once was, as was the author.

In considering the import of the narrator's reading, let us consider Sena's claim, in his preface, for the stories that make up *Os grão-capitães*: "Tudo aconteceu, ou terá acontecido, *quase* asssim. Neste quase, porém, está toda a distância que vai das *memórias* à *ficção*." There is an enormous qualification here. What does that "quase" suggest to this reader of "Homenagem ao Papagaio Verde," or, better still, what avenues does it open up for this reader, one whose response involves intertextuality? Let us set aside, for the nonce at least, that parrots were present in the household when Jorge de Sena was growing up, at least the green one that Sena says was his, and look at parrots in literature, as well as other so-called literary creatures of the air, especially those that, by speaking or singing, convey messages or secrets.

There is the ancient nightingale of Greek mythology, the form given to Philomel after having been raped by Tereus, whose song "jug, jug," according to T. S. Eliot in "The Waste Land," is sung to dirty ears. There are the nightingales of Samuel Taylor Coleridge and John Keats, the latter of which sings, according to Keats's poet (who thinks he perceives the message), of "easeful death." There is Robert Frost's ovenbird that sings of diminished things, making in midsummer sounds resembling the word "teacher." There is the mockingbird of Walt Whitman's "Out of the Cradle Endlessly Rocking" that in singing plaintively of his lost mate leads the young poet to an understanding of grief and an interpretation of the "delicious word death" murmured by the endlessly rocking ocean seas, to which experience he attributes his own birth as a poet. There is Edgar Allan Poe's raven that, persistently questioned by the grieving narrator about his lost love Lenore, answers only "Nevermore," in what seems to be either the only word the bird knows or the only response it uncannily understands will suit his inquisitor, thereby sardonically fulfilling the function attributed to birds in many fairy stories, which is to "confide useful secrets to the heroes" of those stories.[5] There is the green and yellow parrot that shrieks out at the opening of Kate Chopin's novel *The Awakening*. There is the mad speaking bird of John Skelton's "Speke, Parrot" speaking out against the madness of the world; and the parrot that Robinson Crusoe captures, tames, and teaches to speak, offering him the narcissistic pleasure of engaging in parodic conversation ("anthropomorphized subordination," it has been called) in which he hears back his own words mimicked in the sounds and cadence of his own speech.[6] There are the parrots of Jean Rhys's *Wide Sargasso Sea*, Isak Dinesen's *Out of Africa*, Gabriel García Márquez's *One Hundred Years of Solitude* and *Love in the Time of Cholera*, and Derek Walcott's *Pantomime*.[7] And then there is the parrot that makes a grand appearance in Gustave Flaubert's story "Un coeur simple."

"A Simple Heart," probably Flaubert's best-known work after *Madame Bovary*, was published in 1877 in *Trois contes*. The other two stories in the collection are "La légende de Saint-Julien l'Hospitalier" and "Herodias"—the latter being the last work that Flaubert actually completed. I cannot now go into the matter in any depth, but it does seem to me that *Trois contes* must have appealed strongly to Jorge de Sena.[8] "The Legend of St. Julian the Hospitaller" anticipates "O físico prodigioso." In Sena's story, the physician's sexual encounter with Satan, for example, recalls Julian's sensual embrace of the repulsive Leper—"stretch[ing] himself completely over him, mouth to mouth and chest on chest"—which is completed by the Leper's own clasp. With Sena's story in mind, consider Flaubert: "[Julian's] eyes suddenly became as bright as stars; his hair drew out like sunbeams; the breath of nostrils was as sweet as roses; a cloud of incense rose from the hearth, and the waves began to sing. Meanwhile an abundance of delight, a superhuman joy flooded into Julian's soul as he lay swooning; and he who still clasped him in his arms grew taller, ever taller, until his head and feet touched the two walls of the hut. The roof flew off, the firmament unrolled—and Julian rose towards the blue spaces, face to face with Our Lord Jesus, who carried him to heaven."[9] "Herodias," on the other hand, retells the story of St. John the Baptist and Salomé's dance from its source in the biblical Book of Samuel. It will be recalled that in the related stories collected under the title *Genesis*, Sena retells in biblical sequence the story of Adam and Eve in the Garden and the story of Cain and Abel. One might profitably read "Genesis," "O físico prodigioso," and "Homenagem ao Papagaio Verde" as related religious tales, as in the case of Flaubert's three stories some critics have done.[10]

To return to "A Simple Heart." In the 1985 novel *Flaubert's Parrot*, the English novelist Julian Barnes usefully summarizes the plot of Flaubert's famous story. Because Barnes writes better than most of us I shall borrow his summary:

> ["Un coeur simple"] is about a poor, uneducated servant-woman called Félicité, who serves the same mistress for half a century, unresentfully sacrificing her own life to those of others. She becomes attached, in turn, to a rough fiancé, to her mistress's children, to her nephew, and to an old man with a cancerous arm. All of them are casually taken from her: they die, or depart, or simply forget her. It is an existence in which, not surprisingly, the consolations of religion come to make up for the desolations of life.
>
> The final object in Félicité's ever-diminishing chain of attachments is Loulou, the parrot. When, in due course, he too dies, Félicité has him stuffed. She keeps the adored relic beside her, and even takes to saying her prayers while kneeling before him. A doctrinal confusion develops in her simple mind: she wonders whether the Holy Ghost, conventionally represented as a dove, would not be better portrayed as a parrot. Logic is certainly on her side: parrots and Holy Ghosts can speak, whereas doves cannot. At the end of the story, Félicité herself dies. "There was a smile on her lips. The movements of her heart slowed down beat by beat, each time more distant, like a fountain running dry or an echo disappearing; and as she breathed her final

breath she thought she saw, as the heavens opened for her, a gigantic
parrot hovering above her head."[11]

Like Flaubert's green parrot, Jorge de Sena's is an Amazonian—
more specifically, Brazilian—bird. In each case—Flaubert's and
Sena's—the parrot dies. Félicité sacralizes her parrot, praying to its
stuffed body; the adult narrator in Sena's story heroizes the boy's
parrot for him. Though it is no sacred bird (or Devil), the boy's
parrot brings him the word—if not the word of God then the cau-
tionary word of the world. Sometimes the green parrot speaks in
words unfamiliar to the boy or even in unknown tongues—what
the narrator calls "o reportório antigo": "Murmuradamente dizia de
enfiada coisas que eu nunca lhe ouvira, frases, ordens de navegação
e manobra, palavrões, palavras em línguas que eu não reconhecia."
What the narrator knows now, however, is that he learned what he
did not learn in school or the street, namely "os nobres palavrões
essenciais à vida, embora me ficasse, para aprender depois, algum
sentido deles." It is in his last sickness, as he is about to die, however,
that the green parrot reveals to the boy his secret of the world in
words that, in better times, we are told, the green parrot addressed
to "os vendedores que passavam na rua." It, or rather he—for, as
the narrator says, the green parrot "foi a primeira pessoa que eu vi
morrer"—imparts his worldly wisdom. "Filhos da puta!" are the
words Sena's profane parrot, mimicking the giver of tongues, shouts
in the boy's ear.[12] Significantly, these are the only words specifically
quoted by the narrator of the many words (especially "palavrões")
spoken by the parrot and overheard by the boy throughout the years
of his childhood and adolescence, and it is the only time the narrator
quotes them, although he tells us that he had heard the parrot speak
them at other times.[13]

2.

When, recently, I took up my working copy of *Os grão-capitães* to
reread once again "Homenagem ao Papagaio Verde" for the purpose
of writing this piece, I noticed that I had dated my acquisition of

the volume and my first reading of it as July 1980, a year and a half after the appearance, posthumously, of the second edition of *Os grão-capitães*. Moreover, following the date for the composition of the story "(Assis, 3-6-61 e Araraquara, 25-6-62)" that Jorge de Sena appended to his narrative, I had set down notations (somewhat pedantically) on my first reading: "The successful search for a father, the green parrot. A father, a guide, a parent, a 'guardian angel.' Through the parrot's *palavrões* (*filhos da puta*, its last words), something of a story of initiation. Initiation to language, attitudes, death (*morte da primeira pessoa*). Failure of the father, the family, the social structure (if c. 20th, then hangover from c. 19th)."

To these I might have added: Jorge de Sena exploits the literary paradigms of the search for the father, the father's return, and, as Francisco Fagundes subsequently indicated, the Oedipal rejection of the human father.[14] If one looks back through the "palavrão" *filho da puta*, one finds in it the seeds of the question of bastardy or legitimacy, not really familial but nationally historical. It is, in a manner of speaking, the legitimacy or, better, the honesty and integrity of the bourgeois family in early twentieth-century Portugal that Sena excoriates in this story. The story will not parrot the benevolent commonplaces about relationships within the family. In this house there are rooms set off by doors that are locked—especially (and ominously) the door to the parental bedroom—in the attempt to keep certain actions zealously private and, above all, secret. But the sounds of quarrelling are not contained by walls and locked doors, spilling out, as they do, for the entertainment of servants and the bemused edification of the child. If the parrot teaches the boy the "palavrões" essential to life, it is the father and mother, engaged in desperate connubial battles, who teach him, inadvertently, their meanings: "Aliás, este sentido eu ia aprendendo adivinhadamente nas discussões domésticas, à porta fechada, entre minha mãe e meu pai, quando ele, do outro lado da porta, os bradava, e muito explicados em frases elucidativas."[15]

Exposed in "Homenagem ao Papagaio Verde" are the seemingly endemic brutalities of home life. Every three months the merchant

marine captain who is the boy's father ("uma personagem mítica")
returns home from the sea, bearing gifts and purchases (presumably)
of fruits, wine, and fetishes from the various ports of call in Africa,
for a stay of two weeks at home with his wife and son. At the end of
his homeward journey through the streets of the city he greets his
conflicted son, formulaically—"Então como vai o nosso homem?"[16]
He approaches his wife in an awkward, but stylized way. "Parava ao
pé da minha mãe, sem jeito de abraçá-la. Ficavam assim diante um
do outro, a olharem-se, e eu erguendo os olhos por entre eles, até que
meu pai a agarrava pela cintura, o espaço entre ambos desaparecia,
e minha mãe deixava-se pousar a cabeça no ombro dele. Davam-se
então um beijo logo fugido," only to have his mother caution habit-
ually: "Olha o pequeno." The boy's parents repair to the sitting room
where they exchange information about the mother's relatives in
Africa and rehearse the business of the captain's laundry, the father
much of the time listening distractedly, "como uma visita de cer-
imónia," still wearing his hat, his hands resting on the curve of his
cane. This part of the father's ceremonial reentry into the house gives
way to a modicum of endearment when the mother "levantava-se,
como se fosse para despedi-lo, e tirava-lhe da cabeça o chapéu, e das
mãos a bengala." This is followed by a second and closer survey of
the commodities just brought into the hall, additional remarks about
his wife's relatives in Africa, and the father's first, abruptly sexual
move. "Meu pai," says the narrator, "agarrando minha mãe, começava
a arrastá-la para o quarto deles." The father disappears into the room
to await his wife who now busies herself in the kitchen, all the while
becoming more and more discombobulated, as her husband calls
from the bedroom. "A voz do meu pai vinha insistente, cada ver mais
berrada," says the narrator, until the father appears at the door "em
ceroulas de fitas e em fralda." When his wife appears before him
but fails to enter the room, he pulls her inside. Then, the narrator
remembers, "a chave rangia e estalava na fechadura." Significantly,
the narrative then returns to the green parrot and its characteristic
behavior. For the boy, it is as if, locked out of his parents' bedroom
during their periodic couplings, he turns to the one friend he can

count on: the green parrot. "Ninguém é meu amigo, ninguém é meu amigo," as he later says, "Só o Papagaio Verde é meu amigo." The brutality of conjugal sex in this family (representative, arguably, of sexual situations among the middle class of the day) is indicated, not by detailed descriptions of sexual practices, naturally, but by only what the boy would hear emanating from his parents' bedroom— screams, cries, recriminations—and would later see of his mother in tears and his father in anger and rage. Ultimately, this brutalized behavior leads to a scene of confrontation between the boy and his father, an episode that will be taken up later.

But first I would like to call attention to Sena's admiring remarks on the English novel that seem to me to factor somehow into his conception and intentions in his own "family" story. Samuel Butler's *The Way of All Flesh*, published in 1903, shortly after the author's death, has been described as "a thinly disguised account of his own upbringing aimed at exposing the self-righteous hypocrisy underlying Victorian family life and its bourgeois values."[17] Sena, in *A literatura inglesa* (1963), writes that in *The Way of All Flesh*, "[as] relações vitorianas entre pais e filhos . . . seriam objecto da ferocidade de Butler." "Este livro, cuja malignidade vingativa ainda hoje não desceu nas goelas britânicas," he continues,

é um dos grandes romances do século. O seu carácter autobiográfico é patente; e, apesar de, na viragem do séc. XIX, ter havido já, em arte e fora dela, escândalos suficientes, poucas vezes terá sido escrito um tão sangrento e minucioso requisitório das relações de uma família virtuosa, dominada pela religiosidade de um pastor que é a hipocrisia em pessoa. Vinte e tantos anos antes, quando ele fora escrito na hora própria, talvez não tivesse sido possível publicá-lo, tal a crueldade psicológica das suas análises, em que a observação do comportamento das personagens e a adivinhação das motivações que o condicionam se equilibram genialmente. Publicado em 1903, continuava a agredir os apóstolos da respeitabilidade, sem que atraísse devidamente a atenção das vanguardas, por lhe faltarem aqueles ingredientes de vício e de sexualidade, que o esteticismo e o naturalismo haviam posto em moda, indo às vezes muito menos ao fundo das coisas, na sua imitação escolar da literatura francesa da segunda metade do século.[18]

Mutatis mutandis, this is not a bad description of what Jorge de Sena intended to do for the nineteenth-century Lisbon of 1928 (the date he assigns to the events of "Homenagem ao Papagaio Verde"), with sexual violence clearly indicated if not displayed in detail.

3.

"Homenagem ao Papagaio Verde," which can be accurately described as the initial chapter in a Bildungsroman (more specifically, in a Künstlerroman), draws on the structures of both initiation and epiphany. The epiphany, much like Marlowe's in Joseph Conrad's *The Heart of Darkness*—with Kurtz's last words, "The horror, the horror"—obviously lies in the secret imparted by the dying parrot that they are "Filhos da puta!"[19] (It should be pointed out, by the way, that in the novel *Nostromo* Conrad introduces his own literary parrot: "A big green parrot, brilliant like an emerald in a cage that flashed like gold, screamed out ferociously, 'Viva Costaguana!' then called twice mellifluously, 'Leonarda! Leonarda!'"[20]) Not only does the parrot's phrase break open a mystery about humankind that the narrator (along with the author) deems significant enough to single it out of all the parrot's many utterances, but it provides the basis for an ethic and a style. As for initiation, the narrator unfolds a narrative that traces the boy's growing awareness of the true nature of his familial surroundings and his emotional and psychological maturity until he finds that he must rebel against his father's brutal authority. Indeed, with full knowledge and brandishing a knife, he "kills" his father (albeit symbolically) by kicking him in the testicles. Exploiting the psychological value of such a symbolic sacrifice, he substitutes the parrot's friendship and guidance for the father's hitherto unbridled authority. The narrator concludes his account: "A vida, desde então, não me esclareceu muito; mas creio firmemente que, se há anjos-da-guarda, o meu tem asas verdes, e sabe, para consolar-me nas horas mais amargas, os mais rudes palavrões dos sete mares." If this conclusion about the parrot's role in the life of the man who was son to the boy is strangely reminiscent of Félicité's attitude in Flaubert's story toward her own green parrot, there is one great difference. The boy's green parrot's speech, even more than his free-wheeling behavior within and without his cage, is the determinant factor in the life of the fictional boy who would become the fictional author narrating his own fictionally autobiographical tale.

4.

It is a gigantic parrot as paraclete, it will be recalled, that Flaubert's dying domestic servant thinks she sees hovering above her head at the moment of her death. Jorge de Sena has left us no story, comparable to Flaubert's "A Simple Heart," to tell us what the fictional narrator of "Homenagem ao Papagaio Verde" sees or thinks he sees when he comes to die. If the remembered example of the green parrot has sustained him throughout his adult life, as the story's narrator implies, we simply do not know it in the usual way, that is, through another story. Yet it may be surmised that the narrator's life, down to its final months or days, is documented not in Jorge de Sena's fiction but in "Morreu Dom Fuas," one of the poet's very last poems, an elegy for his cat. It will be recalled that at the very beginning of "Homenagem ao Papagaio Verde," the narrator refers to "uma galeria indistinta e confusa de gatos tigrados . . . e todos chamados 'Mimosos' tão onomasticamente como os papas são Pios." Not one of these cats, however, can aspire to "o mais arcaico lugar reservado a uma personalidade animal"—the place reserved for the green parrot. But the Mimosos of the story had given way (in the author's life) to Dom Fuas, it seems; and this cat among animals, now dead, claims his own elegy.

Sena's accounts of the essential qualities of a peerless animal should not be entirely unfamiliar to his readers, for it is presaged in its account of the solitary death suffered by a proud, larger-than-life being, both in the elegy, written in 1972, "À memória de Adolfo

Casais Monteiro"—which begins: "Como se morre, Adolfo? Tu morreste" and ends: "creio que foi pouco / oh muito pouco o que a morte foi capaz de te ensinar"—and in "Homenagem ao Papagaio Verde" itself, even if not one of the many Mimosos—all those cats— merits the poignant attention of the poet, though presumably each one of them has also died in its time.[21] The sorrowful kudos is reserved for the green parrot. Consider this account, partly in the form of a description of the "Papagaio Cinzento," whose cage is in the front parlor:

Este, menos esplendoroso e menos corpulento, menos vaidoso também das suas cores baças, morreu depois do Verde, ave grande, vistosa, transbordante de presunção e dignidade . . . De resto, o Cinzento era sujeito retraído e friorento, que ficava encolhido a resmonear o reportório variado, sem manifestar por alguém qualquer predilecção afectiva; tinha apenas de simpático o olhar nostálgico, melancólico, e a mansidão muito dócil do resignado e acorrentado escravo. O Verde, pelo contrário, era exuberante, de amizades apaixonadas e de ódios vesgos, sem continuidade nem obstinação. Minto: essas amizades e ódios, não continuados nem firmes, faziam parte do seu carácter expansivo e espectacular.

If the boy's early teacher—an exemplary "human being"—was the bird (consider the overlap in the words *papa*, *papá*, *papagaio*) who speaks not in a vale of tears but in this "reino da estupidez," the man's last teacher is the silent, ducal, imperious, but equally exemplary, tomcat. What, then—to end on a question—is one to make of the mature author's desire to spend his posthumous days, sipping coffee and swapping stories with the mythical half man, half beast who is the Minotaur?

4

An "Eichmann" Story

Written in 1961, Jorge de Sena's "Defesa e justificação de um ex-criminoso de guerra (das memórias de Herr Werner Stupnein, ex-oficial superior das S.S.)" first achieved print in *Novas andanças do demónio* in 1966.

1. Notes on Background and Context

On April 4, 1961, the Adolf Eichmann trial opened in Jerusalem to the great interest of an international audience. A week later, in *O Estado de São Paulo*, Luís Martins's daily column, featured a piece on Eichmann under the title "O assassino de milhões."[1] Martins had just read a biography of Eichmann and was shaken by the experience. "A book like Comer Clarke's gives one nightmares and the horribly discouraging feeling that we live in a world where such atrocities do not belong to the fictitious hell of sadistic literature, but that they happened, my God, they happened yesterday, and no one can guarantee that they cannot be repeated tomorrow." He himself was never a partisan supporter of capital punishment, but in Eichmann's case, Martins explains, he would not only support a death penalty but would go further: "I would applaud torture, without any pangs of conscience, I swear, even the most barbaric, savage, necessary torture." It is in this very stance, these extreme feelings, he implies, that we see how the Nazi camps have dehumanized us. "Finally," he concludes, "all of us, everyone, good persons are also victims of Belsen, of Dachau, and of Auschwitz." And even before the historical fact of Eichmann's defense that he was merely the vessel and instrument for the carrying out of orders from his superiors, Martins decides: "The truth is that he consciously integrated himself—and nothing compelled him to do so—in Hitleristic politics, identifying himself with its doctrines and its methods of action. And the mass assassination of the Jews he planned and executed with a genuine enthusiasm that was diabolical, implacable and meticulous. He took pleasure in killing. He was proud of what he had done."

On April 19, 1961, Martins reproduced in his daily column the contents of a letter he had received from Jorge de Sena, writing from Assis, in reaction to his column on Eichmann.[2] Sena praised Martins for his courage in adopting a hard, unsentimental line toward Eichmann and his crimes against humanity, calling for his execution (and torture). He applauded particularly Martins's insight when he concludes: "Finally all of us, everyone, good persons, are also victims of Belsen, of Dachau, and of Auschwitz. Nazi infamy deformed a whole generation." Taking up this idea, Sena cries out: "Undoubtedly the most terrible thing, and that which must be stamped out, is that assent by good people to degradation, which makes them desire punishments that are as horrible as the crimes themselves."

Less than three weeks later, on May 7, 1961, Sena set down, at one fell swoop evidently, his "Eichmann" story. I put the phrase "Eichmann" within quotation marks because only in a genetic sense is this a story about Eichmann, for the name Eichmann nowhere appears in it and the massacres in the death camps in no explicit way figure in the story. Indeed, Sena's indictment of Hitler's ideologies and the barbaric Nazi behavior they gave birth to is given great power through his calculated omission of Eichmann and the Jews.

2. Further Circumstances

The dateline Sena appends to this story is "Assis, 7 May 1961." The trial in Jerusalem of Adolf Eichmann, which was to last until December 1961, began on April 11 of that year, which is to say, less than a month before Sena wrote his story. Sena, who was still in Brazil, having arrived in 1959, was undoubtedly aware of the many rumors circulating throughout the world, but particularly in Brazil and other South American countries, that ex-Nazis were scattered throughout the continent. Eichmann's abduction in a suburb of Buenos Aires on the evening of May 11, 1960, brought considerable credence to those rumors, for here was one notorious ex-Nazi who had been living under an assumed name with his wife and children in Argentina. Even as there would be further credence, years later, when it was discovered that Josef Mengele, Auschwitz's "Angel of Death," had lived and died in São Paulo, the very state in Brazil in which Sena lived from 1959 to 1965. One could readily infer from the date of its composition, that the Eichmann capture and trial, the whole of it lasting nineteen months, was the germ for Sena's story, even if we did not know about Luís Martins's column and the letter from Sena it evoked. But there was also something else percolating in Sena's brain. On June 17, 1961, there appeared a piece by Sena in the literary supplement of *O Estado de São Paulo*. The piece, ostensibly, has nothing to do with Eichmann or Sena's story, but there are at least two intertextual connections that are of some interest. The piece, collected in *O reino da estupidez* (1961), is entitled "O culto do 'autêntico' ou a crítica pelo buraco da fechadura."[3] The title of the article does not do justice to the far-ranging examination of "authenticity" and its modern uses that the piece actually performs. It is not without relevance that Sena's story ends with a reference to a "more authentic future." I shall come back to this essay.

On June 11, 1961, Sena wrote another first-person account, this time a poem, "Camões dirige-se aos seus contemporâneos."[4] Here are the words of a victim, not those, as is the case in "Defesa e

justificação . . . ," of the authoritarian oppressor. Both the poem and
the story, coming at it from opposite sides, bring up the matter of
the exercise of authority and resulting injustices. It may have been
around this time that Sena wrote his essay "Maquiavel e o 'Príncipe,'" in which he asserts that Machiavelli's great gift to man was
that he "restored to him his responsible dignity," and he did this by
"taking away from him the excuse to attribute to himself the right
to be monstrous on a grand scale."[5] No longer allowed to look outward or upward for external sanctions on his behavior, man was now
responsible to himself for his everyday and his ultimate actions. It
was a call for a bare humanism that would cause man to see himself
as he is. Machiavelli practiced what he preached, in proclaiming that
"all things human must be studied as they are and not as they should
be." At first blush, one might say that Sena's "ex–war criminal" is
merely following to an extreme Machiavelli's principles. But one
comes to realize that his monstrosity is not the result of Machiavellian humanism (however arid that humanism might become in
the extreme) but of the tragically misplaced faith in a stronger, if not
higher, power: the "German ethic," in which "what is moral is the
conjunction of practical rules, worked out through the experience of
the species in its selective battle to survive and to conquer." From the
point of view of the humanist, this is monstrosity on a grand scale;
from the point of view of one who would follow the teachings of the
Führer, this is the fulfillment of biological and racial destiny.

For Sena, to whom "nothing human was alien"—including the
beliefs and behavior of an "ex–war criminal" like his memoirist,
one must presume—Eichmann and his fellow criminals must have
posed an extreme test. In short, the artist in Sena worked as a true
Machiavellian, describing and dramatizing his criminal as he was
and is. But the humanist in Sena, who is not unlike the humanist he
finds in Machiavelli himself in his other writings, especially when he
is not being "objectively" descriptive of behavior—it was not Machiavelli's fault that he was blamed for prescribing a form of behavior
that was in existence, as he well knew, long before his own lifetime

and (there was Machiavellianism before Machiavelli, Sena notes)—
could not help but keep his apologizing memoirist at arm's length.
Sena's true judgment of the Nazi criminals can be readily inferred
from something he had written before the capture of Eichmann
in 1960. The poem "Carta a meus filhos sobre os Fuzilamentos de
Goya" is dated "Lisbon, 25 June 59"; the entire poem is relevant, but I
shall limit myself to quoting only a few lines:

> there is no counting the number of those . . .
> who loved their fellow-creatures for what made them
> unique, uncommon, free, and different,
> and who were sacrificed, tortured, beaten,
> and delivered hypocritically to secular justice,
> so that they could be liquidated with "the greatest pity and no
> bloodshed."
> For having been faithful to a god, to a thought,
> to a country, to a hope, or to nothing more than
> the unanswerable hunger that gnawed at their insides,
> they were eviscerated, flayed, torched, gassed,
> and their bodies stacked up anonymously, even as they had lived,
> and their ashes dispersed so that no memory of them would survive.
> Sometimes for belonging to a race, at other times
> to a particular class, they expiated
> all the errors they had not committed or had no awareness of
> having committed.[6]

Here the poet is concerned with globalizing victimization of individual human beings down through history, rather than the group
singled out in Goya's startling painting. And though it might be
legitimately inferred that the reference to those who were "gassed"
identifies the Jews (and gypsies, as well as some others, though the
Jews so victimized predominated by a huge margin in numbers),
Sena is really concerned with the crimes against humanity everywhere and overall for whatever reason or in whatever cause. It is this
concern with seeing Nazi criminality on the largest human scale, and

not as a crime against primarily the Jews, but as a crime against the very essence of what makes a human being human, that must have impelled him to write his story about a functionary near the Russian front who practiced his indecencies against a civilian population of Slavs and Ukrainians but a population that is never identified racially. It is enough that the Nazis considered those populations inferior in every way to the Germans, that it was therefore impossible for them to share in the German ethic. Remember that the memoirist, even in his utterly safe retirement (though criminal and war courts have found him guilty of crimes, they did not find him guilty, he is quick to point out, for his beliefs and ideas), continues to believe that he was part of "one of the highest and most legitimate culminations of human consciousness (as well as conscience) on the way to its most authentic future."[7] But in "Letter to My Children" Sena had put his objection to all such ideological rationalization for murder: "Believe it, that no world, that nothing or no one / is worth more than one life and the joy of having that life. / This is what most matters—that joy. Who will resuscitate those millions, who will restore / not only their lives, but all that was taken from them? / No Last Judgment, my children, can give them / the instant they did not live, that goal / they did not bring to fruition, the gesture / of love they would have made 'tomorrow.'" The poet ends with the statement that each one of us is the guardian "of the love / that others did not love because it was stolen from them." Interestingly enough, "Camões Addresses His Contemporaries" begins with an imprecation: "Rob me blind." It is the theft of that "humanity" that is that "joy," whether that theft be from a Camões or an unknown, merely numbered Ukrainian on the bloody path to the battle of Stalingrad, that Sena sees as the highest of crimes against mankind.

3. First Person

One of the marvels of this story is that Sena could so thoroughly channel his repugnance at what the Nazis did into the dramatization of a Nazi's mind as it unfolds itself, not in remorse or as a confession of culpability, but as an unabashed account of what he did and what he believed and still believes. Nowhere does Sena break the illusion that the memoirist is speaking in order to point an authorial moral or draw a conclusion. Actually, it is an astonishing fact that a reader who held fast to the same ideology expressed by the memoirist would find nothing to disagree with in the story. This show of authorial restraint, this ability to get within his own imagined character and to stay within that mind, never once to stray toward an extranarrative evaluation or final judgment, could not have come easily to a writer who said of himself, in his preface (1977) to *Poesia—II*, that to him "what is most important" is "the comprehension of freedom, justice, and human dignity, for which I have always fought in prose and poetry, as in life."[8] Only the writer's pleasure in creating and in getting something down exactly right in the words natural to the thing itself could account for the energy in the ex–war criminal's fascistic claim: "I never preached freedom, but order; I never preached equality, but hierarchy; I never preached brotherhood, but the free arbitrariness of the race that has purified itself so as to have it." In fact, he continues, "What the next person does cannot be indifferent to us, because our only reason for being derives from that ascendant and selective sense of Life. Democratic indifference blindly and criminally ignores the ludic character of cruelty, one of the most innocent manifestations of the vital instinct. A child that tortures a bird, a cat that plays with a rat—that's ethical. It is the only ethic." Now, even Hitler in *Mein Kampf* had come up short of employing the pleasure principle as inherent in his ethic of superiority, oppression, and racial evolution. When Hitler said merely (and I astonish myself by having to write that "merely"): "No fox will ever be found possessed of a fancy after the human manner with regard to a goose, just as likewise no cat exists with a friendly inclination towards mice," he had in mind, not any ludic element, but that the great truth of Nature, according to the Führer, was that "every animal pairs exclusively with a mate of the same species as itself."[9] "If it does otherwise," writes Wyndham Lewis (who in 1931 was writing to understand Hitler, he said, not to attack or support him), "Nature registers her protest by causing her offspring to be barren, or else by robbing them of Widerstandsfähigheit, against sickness or enemy attack."[10] Sena's memoirist went further, of course, seeing that for human beings pleasure was not to be divorced from the imperative to follow Nature's own ethic, but that it was the natural human development of the superior race. But to return to the memoirist's notions about "the next person." In his essay on "The Cult of the 'Authentic'" Sena had defined his own contrary position: "outside of the democratic criteria of freedom and responsibility for everyone, no one has, or should have, anything to do with the relative 'serenity' of the next person, so long as that person does not interfere with one's own serenity (and even this interference should not be understood as being on the plane of repugnance which, like non-repugnance, will be, among well-balanced individuals, personal and untransmittable)."[11] Obviously, this statement about the rights of others in a democracy comments on the ex–war criminal's totalitarian position on the rights of the individual to freedom and privacy. Sena's position is not explicit in his story, but we are to infer it from what is, for most of Sena's readers, one presumes, the ex–war criminal's obnoxious defense of "interference" with the next person as a right and duty of the "higher" race that has so purified itself that it has earned them.

4. To Kill or Not to Kill

What might be an important question in the judgment of any SS official, whether Adolf Eichmann or Sena's fictional memoirist, when translated into the past tense—did they kill or did they not kill—is answered significantly in the very same way by both the historical Eichmann (whose favorite occupation, incidentally, was to write his "memoirs") and by the fictional Herr Werner Stupnein.[12] Their statements are interchangeable. Eichmann, who was accused of killing millions of Jews, replied: "With the killing of Jews I had nothing to do. I never killed any human being. I never gave an order to kill either a Jew or a non-Jew; I just did not do it."[13] Sena's fictional memoirist, who was accused of "having personally directed the assassination of 2754 creatures of both sexes of various ages and races," replies: "I never assassinated anyone, directly or indirectly. During my administration there died, under differing circumstances, and in accordance with the administrative principles that were not unknown to the enemies of the Reich who never openly condemned them, 1893 creatures of the human genus." In broadening the charge—that is, to accuse his ex–war criminal of killing various people (and not just, or primarily, Jews), Sena anticipates Hannah Arendt's position, namely, that Eichmann's crime was really against all mankind and that it should have been so construed from the outset for both legal and moral purposes. That Eichmann and the other Nazis committed their crimes against humankind and that that would have been their greatest crime even had they killed only Jews or only gypsies or only Slavs is a position that Sena, acting consistently, would have sustained. We can certainly infer this from the poem "Carta a meus filhos sobre os Fuzilamentos de Goya." His words would not have been in disagreement, I think, with those words that would conclude Arendt's book *Eichmann in Jerusalem*, in which she addressed (the now-dead) Eichmann:

> Let us assume, for the sake of argument, that it was nothing more than misfortune that made you a willing instrument in the organization of mass murder; there still remains the fact that you have carried out, and therefore actively supported, a policy of mass murder. For politics is not like the nursery; in politics obedience and support are the same. And just as you supported and carried out a policy of not wanting to share the earth with the Jewish people and the people of a number of other nations—as though you and your superiors had any right to determine who should and who should not inhabit the world—we find that no one, that is, no member of the human race, can be expected to want to share the earth with you. This is the reason, and the only reason, you must hang.[14]

5. The Ex–War Criminal's Library

One of the striking discoveries made by Arendt was that Eichmann was a perfectly ordinary human being, with no pretensions to education or to high culture. In fact, he (and so many others like him) was "terribly and terrifyingly normal."[15] Sena's memoirist, on the other hand, does not consider himself to be ordinary in any way. He sees himself as superior to his fellow SS officers. He is not guilty (as was Eichmann himself) of "Rassenschaude, sexual intercourse with Jews . . . probably the greatest crime a member of the SS could commit."[16] As he says, "I never harbored secret passions for Jewish women or Jewish boys, something that not all of my superiors, or my rival, could boast of. [. . .] My purity of blood was beyond any suspicion whatsoever." And he considers himself superior, even to his fellow officers, in that he possesses a library, actually two libraries: the main one that he must leave behind in Berlin when he is sent to the Russian theater of war, and the smaller one—a selection of his books from the larger library in Berlin—that he has packed and sent on to Liublionovgrad. The selective, smaller library disappears. It never reaches him, and now, years later, he still laments its loss, even as he laments the loss of the main library, which, he would learn later, was destroyed in the Berlin bombings. What one day does arrive in Liublionovgrad, instead of his carefully packed boxes of personal books, is a truck full of boxes containing other books, copies of *Mein Kampf*, volumes of the Führer's speeches, works by Rosenberg (Hitler's theorist of race), and books by others, writers such as Ernest Junger (whom he admits admiring). The books are all in German, he observes. There is an implied complaint in this observation in that it is made by a man who finds himself to be culturally superior to all those under his command. "What did I want with all that," he asks, "instead of my cherished companions, my books?" Sena does not have his memoirist reveal any of the titles in his personal library. We are to infer only that it is the library of a cultured man, a cultured man who, it might be inferred from his disappointment that the books sent him were all in one language (even if that language is German), has access to books written in languages other than his own. I am reminded of a television interview in Brazil at the time of the discovery that Josef Mengele had lived and died in the state of São Paulo. Among those interviewed was a man who had permitted Mengele to live in his house for some few years. He had not known who his tenant was, he claimed, but he had always enjoyed and profited from sharing his quarters with him. His tenant was obviously a man of learning and great culture, he insisted, and talking with him over the years had always been informative and enlightening. All this he said with an equanimity that would seem to belie the facts about the identity of his tenant that were then being sensationally revealed in the newspapers, on radio, and on television. Would his attitude toward his tenant have been different at the time had he known his true identity? he was asked. No, he answered. Did the new revelations change his attitude now? No, he again answered. Obviously, this man had known one Mengele, the one with the engaging voice that spoke to him of knowledge and culture. He had not known the voice of the "Angel of Death" at Auschwitz. It is this astonishingly clear-cut cultural and moral schizophrenia in the Nazi character—the embodiment of a high refinement and the atavistic reversion to unconscionable murder—that Sena has so well captured and dramatized.

6. Sex and Rape

One of the major problems facing the Nazi commandant of Liublionovgrad, recalls the memoirist, was the unavailability of women to satisfy the sexual needs of the men under his command. He found no women in the fullness of life or of nubile age. Bringing in German women was of course out of the question, since "German morality most justly did not permit, except for copulations destined eugenically for the production and propagation of a superior and authentic race, that our young German women constitute such an auxiliary corps for the military." To solve his problem he hit on what was to him the happy device of the "hunt"—"carefully organized, prolonged, artful expeditions that inebriated my men and which, I confess, I very much liked to conduct personally." He tells generally of those forays in search of vessels appropriate to the sexual use of German men. He boasts of never being tempted, except once. And on that occasion he could not resist raping a fifteen-year-old girl, "dirty and in rags, but with what eyes, what breasts!" Apparently he is immediately attracted to her but what takes him beyond his resolve never to engage in the rapes attendant to these periodic "hunts" is that while his two "companions" are holding her, she is incontinent, the urine running down her legs. With the help of his companions, who hold the girl down, the commandant rapes her; and then, out of "fairness" to his underlings, he makes her available to them. Even now, years later, he remembers that despite the fact that she had to be held up by his men, that her clothing was fully in tatters, and that she was in tears, he nevertheless saw that "in her eyes, illuminated by the golden, green, orange light of the sunset, which lit up the steppe, there was a new splendor: such is the revelatory power of sex, when it is carried out by superior men, free from sentimental scruples." The incident illustrates perfectly the memoirist's point, spelled out elsewhere, that whatever acts are performed against (or even with) individuals of the lower orders are fully within the German ethic. No one of the lower orders can be depraved by such actions, because from "the point of view of biology and philosophy, such depravity and such degradation" is not "possible." This single instance of rape recalls, in a way, the reports that once and only once did Eichmann kill a Jew. He coldly shot a child—a male—to show a subaltern how and what needed to be done. It does not matter that the prosecution was never able to prove that the incident with the Jewish child ever took place. What is important, for us, is that the fictional rape and the putative shooting both serve as a "showing of the way" by superior SS officers.

7. Gilles de Rais

Part of the memoirist's rationalizations involve sexuality, that of his men, as we have seen, and that of himself. I shall not go very much into the way in which Sena brilliantly handles his German officer's thinking on the subject, but some things can be pointed to. The nub of his principles on the matter is that what might be seen by some persons as perverted sexual relations when occurring between German and German—those of client and prostitute, male and male, adult and child—do not at all signal perversion when they occur between a German and someone of a lower order. "It is a crime for one German to harm another pure German, who, like him has an equal right to contribute to and participate in this progress," he claims—"the progressive evolution of the human species, represented by the destiny of the Germans." What those beings of the lower orders did among themselves, of course, did not matter unless they brought about public scandal by their publicity or through excesses. It is with a show of admirable equanimity, he would have us believe, that he handled one case of a sadist who was guilty of gross exaggeration in his appetite for small children. What he was doing to them was not in itself reprehensible, it seems—"he consumed three to four children per week, by the Chinese method of 'ducks and geese,' or, if you will, that of the Marshal of France, Gilles de Rais, a precursor of genius, to whom was lacking both the culture and historical moment." The mention of Gilles de Rais (1404–1440) is resonant, for at his trial Rais was called "a heretic, an apostate, a sorcerer, a sodomite, an evoker of evil spirits, a diviner, a torturer and murderer of innocent children, a criminal, a backslider and an idolater who has deviated from the faith and who is illy disposed toward it."[17] (It is only as a torturer and murderer of children, however, that Rais is invoked admiringly by the German ex–war criminal.) Here is an excerpt from the testimony against him:

> Gilles de Rais abused these boys and girls in the heat of his lust in a unnatural manner according to his abominable custom: first he took his own penis or virile member in one or the other of his hands, rubbed it or stretched it out, then put it between the thighs or legs of these boys and girls while avoiding the natural vessel of the girls; he rubbed his penis or virile member on the belly of these boys and

girls with great pleasure, ardor and depraved concupiscence until he emitted his sperm on their belly. . . . Before Gilles de Rais perpetrated these shameful acts with the said boys and girls, he sometimes hanged them himself while at others he had someone else hang them by the neck with a rope in his room and left them for a brief time hanging from a hook in order to keep them from shouting or to prevent any shouts from being heard; that then he took them down or had them taken down and cajoled them or pretended to comfort them; that he claimed that he did not want them to be hurt or for them to receive any harm, that, on the contrary, he had only been playing with them; and that in this way he kept them from crying out.

After Gilles had done this, he shamefully, horribly and disgracefully committed with these boys and girls the sin of luxury, as described above, and consequently he murdered them or had them murdered.[18]

Now, it is interesting that the German concentration and Nazi murder camps are never mentioned by Sena's memoirist. Such references are strategically left out of the story. But that they were on Sena's mind at the time, naturally enough given the continued publicity the Eichmann trial received, is evident from a paragraph in Sena's essay on the cult of "authenticity," written and published, as we have seen, at just about the same time as the story. Remember that throughout Sena talks ostensibly about tendencies and practices in literary criticism:

> Recently the situation has changed. All that was *piquant* in literary criticism, the opportunity for each one to exhibit his largeness of spirit, his moral neutrality in matters of aesthetics, almost completely dissolved itself. Wilde, Proust, Gide all lost their attractiveness and turned themselves into the most intolerably bourgeois banality. And it became necessary for the romantic myth of the exceptional— despite the sumptuous banquet that were, in every way, the Nazi concentration camps—to discover Jean Genet, resuscitate the Marquis de Sade, and to publish in their entirety the proceedings of the trial of the "Constable" of France, Gilles de Rais, the Bluebeard of history, not of legend.[19]

Here again Sena refers to Gilles de Rais as a murderer, which the memoirist sees as aberrational only when the perpetrator of such horrors has acted excessively, "having forgotten," as the memoirist says, "that supplies (of such children) were not limitless and which circumstances did not permit organization of production on a large scale, and having forgotten as well of the solidarity he owed to those others interested in the same style of gratification." It will be recalled that it was Eichmann's job to so organize the collecting of human beings and the shipping of them to the death camps that those interested in that particular kind of murderous gratification would be satisfied. It is significant, too, that Sena, long before Hannah Arendt subtitled her work on Eichmann's trial as "A Report on the Banality of Evil," should have used the word "banality" in conjunction with the "romantic myth of the exceptional" that should have been monstrously satisfied with the sumptuous feasts of the death camps, but apparently was not. What Sena does not make explicit either in his essay or his story is that Gilles de Rais was deeply involved in the black arts, that is to say, he was of Satan's party. Obviously, a direct reference to Satan would be out of keeping in the first-person memoir of an unrepentant ex–war criminal, but the reference to Rais puts the Black Man there nevertheless, if silently. The most recent edition in English of the testimony at the trials of Gilles de Rais is entitled *Laughter for the Devil.* The phrase might serve as Sena's judgment of the murderous ideology the memoirist will espouse boastfully, it is apparent, until the day of his death.

8. First Word

Liublionovgrad, the city in which the memoirist has spent his World War II command, is a place in the Ukraine ("a miserable city"). A quick check of the atlas does not turn up any such city. If there was no such city in the early 1940s (to that extent the past was illusory), then the last word of the story, "future," may also be something illusory. Whether made up or not, however, Liublionovgrad would seem to have been a city well on the road to Stalingrad. As such, it would have been taken during the German offensive and actually, as the memoirist observes, "overrun" by the army. The memoirist commands, then, a force of occupation. He is an administrator rather than a frontline soldier. He is, in fact, as he claims proudly, "a competent and dedicated functionary," adding that his "purity of blood was beyond any suspicion." As the commandant administering the occupied city, he sees as his job both the carrying out of orders and the rationalizing of those orders in accordance with his ideological beliefs, which were always in line with the teachings of the Führer. Even now, years later and long after everything about the Führer's plans for the Third Reich has been historically washed away, he writes:

> Now that everything has passed away, I can acknowledge what I always knew: how insufficient the teachings of the Führer were without his magical presence. What a cheap philosophy for such grand destiny! The truth is, though, that if that philosophy were more expensive, it would not have enraptured, as it did, so many of those idiots, those inferior to me. I, in effect, accepted it as an act of intelligence, recognizing in it and valuing it by the importance with which it was imbued, elaborating it to its extremes—that which it did not reach— of logical dignity.

9. Epigraph

"Afraid? Of whom am I afraid?" is the first line of a poem, as the author says, by Emily Dickinson, the nineteenth-century American poet. There are two questions to start out with. Why does the author quote the line in English, especially when he knows English not only well enough to read it but to translate it? Indeed, as early as 1961 (the year in which "Defense and Justification" was written), Sena was announcing as "in press" a book of translations entitled *61 poemas de Emily Dickinson*.[20] (By the time the book appeared, posthumously, in 1979, its title was changed to *80 poemas de Emily Dickinson*.) And why does the author quote only the first line of what is a twelve-line, three-stanza poem? (The entire poem appears in translation in *80 poemas.*) If the epigraph asks a question that the memoirist might himself ask and then answer, it is fitting that only the first line be quoted, for Dickinson's poem goes on bravely to consider what the poet might fear, all the while denying that she has anything whatsoever to fear. Should she fear death? Life? Resurrection? No, not any of them because hers is a poem of consolation and promise:

> Afraid! Of whom am I afraid?
> Not Death—for who is He?
> The Porter of my Father's Lodge
> As much abasheth me!
>
> Of life? Twere odd I fear (a) thing
> That comprehendeth me
> In one or two existences—
> Just as the case may be—
>
> Of Resurrection? Is the East
> Afraid to trust the Morn
> With her fastidious forehead?
> As soon impeach my Crown![21]

Here, of course, is a statement of belief in a God, that is to say, belief in something external to the strictly humanist experience. As a poem of faith, these lines put all trust in things as they are: the existence and necessity of death, the naturalness, understandingly, of life that "comprehendeth" the self in the two existences—here and the hereafter, with the possibility of the second, eternal life. Sena's memoirist shows no sign that he will consider even the possibility that there is a power beyond the power of the proper evolution of the human race, that is, of the evolution of the German people properly understood. Given his unflinching commitment to that evolutionary principle for the German people and his conviction that he has embodied it in its purest form, he fears nothing, he fears no one. His religious instinct, unlike Dickinson's, is satisfied by his commitment to a greater force (and concomitant cause): the purification of the

German people. Sena's memoirist puts it squarely: "The dilemma of this world . . . consists in knowing if there is any natural sanction that militates against the affirmation of a biological supremacy. I firmly believe that there is not."

10. Title

The title is a trifle ambiguous. Intentionally so. Let us recall, first of all, that the story is written in the first person, not as a confession (which would have made it Poe-like or Dostoyevsky-like) but as a memoir of a particular period in the ex-officer's life in the Russian theater cum revelations of his personality and expressions of his ideology. As a memoir it need not ipso facto be either a defense or a justification, and in fact this memoir functions more as an explanation (apologia) for actions taken rather than thoughts Mr. Werner Stupnein still believes in though it has been years since he was a high official in Hitler's SS. It is a nice touch to reflect in the title the memoirist's own attitudes by calling him an ex–war criminal. A question occurs. When does a (war) criminal become an ex– (war) criminal? Perhaps the phrase is intended to reflect the memoirist's own view of the matter. But no. Nothing in his statement suggests that he has ever thought of himself, either during his service in the Ukraine or at any time thereafter, as a criminal. He is not only not repentant, but he does not think that he has ever done anything to be repentant about. He lives at the end with undaunted sureness that, even if others have fallen away from the high cause of the Third Reich, he "shall die certain and confident that he was one of the highest and most legitimate culminations of human conscience, on the way to his most authentic future." Subsequent history—take Kurt Waldheim as an example—has done nothing to shake the accuracy of Jorge de Sena's zeroing-in on the essential nature of the mentality of the "ex–war criminal."

5

The Case for Camões

Camões sem comemorações, necessárias a vários outros respeitos, é
para nós mesmos neste momento, como nós seremos mais tarde ou
mais cedo, uma sombra . . .

—Óscar Lopes (1995)[1]

José Régio was asked to take the time to travel to Lisbon to record
some of his poetry for dissemination at the International Colloquium on Luso-Brazilian Studies scheduled to take place in Washington, DC, in October 1950.[2] The much-esteemed writer refused
to do so. He was not disposed to do any such thing, he informed
Adolfo Casais Monteiro, his erstwhile colleague in the editing of
the journal *presença*, who had decided, mistakenly, it turned out,
that Régio's reluctance to participate in the venture was due to his
proverbial shyness or timidity. Under renewed pressure, Régio felt
obligated to elaborate on his reasons for refusing:

> Embora obscuramente (e tanto melhor se um bocadinho de populari-
> dade do meu nome pudesse tornar tal reacção menos obscura!), lutarei
> contra certas *americanices* do mundo moderno. Pois Você pensa que
> esses discos poderão, *realmente*, contribuir para qualquer *real* interesse

da América pela nossa Literatura? Poderão ser *real* testemunho de tal interesse?! Deus me valha! A única maneira eficaz, autêntica, séria, de os Estados Unidos manifestarem qualquer interesse pela nossa Literatura—seria juntar, nas suas Bibliotecas, livros nossos, (como, aliás, creio que em parte estão fazendo); depois promover a expansão, por todos os meios, desses livros: mas uma expansão real, fundada no seu conhecimento, e não em reclames que dispensam o conhecimento da própria coisa reclamada, e, sobretudo, traduzir aqueles dos nossos livros que disso fossem julgados dignos, e espalhar essas traduções. . . . Isto sim, será obra séria; *seria* obra séria.[3]

Echoing countless numbers of writers before him—in Portugal and, of course, elsewhere—Régio makes his point. Reader neglect, though not just abroad—other countries, other languages—is the durable theme and chronic complaint of poets and writers in all languages. In Régio's case, over a half century since he voiced his complaint, his work is virtually unknown in the United States, apart from academic circles, and then only, one suspects, by those professionally involved with the literature of Portuguese expression. Surely such complaints have lost some of their force in Fernando Pessoa's case, at least in recent decades, which have seen an impressive growth of interest in the United States. And in all fairness, they cannot be made about Camões, especially not beginning with the early nineteenth century. For although it is true that Camões has never been much celebrated in the United States (at least not ceremonially or in pageant-like fashion), it is equally true that Camões and his major work have been more widely appreciated than is commonly thought.

As I have tried to show elsewhere, principally in *The Presence of Camões: Influences on the Literature of England, America, and Southern Africa*, published in 1996, while Camões's work was known to writers working in the English language in the seventeenth and eighteenth centuries, it was in the nineteenth century that his work was most influential. In that century he was read by, among others, Joel Barlow, Edgar Allan Poe, Herman Melville, Henry Wadsworth Longfellow, Thomas Wentworth Higginson, Walt Whitman,

Emily Dickinson, and Richard Henry Wilde (a poet and scholar who not only translated some of Camões's sonnets but also wrote an important book on Camões's kindred spirit, Torquato Tasso). Remarkably, however, there was no full translation of *Os Lusíadas* published in the United States until the exact middle of the twentieth century, when the Hispanic Society of America brought out the fine version by the poet-critic Leonard Bacon. And while there are dozens of poetic tributes to Camões in English, only Melville, Kermit Roosevelt, and Leonard Bacon, among the Americans, have been identified to date as having written poems about Camões. As for public celebrations of the third centennial, there was certainly not only nothing to compare with what took place in the British Empire, Brazil, or elsewhere, but there was simply none whatsoever. Searches of the major newspapers and journals of the day turn up nothing regarding such celebrations. A search of Portuguese-language newspapers should turn up information regarding utterly local commemorations in social clubs or the like if any commemorations took place.

In the Romance and modern language departments of a small handful of universities, things were somewhat better. (Although it must be said, parenthetically, that there seem to have been precious few doctoral dissertations devoted to Camões in their entirety or in appreciable part defended in American universities. A quick count of the titles contained in the most complete listing to date of doctoral dissertations on Portuguese themes in United States universities turned up, as of mid-1995, only three certainties, and in one of those three, the name of Camões does not appear in the title.)[4] As a professor of languages teaching at Harvard University in the 1840s, the poet Henry Wadsworth Longfellow had anthologized both Camões's lyric poetry and, in excerpt, his epic poem. His impressively inclusive (for the time) *Poets and Poetry of Europe* was first published in 1845 in Philadelphia and achieved several additional printings throughout the rest of the century.

In the late nineteenth and early twentieth century both Yale University and Harvard University had renowned scholars interested in

Portuguese poetry—J. D. M. Ford at the latter, and Henry Roseman Lang at the former. And at Columbia University—it was announced in the *New York Times* in 1901—

> A series of lectures on Portuguese poetry, which is thought to be the preliminary step toward the foundation of a course in Portuguese at Columbia, will begin at the university on Wednesday. The series will be given by William Tenney Brewster. It will consist of four lectures, which will be given as follows: April 3, "Portuguese Popular Poetry"; April 10, "The Predecessors of Camoens"; April 17, "Camoens"; April 24, "Portuguese Poetry After Camoens."[5]

It is interesting to me that Brewster was a member of the Columbia University Department of English, and that, in 1931, as reported in the *New York Times*, he donated to the university his "volumes of Portuguese literature," along with—thoughtfully—"a fund for binding part of the collection."[6]

When, in the early years of the twentieth century, the Brazilian Joaquim Nabuco, a student of Camões and lifelong promoter of all things Camonean, found himself in Washington as his country's ambassador to the United States, he took upon himself to give lectures on Camões at two major American universities in the East, Cornell and Yale, and at Vassar College. At the time of his death he was preparing a similar lecture for delivery at Harvard University. At Yale, Nabuco departed from his prepared text for a moment to implore Henry Lang, who was in his audience, to undertake a translation of *Os Lusíadas*. No such translation was ever published, and my own look into Lang's archive, admittedly not exhaustive, did not turn up any evidence that he ever attempted such a translation. What seems most significant to me about Nabuco's U.S. lectures on Camões is that major American institutions such as Yale, Cornell, Vassar, and Harvard were receptive, not only to Nabuco, but to the subject he had chosen—a *Portuguese* poet of the sixteenth century— one that must even then have been considered a bit offbeat for a *Brazilian* diplomat. That was a different time, of course; it is hard to imagine anything similar happening today.[7]

Interest in Camões was expressed by another member of the Columbia University faculty when, in 1910, George Edward Woodberry, a professor of comparative literature, devoted a chapter to Camões, "the maker of the only truly modern epic," in his well-received book, a collection of essays on the theme announced in his title, *The Inspiration of Poetry*. Of the man who wrote the first modern epic, Woodberry says: "Camoens shows in his verse as he was in life, with a naturalness and vigor, with an unconscious realism, a directness, an intensity and openness that give him to us as a comrade."[8] The critic's notion of Camões as a "comrade" would be echoed elsewhere over the years, notably in singular poems by Kermit Roosevelt (President Theodore Roosevelt's adventurous son) and Roy Campbell, the Lusophilic South African whose fine sonnet entitled "Luís de Camões" was translated into Portuguese by Jorge de Sena in 1952. Woodberry's book was followed, three years later, by an edition of *The Book of the Epic*, H. A. Guerber's survey of the world's great epics, ranging from the Greeks' *Iliad* to the Indians' *Mahabharata*. Besides the usual biographical account of Camões's life, Guerber offers a useful book-by-book summary of *Os Lusíadas*.[9]

In 1924, commemorating the quadricentennial of the birth date most commonly assigned to Camões, there appeared important essays in two of the major newspapers in New York. In "Camoens, 1524–1924," an essay that appeared on the first two pages of the *New York Evening Post Literary Review* in September, Merritt Y. Hughes discusses Camões's great poetic achievement, partly in the context of his having influenced John Milton's poem *Paradise Lost* and Herman Melville's sea fiction, most notably *White-Jacket* and *Moby-Dick*. He also notes that "toward 1850 the Latin countries united to canonize him a literary saint, and even in New York City a statue has been put up in his honor." It was Camões's singular achievement, according to Hughes, to be "the only man of the Renaissance, when everyone was writing epics and when Europe was appropriating Asia and the Americas and fighting its wars of religion, who made a successful

attempt to write an epic about a contemporary subject. That itself
would be a good claim to fame, but in addition 'The Lusiads' fore-
shadows modern ethical, political and economic ideas, and suggests
much that is usually believed to be characteristic of the nineteenth
and twentieth centuries in poetry."[10]

In "Portugal's Poetical One-Eyed Devil," an essay in the *New York
Times* in July 1924, Eva Madden, a writer of some popularity at the
time, rehearses, in loving detail, the "facts" of the poet's romantic
and, as we know, romanticized biography. In the recent biography of
Camões by Aubrey Bell, she tells us, "at last the world is to know all
there is authentically to know of the adventures of the most daring
and active poet of all literature. No figure of letters can even approach
him as Munchausen-like adventurer, for Camoens himself actually
went through the thrilling events of the many chapters related of
him." She concludes her genial piece with an assessment of Camões's
English-language translators (though she makes mistakes in two of
the names): "The 'Lusiad' was first put into English by Robert [actu-
ally Richard] Fanshawe in 1665; then by Mickles [Mickle] in 1776.
A third version, and the last, was made by Sir Richard Burton—
with more accuracy than mellowness of rendition—none of the
three having caught with any too great felicity the poetic vigor, the
Portuguese voluptuousness of expression, of the amazing original."[11]
It is worth mentioning in this context that toward the end of his
long career at Harvard University, in 1940, Jeremiah Ford published
a facsimile edition of Fanshawe's 1655 English version of *Os Lusíadas*, followed, a few years later, by a scholarly, well-annotated textual
edition—the first ever in the United States—of Camões's epic.

The academic study of Camões in the United States received an
appreciable boost when, in 1965, the poet, critic, and all-round man
of letters Jorge de Sena left Brazil for the United States. He did not
return to Brazil. For the next thirteen years he taught in the United
States, first at the University of Wisconsin at Madison and then, for
the remaining years of his life, at the University of California, Santa
Barbara. Right off, he participated in the VI Colóquio Internacional

de Estudos Luso-Brasileiros, held in September 1966—partly in Cambridge, Massachusetts, on the watch of Francis M.

Rogers, Harvard University's Nancy Clark Smith Professor of the Language and Literature of Portugal, and partly in New York under the auspices of the Hispanic Society of America. And in December of the same year, at meetings of the Modern Language Association held in the city of New York, Sena delivered a paper entitled "Camões revisitado."[12] In 1969 he published his provocative and controversial study of *Os sonetos de Camões e o soneto quinhentista peninsular*, a work that applied an arithmetical method of his own devising to solve the problem of which sonnets truly belong in the Camonean canon, followed a year later by the collection of essays entitled *A estrutura de "Os Lusíadas" e outros estudos camonianos e de poesia peninsular do século XVI*. It was altogether fitting, then, that Sena was invited to be the featured opening speaker in a two-day symposium on Camões to be held on April 21–22, 1972, at the University of Connecticut, Storrs. The invitation was extended by the organizer and administrator of the symposium, Dr. António Cirurgião, recently appointed to the university's faculty. Sena entitled his keynote talk "Camões—New Observations on His Epic and His Thinking." He talked for more than two hours (over twice the allotted time), and then he followed his talk with a reading of the entry on Camões he had just written for the *Encyclopædia Britannica*, itself amounting to a second lecture. The other speakers on the first day were Heitor Martins (Indiana University), whose title was "Camões, beyond Vergil: An Investigation of the Epic"; and Charles Boxer (Yale University), whose proposed topic was "Christians and Spices in *Os Lusíadas*" (but who, because, as he explained, he "could not find sufficient material" for his "suggested paper," spoke, rather, on "Camões and Diogo do Couto: Brothers in Arms and Literature").[13] On the second day the two speakers were Wilson Martins (New York University), whose title was "Camões and the Super-Camões," and Louis L. Martz (Yale University), who spoke on "*Os Lusíadas* in England: Camões and Milton."[14] It was an international cast, overall, with featured participants hailing from countries such as Brazil, Portugal, and the United Kingdom. Of the contributors to the special issue of *Ocidente* that grew out of the conference, four hailed from Portugal and Brazil—Sena, Wilson and Heitor Martins, and Frederick C. H. Garcia—although all of them were then teaching at universities in the United States. Of the three contributors from the United Kingdom—Boxer, Frank Pierce, and Roger M. Walker—one, Boxer, was then teaching in the United States. The remaining eight— Martz, Thomas and George Hart, Neil Miller, Anson C. Piper, George W. Reinhardt, Jack Schmitt, and James H. Sims—were Americans teaching at universities in the United States.

Tied into the theme of the symposium was a production by the university theater group of Henri de Montherlant's *La reine morte*, given in English as *The Queen after Death*. Chosen to complement the symposium, this play on the theme of Inês de Castro was attended by the conference participants on the evening concluding the first day of the meetings. According to Cirurgião, Sena judged this college production of Montherlant's play to be "an improvement over the original." "Sena didn't like Montherlant," explained Cirurgião.[15] The production ran for a week.

The lectures given at the symposium, along with a number of other pieces, including a bibliography of Camões in English translation, were published in November of that same year in a special number, running to 223 pages, of volume 35 (new series) of *Ocidente*, the venerable, but soon to be lamented, "Revista Portuguesa de Cultura." Included were papers on Richard Francis Burton as Camões's translator (Garcia), the idea of history in *Os Lusíadas* (Hart), *Os Lusíadas* and the *Cancioneiro Geral* (Miller), Camões and Inês de Castro (Pierce), teaching *Os Lusíadas* in Leonard Bacon's 1950 translation (Piper), August Graf von Platen's admiration for Camões (Reinhardt), the nineteenth-century American novelist Herman Melville's admiration for, and indebtedness to, Camões (Schmitt), *Os Lusíadas* and John Milton's *Paradise Lost* (Sims), the symbolic uses of Bacchus and Venus in *Os Lusíadas* (Walker), and Camões

in English—a bibliography (Hart). Missing was Heitor Martins's
paper on Camões and Virgil, a summary of which was given as an
abstract. Sena also participated, along with Norwood Andrews, Jr.,
and Alberto Machado da Rosa, in a one-day quadricentennial commemoration of the publication of *Os Lusíadas* held at the University
of California, Los Angeles, on May 12, 1972.

It is not coincidental, moreover, that shortly after his participation
in the symposium in Connecticut and the commemoration in California, Sena chose, in May, to share with the readers of the *Diário
popular* his thoughts on the Camonean celebrations then going on,
internationally and locally in Portugal. His is a warning against the
provincial and chauvinistic misuses of Camões and his work:

> Assim, celebrem-se *Os Lusíadas* e o seu autor. Mas sem esquecer
> que eles não são propriedade exclusiva de Portugal. Assim como nos
> Estados Unidos ninguém pensa que Shakespeare não é "americano,"
> no Brasil ninguém pensa que Camões não seja "brasileiro," porque é
> parte gloriosa da língua portuguesa. Do mesmo modo, tenha-se sem-
> pre presente que é o valor universal de Camões e da sua obra o que
> mais importa celebrar, pôr em relevo e difundir. Mas, repita-se, *a obra*,
> de que *Os Lusíadas* são uma parte sem dúvida extremamente impor-
> tante, mas não mais importante do que a obra lírica, nem separável
> dela: o homem que escreveu essa epopeia, e que nela constantemente
> se intromete, está inteiro, tragicamente inteiro, nas meditações dolo-
> rosas da obra lírica.[16]

It was also António Cirurgião's happy idea to suggest to the editor
of *Hispania*, Irving P. Rothberg of the University of Massachusetts
at Amherst, that, as the single journal devoted to scholarship and the
teaching of Spanish and Portuguese in the United States, *Hispania*
devote an issue to Camões on this occasion. One is happy to report
that Rothberg agreed. But the idea had its formidable opponent.
Having learned of the symposium proposed, along with the possibility that *Hispania* would commemorate Camões in the same year,
Harvard's Francis Rogers took it upon himself to issue a warning, in
a letter to Rothberg. Here is its opening paragraph:

I am writing to express to you my views concerning "commemorations" in general and specifically the commemoration of the fourth
centenary of the publication of the *Lusíadas*. I tend to place commemorations in general in the same hopper as honorary degrees and
decorations from foreign governments. In principle, they are very
nice, but they are fraught with hidden dangers. This is particularly
true with a commemorative volume concerning the *Lusíadas*. I have
a great deal of affection and respect for this poem and its author.
Indeed, I have taught both for many years and directed one splendid
thesis by a Brazilian Jesuit on the poetry of the poem. Unfortunately,
down through the years, the *Lusíadas* has been used, or misused, as
a prime document of political rhetoric. It has been misused in other
ways as well. Thus, we have had studies on the fauna, the flora, nau-
tical astronomy, law, and much else in the poem. Unfortunately, we
have had very few studies of the poem as a poem, those few having
been made by such people as Woodbury [*sic*], Ezra Pound and C. M.
Bowra. I feel that a commemorative volume concerning the *Lusíadas*
to appear in 1972 could well give rise to a plethora of studies concerning the poem which would have nothing to do with the poem as a
poem. Some of the articles submitted would be written by individuals
whom only the most callous of editorial boards could turn down. The-
oretically, I believe a well edited commemorative volume is possible.
In practice, in these years, I am doubtful.[17]

Fortunately, Rogers's ominous words did not dissuade Rothberg
from his plan to commemorate Camões, and *Hispania* ultimately
published a collection of five essays, contributed by distinguished
scholars, in its May 1974 issue, in time to honor the four hundredth
anniversary of the poet's death. The essays are "Camões' Shipwreck"
(by Gerald M. Moser, Pennsylvania State University), "Ancient
History in *Os Lusíadas*" (Frank Pierce, University of Sheffield),
"The Feminine Presence in *Os Lusíadas*" (Anson C. Piper, Williams
College), "The Epic Similes of *Os Lusíadas*" (Roger Stephens Jones,
Carleton University, Ottawa), and "Joaquim Nabuco e Camões" (C.
Malcolm Batchelor, Yale University). (Piper and Pierce, it will be
recalled, had also contributed papers to the 1972 special issue of

Ocidente devoted to the conference on Camões at the University
of Connecticut.) In his capacity as editor of *Hispania*, Rothberg
wrote:

> The year 1972 saw a number of impressive observances of the 400th
> anniversary of the publication of Luís de Camões' *Os Lusíadas*, the
> greatest epic poem of the Renaissance. It is with pleasure that we
> now—somewhat after the fact—dedicate the present issue of *His-
> pania* not only to this enduring masterpiece but to the 450th anniver-
> sary of its poet's birth who is generally believed to have been born in
> 1524. The editor's deep thanks are offered to the authors of the articles
> that follow who obligingly wrote them at the editor's request.[18]

Aimed at a limited audience of specialists in Iberian literature, the
essays on Camões in *Hispania* nevertheless warrant further attention. Moser adduces accounts of shipwrecks in three contemporary
letters to support his belief that Camões's two references to shipwreck in *Os Lusíadas* are reliably autobiographical. Moser ends his
piece as follows: "In 1880, when as in 1972, the Portuguese-speaking
countries celebrated Camões as the author of their national epic,
Machado de Assis wrote a series of four sonnets for the occasion."
Moser then quotes the last four lines of Machado's sonnet—which,
in its entirety, reads:

Um dia, junto à foz de brando e amigo
Rio de estranhas gentes habitado,
Pelos mares aspérrimos levado,
Salvaste o livro que viveu contigo.

E êsse que foi às ondas arrancado,
Já livre agora do mortal perigo,
Serve de arca imortal, de eterno abrigo,
Não só a ti, mas ao teu berço amado.

Assim, um homem só, naquele dia,
Naquele escasso ponto do universo,
Língua, história, nação, armas, poesia,

Salva das frias mãos do tempo adverso.

E tudo aquilo agora o desafia.

E tão sublime preço cabe em verso.[19]

In "Ancient History in *Os Lusíadas*," Frank Pierce, who would a few years later publish an excellent edition of the poem, looks anew at Camões's use of history as "subject-matter rather than style." The "company of Alexander, Julius Caesar or Hannibal," he decides, "was an inevitable component of any attempt to write public poetry on one's country and its past," and Camões was no exception in this. Yet it is the Portuguese poet's success in making the reader see the events of Vasco da Gama's voyage "as something that is taking place before our eyes without any special narrator to interpret it for us" that gives the poem the "freshness and immediacy which set *Os Lusíadas* apart from most examples of the literary epic."[20]

Anson C. Piper's subject is "The Feminine Presence in *Os Lusíadas*." "A close study of the poem," he writes, "furnishes ample evidence of the fact that the feminine presence which pervades *Os Lusíadas* constitutes one of the major literary and psychological motives of this highly sensuous Renaissance masterpiece." For "the fact that [Camões] wrote under the powerful spell of Renaissance humanism required him to pay his courtier's debt to the current concept of love as a highly formalized standard for measuring human conduct." In short, Camões "strove in his poetry to join his humanistic learning to the chivalric ideal of perfect manhood 'fused with female grace.'"[21]

Camões's use of epic similes is Roger Stephens Jones's subject. Distinguishing between Homeric similes, which support the celebration of "the grandeur of a warrior-hero," and Virgilian similes, which help to define "the grandeur of a moral hero," Jones decides that, on balance, *Os Lusíadas* is a Virgilian epic (with Homeric elements).[22]

In the final essay of the unit on Camões in the May 1974 issue of *Hispania*, C. Malcolm Batchelor rehearses the matter of the Brazilian Joaquim Nabuco's profound devotion to the promotion of the Portuguese poet in Brazil and, later, in the United States. As a twenty-three-year-old, Nabuco published *Camões e os Lusíadas* (1872). As a thirty-year-old, he would proclaim, during the 1880 celebrations in Rio de Janeiro to an audience of four to five thousand listeners, "O Brasil e *Os Lusíadas* são as duas maiores obras de Portugal."[23] Batchelor's detailed account makes the point that central to Nabuco's sense of his own spiritual and intellectual worth was his conception of Camões's exemplary greatness.

Two other items, by Americans in 1972, merit attention. Contributing to the festivities devoted to Camões that year, one that has been largely ignored, but well worth noting, is Edgar C. Knowlton Jr.'s prose translation of Almeida Garrett's canonical poem *Camões*. Knowlton, a university teacher who was born in New Bedford, Massachusetts (the location of an important Portuguese-American enclave), has spent most of his professional life in Hawaii. Contributing to the obscurity into which Knowlton's translation has fallen, no doubt, is the fact that it appeared in Macau, in a double issue (numbers 1 and 2 of volume VI) of the *Boletim do Instituto Luis de Camões*.

The second of these 1972 items is a piece in the autumn issue of that year in the well regarded and, at the time, highly popular middlebrow journal *Horizon*. Contributed by Edmond Taylor, a distinguished historian (he was the author of *Richer by Asia* [1947], *The Fall of the Dynasties* [1963], and *Awakening from History* [1969]), this illustrated essay of eight pages argues the controversial thesis that Camões, the "one-eyed author of *The Lusiads*[,] wrote—and lived— the national epic of Portugal, but his countrymen missed the moral: that the paths of imperial glory lead to the grave of the spirit."[24] Beginning his essay with an epigraph—lines from the old man's dire warning (Canto IV, 95, 97)—Taylor puts the matter forcefully right at the outset:

> To the contemporary American taste, Camoëns is probably the least readable among the schoolroom classics of Western literature. He comes surprisingly alive, however, if one rereads him in his native

Lisbon, the seat of West's first overseas empire, which has now become the last, defiant, though somehow dejected, bastion of Western colonialism. The tragic, beautiful city, scarred by so many disasters, where the poet was probably born and where he unquestionably lived out his years after a long, adventurous, unprofitable career as a colonial swashbuckler, is haunted by the delusions and lucidities of his genius in almost the same way the passions and afflictions of a syphilitic haunt his descendants.[25]

Cleverly using the legendary and virtually mythic story of the poet's life and writings as told in "a pictorial biography, in gaudily colored comic-book format"—Camões (colecção de 124 cromos)—Taylor "corrects" the story, point by point, by incorporating the latest demythologizing scholarship on the subject. The historian has two principal aims: (1) to tell the story of the poet and his work ("Since Homer, few single poems have more effectively crystallized the deepest emotions, aspirations, and delusions of a whole people—even, perhaps, of an epoch"); and (2) to deplore Portugal's dictatorship's stubborn and disastrous refusal to give up its possessions in Africa ("Those fictitious 'provinces' of an anachronistic colonial empire camouflaged as a modern nation could someday prove to be the final grave, not merely of Portuguese imperialism, but of what up to now has remained a Christian and noble civilization—that of Portugal itself, Camoëns's own").[26]

The participation of Jorge de Sena—by then settled permanently, as it turned out, at the University of California, Santa Barbara—at the University of Connecticut's commemorative symposium in 1972 fit in perfectly with his own professional interest in promoting all matters Camonean over his entire literary and professional careers. During 1972 he took part in several congresses in Europe with major speeches and important papers that were in due course published in the appropriate proceedings. He published essays in the newspaper Diário popular, along with the poem "Camões dirige-se aos seus contemporâneos" in the November 1972 issue of the journal Ocidente. Indeed, it can be said that Sena's work on Camões, which included a doctoral dissertation and several other books, as well as numerous essays, reviews, and newspaper articles, not to mention the brilliantly realized bio-critical story "Super flumina Babylonis," which ends with the sick and improvident Camões setting down the first line of his famous poem "By the Rivers of Babylon," came, publicly, to a head in the early 1970s. (Interestingly enough, an advertisement for what appears to be among the earliest, if not the first, film made about Camões also focuses on Camões's final days. Produced by the internationally known Gaumont Company founded by Léon Gaumont [1864–1946] in Paris, this historical drama was released on December 9, 1911, and distributed in the United States by George Kleine of Chicago, Illinois, under the title "Camoens, the Portuguese Shakespeare."[27])

During the period of 1972–73 Jorge de Sena made major contributions to the dissemination of information on Portugal's great poet. On March 9, 1972, at the Centro Cultural Português Fundação Calouste Gulbenkian, in Paris, he spoke on "Camões: Quelques vues nouvelles sur son épopée et sa pensée," which, later that year, appeared in the proceedings of those meetings, *Visages de Luís de Camões: Conférences.* In April Sena presented, in English, a version of his Paris speech at the University of Connecticut in Storrs. The Portuguese version of this lecture appeared, as we have already noted, as "Camões: Novas observações acerca da sua epopeia e do seu pensamento," in November in the well-established and highly influential Lisbon journal *Ocidente.* This piece, Sena made a point of explaining, he had himself translated "do original ingles." It offers a taste of a forthcoming book, one that he is putting the finishing touches on. In it, he will take up, as the necessary and complementary study to his previous investigation of the "architecture" of Camões's epic, an interpretation of the poem's texture (*textura* or *tessitura*). He will interpret language—the frequency, sequence, and context of words such as *natura, amor, santos, milagre, pai, mãe, filhos, virtude, Judea,* and so forth—as the key to interpreting not only the poet's intentions but his ideas, beliefs, and purposeful omissions as well. Here is the abstract of Sena's essay prepared editorially:

The Lusiads became such a symbol of Portuguese imperial glory that many believe it still weighs too heavily on Portuguese life. To foreigners, always suspicious of Portuguese colonial proclivities, celebrating *The Lusiads* is just a cover for dark intentions. It is difficult to separate the epic from what men have made of it for centuries. Even today eminent critics are unwilling to acknowledge the courage and coherence shown by Camões in his masterpiece. The Author had a manifold purpose when he tried to elucidate the "structure of *The Lusiads*." Now he intends to study its *texture*. No ideas, however great, serve a poet's true greatness unless they come to us perfectly embodied in the very texture of his works. By studying this texture the Author tries to read the poet's *intentional meaning*, revealing complex Camonian inner thought and daring intention, and has selected some definitely important or controversial areas in order to probe it.[28]

On June 8, 1972, Sena published an article entitled "Camões em 1972" in the supplement *Quinta-feira à tarde* of the *Diário popular*. In the *Actas da I reunião internacional de camonistas* (Lisboa, 1973) appeared another of his conference talks, one that he was unable to deliver in person due to illness—"Aspectos do pensamento de Camões através da estrutura linguística de *Os Lusíadas*." He contributed the entry on Camões to the fifteenth edition of the *Encyclopædia Britannica*, which appeared in 1973. He prepared a substantial introduction, dated October 22, 1972, to a facsimile edition of the 1639 edition of *Lusíadas de Luís de Camões comentadas por Manuel de Faria e Sousa*. The next month he composed the preface for a facsimile edition of the edition of 1685 of *Rimas várias de Luís de Camões comentadas por Manuel de Faria e Sousa*. Sena aims his remarks on this occasion at Camões scholarship down the centuries, which had denigrated Faria e Sousa's work while availing itself of his insights and observations. Faria e Sousa's work is simply, according to Sena, "o mais rico repositório de comentos sobre a epopeia, a fonte semiclandestina de mais de três séculos de erudição camoniana, um dos mais extraordinários monumentos erguidos por alguém, devotadamente, a um poeta e a uma cultura, eis o que regressa aberta e publicamente ao mundo português, que é o seu."[29]

At the same time Sena also arranged with his publisher in Porto to bring out a limited edition of a composite work entitled *Camões dirige-se aos seus contemporâneos e outros textos.* The publication collects three works: Sena's 1966 story "Super flumina Babylonis" (taken from the collection *Novas andanças do demónio*), "Camões dirige-se aos seus contemporâneos" (a poem from his 1963 collection *Metamorfoses* that references the elaborate ceremonial translation of the poet's putative remains to the Jerónimos monastery in 1880—"Nada tereis, mas nada: nem os ossos, / que um vosso esqueleto há-de ser buscado, / para passar por meu"), and "Camões na Ilha de Moçambique," an unpublished poem written on July 20, 1972, in Moçambique, where Sena was lecturing on Camões. The Moçambique poem is worth recalling for its frankly stated humanizing and universalizing image of Camões as an earthy creature of nature:

> É pobre e já foi rica. Era mais pobre
> quando Camões aqui passou primeiro,
> cheia de livros a cabeça e lendas
> e muita estúrdia de Lisboa reles.
> Quando passados nele os Orientes
> e o amargor dos vis sempre tão ricos,
> aqui ficou, isto crescera, mas
> a fortaleza ainda estava em obras,
> as casas eram poucas, e o terreno
> passeio descampado ao vento e ao sol
> desta alavanca mínima, em coral,
> do onde saltavam para Goa as naus,
> que dela vinham cheias de pecados
> e de bagagens ricas e pimentas podres.
> Como nau nos baixios que aos Sepúlvedas
> deram no amor corte primeiro à vida,
> aqui ficou sem nada senão versos.
> Mas antes dele, como depois dele,
> aqui passaram todos: almirantes,
> ladrões e vice-reis, poetas e cobardes,

os santos e os heróis, mais a canalha
sem nome e sem memória, que serviu
de lastro, marujagem, e de carne
para os canhões e os peixes, como os outros.
Tudo passou aqui—Almeidas e Gonzagas,
Bocages e Albuquerques, desde o Gama.
Naqueles tempos se fazia o espanto
desta pequena aldeia citadina
de brancos, negros, indianos, e cristãos,
e muçulmanos, brâmanes, e ateus.

Europa e África, o Brasil e as Índias,
cruzou-se tudo aqui neste calor tão branco
como do forte a cal no pátio, e tão cruzado
como a elegância das nervuras simples
da capela pequena do baluarte.
Jazem aqui em lápides perdidas
os nomes todos dessa gente que,
como hoje os negros, se chegava às rochas,
baixava as calças e largava ao mar
a mal-cheirosa escória de estar vivo.
Não é de bronze, louros na cabeça,
nem no escrever parnasos, que te vejo aqui.
Mas num recanto em cócoras marinhas,
soltando às ninfas que lambiam rochas
o quanto a fome e a glória da epopeia
em ti se digeriam. Pendendo para as pedras
teu membro se lembrava e estremecia
de recordar na brisa as croias mais as damas,
e versos de soneto perpassavam
junto de um cheiro a merda lá na sombra,
de onde n'alma fervia quanto nem pensavas.
Depois, aliviado, tu subias
aos baluartes e fitando as águas
sonhavas de outra Ilha, a Ilha única,

enquanto a mão se te pousava lusa,
em franca distracção, no que te era a pátria
por ser a ponta da semente dela.

E de zarolho não podias ver
distâncias separadas: tudo te era uma
e nada mais: o Paraíso e as Ilhas,
heróis, mulheres, o amor que mais se inventa,
e uma grandeza que não há em nada.
Pousavas n'água o olhar e te sorrias
—mas não amargamente, só de alívio,
como se te limparas de miséria,
e de desgraça e de injustiça e dor
de ver que eram tão poucos os melhores,
enquanto a caca ia-se na brisa esbelta,
igual ao que se esquece e se lançou de nós.[30]

This is an imagined scene, of course, one presenting, at an earlier
time, the Camões who is destined to endure even greater hardships
after he has returned home to Lisbon, difficulties that even the publication of his great poem will only temporarily assuage. The poem
is part of Sena's project to demythologize the romanticized life of
Camões inherited, largely, from the late eighteenth century.

The publication of the collection *Camões dirige-se aos seus contemporâneos e outros textos* was delayed for several months, appearing
only in 1973.[31] It is also of interest that it was precisely in the autumn
of 1972 that Sena wrote the remarkable poetic meditations that he
collected under the indicative title "Sobre esta praia," pointing back
to the opening words of Camões's great poem: "Sobre os rios."[32]
"Note-se ainda, de uma vez para sempre," as Sena writes in his guise
as scholar, in an essay titled "Babel e Sião," "que o 1° verso é *Sobre os
rios que vão* e não *Sóbolos*, como aparece na 2ª edição, 1598, à conta
das prosódicas emendas que provámos espúrias."[33] Not to put too
fine a point on it—that there is an obvious link between "Sobre esta
praia" and Camões—let me just say that in these eight meditations
on almost clinical analysis of the nexus of nude bodies and sexuality

by the Pacific Ocean, Sena draws not only on Camões's poem "By
the Rivers of Babylon" but from, "modernizing" it as he goes along,
the episode of the Isle of Love in Book IX of *Os Lusíadas*.
It was at approximately the same time that Sena submitted his
entry on Camões to the fifteenth edition of the *Encyclopædia Britannica* (copyright 1974). When Mécia de Sena collected this piece in
Trinta anos de Camões in 1980, she wrote in explanation:

> Esta é, em tradução, a primeira versão destinada à 15.ª edição da
> *Enciclopédia Britânica*. Nada tem em comum com o que foi publicado
> senão, evidentemente, o que é factual. O que na *Enciclopédia* saiu
> foi uma versão tornada estilisticamente incolor e rearrumada pelos
> serviços da mesma Enciclopédia. Aliás, nunca correspondera ao
> desejo da mesma—queriam a "entrada" dedicada mais exclusivamente
> à biografia do Poeta, o que, como é sabido, só usando de muita fanta-
> sia se poderia fazer.[34]

Sena's essay ran to close to 4500 words, but the published entry ran
to about 2800 words, in addition to listings of Camões's major works
and selected biographical-critical bibliography running to some
seventy lines. Besides flattening Sena's characteristically rhetorical
style and rearranging material, the Britannica's editors made two
major changes in content. They dropped most of Sena's discussion
of the accumulated scholarship on Camões and his work, and they
dropped his comparisons of Camões with other writers, notably
Shakespeare. Here, for example, is a passage omitted in the *Britannica* but restored in *Trinta anos de Camões*:

> O caso de Camões é, como grande e internacional figura, o reverso
> do de Shakespeare. Muito se sabe da vida de Shakespeare, em com-
> paração, mas ninguém aceita que ele não tivesse sido um mínimo de
> génio "romântico" na sua vida privada; quase nada se sabe ao certo
> sobre Camões e tudo aponta para que tenha sido um homem bem
> pouco comum (no entanto em acordo com a sua posição na vida social
> do seu tempo e na sua era de aventuras imperiais), que, ao contrário
> de Shakespeare, nunca casou ou foi pai de sabidos filhos (apesar da
> sua ostentação de casos amorosos, ardente erotismo e até adolescente

gabarolice nas suas obras—ou talvez demasiado de tudo isto). Os eruditos têm discutido largamente as ideias de Shakespeare, que ele encerra nas declarações teatrais feitas pelas suas personagens em situações dramáticas; das ideias de Camões, dos seus sentimentos, esperanças e tristezas, estejam como estiverem disfarçadas sob os modos e tonalidades da sua época (e também por causa dos perigosamente repressivos tempos em que vivia), tudo sabemos, já que não muitos grandes poetas, no mundo da literatura, escreveram tanto acerca de si mesmos como ele fez obsessivamente, até no seu poema épico. A crítica sobre as suas obras (especialmente a épica) tem sido imensamente enganada pelo orgulho e preconceito políticos ou religiosos portugueses, que pondo em relevo o carácter nacional do poema épico, reduziram a mais larga visão do pensamento de Camões.[35]

Surely, in the early 1970s, no one's efforts exceeded those of Sena, scholar or poet, to bring attention to Camões in the quadricentennial year of the publication of *Os Lusíadas*. As for the real effect of the celebratory events of 1972, that, too, was assessed by Sena, in 1975:

When, in preparation for the celebrations of the 3rd centennial of his death, in 1880, his [Camões's] Portuguese admirers looked for the remains, everything was most uncertain. And the bones transferred with pomp and circumstance to a lavish tomb placed in the "Jerónimos" monastery, a splendid building erected in Lisbon at the beginning of the 16th century near the beach from where Vasco da Gama (the hero of *The Lusiads*) left for his glorious voyage to India, and to celebrate the great event—those bones are for sure not his. So there happened with his remains what had happened with his life, with his lyrical poetry left scattered and unpublished when he died, and, we can say, with his poetical personality at the hands of many biographers and critics. Now (and paradoxically the celebrations of the 4th centennial of *The Lusiads* in 1972 have helped) Camões is rising from the dead like the phoenix.[36]

In 1980, two years after Jorge de Sena's death, his spirit was still very much present at the "Colóquios Camonianos" commemorating the quadricentennial of the death of Camões, held at the University of California, Santa Barbara, on April 25–26, 1980. Nineteen of the more than two dozen papers presented were selected for the proceedings volume published as *Camoniana Californiana* under the editorship of Maria de Lourdes Belchior and Enrique Martínez-López in 1985.[37] The entire effort, the colloquium and its published proceedings, was intended, according to the editors, to run counter to the pessimism expressed by Sena's famous poem (quoted in the book's preface):

> Podereis roubar-me tudo:
> as ideias, as palavras, as imagens,
> e também as metáforas, os temas, os motivos,
> os símbolos, e a primazia
> nas dores sofridas de uma língua nova,
> no entendimento de outros, na coragem
> de combater, julgar, de penetrar
> em recessos de amor para que sois castrados.
> E podereis depois não me citar,
> suprimir-me, ignorar-me, aclamar até
> outros ladrões mais felizes.[38]

A list of those participants whose papers were included in the published proceedings, along with their institutional affiliation, will give an indication of the scope of this international gathering in California, on the shores of the Pacific Ocean. Included were José Martins Garcia (Brown University), Kenneth David Jackson (University of Texas at Austin), Maria de Lourdes Belchior (University of California, Santa Barbara, and University of Lisbon), Stephen Reckert (King's College, University of London), Maria Leonor Machado de Sousa (New University of Lisbon), Bryant Creel (California State University, Los Angeles), Augusto Hacthoun (Wheaton College), Gordon Jensen (Brigham Young University), Frederick G. Williams (University of California, Santa Barbara), Leodegário A. de Azevedo Filho (PUC Rio de Janeiro), Rebecca Catz, Joaquim-Francisco Coelho (Harvard University), Eduardo Mayone Dias (University of

California, Los Angeles), Nelly Novaes Coelho (University of São
Paulo), Davi Traumann (University of California, Santa Barbara),
Vergílio Ferreira, António Cirurgião (University of Connecticut),
Gilberto Mendonça Teles (PUC Rio de Janeiro), and Ronald S.
Sousa (University of Minnesota). It is interesting to note that there
are twelve American universities represented in this list, as opposed
to two Brazilian, two Portuguese, and one British. It is a curiosity that Francis Rogers of Harvard did not attend the meetings
although he did send a paper. It was not included in the commemorative volume.

Later in the same commemorative year, a three-day multidis-
ciplinary conference on the subject "The Portuguese World in the
Time of Camões: Sixteenth-Century Portugal, Brazil, Portuguese
Africa, and Portuguese Asia" was held at the University of Florida
(September 29–October 1, 1980). Of the twenty-six presentations,
eighteen were included in the proceedings volume, *Empire in Transition: The Portuguese World in the Time of Camões*, edited by Alfred
Hower and Richard A. Preto-Rodas and published in 1985, which
included a goodly number of papers dealing entirely or substantially
with Camões.[39] It will be observed that between the participants in
the Santa Barbara and Gainesville conferences in 1980 there were
some fifteen different United States universities represented, only
two of which were represented in 1972 in the *Ocidente* volume or
in the *Hispania* issue of 1974. Notably, in its winter 1980 issue, the
scholarly journal *Luso-Brazilian Review*, published in Madison,
Wisconsin, collected a half dozen articles under the commemorative
heading "Camões and His Centuries," with contributions by Gerald
M. Moser, Joseph A. Klucas, Norwood Andrews, Jr., Clementine
C. Rabassa, Kenneth David Jackson, and Alexandrino E. Severino.
Finally, to bring the matter closer to date, it can be noted that a major
international conference, "Post-Imperial Camões," was held at the
University of Massachusetts Dartmouth on October 11–12, 2002.[40]

The accumulation of names and wide range of institutional affil-
iations associated with the various conferences on Camões held in

the United States, beginning with the 1972 gathering at the University of Connecticut, seem to indicate—hardly a surprise—that Camões's literary reputation is now largely in the hands of scholars and translators. In 1965 Sena had written of the Camões who had "deixado / a vida pelo mundo em pedaços repartida, como dizia / aquele pobre diabo que o Minotauro não leu, porque, / como toda a gente, não sabe português."[41] The efforts of Jorge de Sena, culminating in a series of essays, poems, and books in the 1970s, earned him a central place in the campaign to make Camões and his work better understood and more widely read not only in Portuguese-speaking countries but in the United States and the United Kingdom as well. He concluded his 1975 essay "Camões: the lyrical poet," written to accompany the publication of a small handful of translations of Camões's poems, in this way:

> Let us hope that this selection of his poems will start his resurrection as a great lyrical poet for English readers. Much has aged for our time in his epic poem, which still is, nevertheless, an extraordinary achievement whose fascinating secrets (very different from the "official" interpretations) are yet very far from being unraveled. But nothing has aged in his lyrical poems, except superficial modes and turns of style: and there, as in many passages of the epic poem, we have a man, and a complex human being at that, talking to us, in the way only great poets do, about anguishes, hopes and despairs very much akin to our own today.[42]

To the same end, that of making Camões better and more accurately known to the English-speaking world at large, Sena (I was told by an editor at G. K. Hall in the late 1970s) had agreed to write the biographical-critical volume on Camões for Hall's series on "World Authors." If he ever made such a commitment, it was not his destiny to fulfill it, for Jorge de Sena, the scholar of his generation best fitted to promote the cause of Camões, died in 1978 at the age of fifty-eight.[43]

6

Portugal in "Figura"

Eis aqui se descobre a nobre Espanha,
Como cabeça ali de Europa toda,
Em cujo senhorio e glória estranha
Muitas voltas tem dado a fatal roda;
. . .
Eis aqui, quasi cume da cabeça
De Europa toda, o Reino Lusitano
Onde a terra se acaba e o mar começa
E onde Febo repousa no Oceano.

—Luís de Camões, *Os Lusíadas*, III, 17, 1–4; 20, 1–4

She waited for her Sebastian, till her hope grew dim. Her remaining strength, if strength she had, has gone out into the young empire of Brazil; and she sits with her dark and sweet-voiced children around her, a widow, clad in life-long sables, and weeping eternal tears.

—Thomas Wentworth Higginson (1856)[1]

A tristeza lusitana é a névoa d'uma religião, d'uma filosofia e d'um
Estado, portanto. A nossa tristeza é uma Mulher, e essa mulher é de
origem divina e chama-se Saudade.

—Teixeira de Pascoaes (1911)[2]

Escrevi, até às 4 de manhã, um conto: Super flumina . . . que não
esperava.

—Jorge de Sena (March 27, 1964)[3]

In an unpublished note found among his papers, Fernando Pessoa
lists the writer-philosopher Miguel de Unamuno among the Spanish writers and intellectuals who may possess "grande talento" but
are not "figura[s] de real destaque genial."[4] This dismissive assessment dates from 1914, suggest Pessoa's editors, and thus precedes
Pessoa's attempt to communicate directly with Unamuno in a letter
dated March 26, 1915. Sending along a copy of the first issue of
Orpheu, published in January, Pessoa invites Unamuno to comment
on the new venture. Obviously aware that the Spaniard was a great
champion of the Portuguese and their accomplishments, Pessoa
permits himself to hope that Unamuno will see fit to applaud
Orpheu as the original work of the "nova geração portuguesa," that
he will see the journal as expressive of a genuine effort to reach out
across borders to Spain.[5] Unamuno was not invited to contribute to
future issues of *Orpheu*. He did not reply to Pessoa's letter. His possible motives for not doing so have been the subject of speculation
without certitude:

Estas palabras [those of Pessoa's letter], incendiarias con respecto al
pasado reciente de la literatura portuguesa y terriblemente provoca-
tivas y presuntuosas, debieron sin duda acalorar al rector salmantino
quien, probablemente, pensase que la mejor solución para "castigar" a
tan atrevidos jóvenes sería someterlos al más rígido silencio, a la más
oscura de las marginaciones. Es bien probable que Unamuno, con la

experiencia de los envíos de Sá-Carneiro en su haber, tomase la carta como una ofensa premeditada contra los hombres de su generación, razón que (debería pensar Pessoa) probablemente le condujese a plasmar su opinión sobre la revista en la prensa española, fuese cual fuese esa opinión, como afirma desafiante. La carta adopta, así, formas cercanas a la actitud de la vanguardia, como sucede con la exposición de la propia conciencia de su misión poética (original y elevada, como indica Pessoa) y la adopción de un riesgo inherente a este tipo de expresiones, asumido con cierto carácter altivo e con la certeza de que la "agitación de ideas" sería uno de los rasgos más válidos ante semejante figura.[6]

Such an explanation for Unamuno's behavior toward Pessoa, plausible though it might appear at first, seems less likely when one discovers that Unamuno left no record whatever, not even in his letters, of his reaction to the venture that was *Orpheu*, the contents of its first issue, or its editor's temerity in addressing to him a promotional letter. Had Unamuno felt at all insulted or that his generation had been maligned in the matter, he would in all likelihood, one would have thought, have mentioned it to someone else. That there is nothing along these lines in his correspondence with Teixeira de Pascoaes, who had already published both Unamuno and Pessoa, is strong evidence that Unamuno was simply not interested by what Pessoa had sent him—letter or journal.

If *Orpheu* did not find a place among the Portuguese things and ideas that Unamuno held in high regard, the work and sentiments of Teixeira de Pascoaes did. There was an exchange of visits and some correspondence before the Portuguese poet approached Unamuno for a contribution to the journal *A Águia*, an organ for the patriotic movement called "Nova Renascença." For twenty years, beginning in 1910, this journal would promote *saudosismo*, celebrating the glories of Portuguese history even as it hoped to infuse the present and shape the future with a renewed spirit of accomplishment. One of its rallying cries was that a new and powerful literature would revitalize Portuguese civilization.

Unamuno had on hand "Portugal," a poetic draft he had composed in Porto on June 26, 1907:

PORTUGAL
Portugal, Portugal, tierra descalza,
acurrucada junto al mar, tu madre,
llorando soledades
de trágicos amores,
mientras tus pies desnudos las espumas
saladas bañan,
tu verde cabellera suelta al viento
—cabellera de pinos rumorosos—
los codos descansando en las rodillas,
y la cara morena entre ambas palmas,
clavas tus ojos donde el sol se acuesta
solo en la mar inmensa,
y en el lento naufragio así meditas
de tus glorias de Oriente,
cantando fados quejumbrosa y lenta.[7]

This fragment echoes lines in a poem by the late romantic Thomaz Ribeiro, quoted here in Aubrey Bell's English translation: "Why by the waters dost thou mourn and brood, / Poor—mistress thou of lands beyond the sea, / Dreaming for ever, in sad, wistful mood / Of days that were?"[8] But the poem also reflects aspects of Unamuno's mood and spirit customary during his frequent travels in Portugal. In March 1907, for example, he had written: "Hago un viaje allá por lo menos una vez al año, y cada vez vuelvo más prendado de ese pueblo sufridor y noble."[9]

In 1911 Unamuno contributed two unpublished sonnets to *A Águia*, which were to be published in the review before being collected in *Rosario de sonetos líricos*. One was a lyric built on a motto— "Na mão de Deus, na sua mão direita"—drawn from Antero de Quental's famous poem. The other one was "Portugal," a revised version of the 1907 poem bearing the same title. Significantly, Unamuno had recently published *Por tierras de Portugal y de España*. Foreshadowed obliquely at several moments in that book, his new version of "Portugal" reflected closely what he had written in 1908 about the fishing community of Espinho:

> Hermosa evocación! El sol muriendo en las aguas eternas y los peces en la arena, los hombres mercando su cosecha marina, el mar cantando su perdurable fado, los bueyes rumiando lentamente bajo sus ornamentados yugos, a allá, a lo lejos, las oscuras copas de los pinos empezando a diluirse en el cielo de la extrema tarde. Y junto a los pinos, en la costa, unos cuantos molinos de viento, sobrevivientes también de una especie industrial que empieza a ser fósil, moviendo lenta y tristemente sus cuatro brazos de lienzo.
>
> Esta contemplación de la puesta del sol marino brisado por la canción oceánica es una de las más puras refrigeraciones del espíritu; pero al detenerme así a mirarle con interés, temo que saque de entre las olas un brazo de luz, extendiéndomelo, exclame quejumbroso: *dez reisinhos, senhore!*[10]

Here is the version of the sonnet "Portugal" that Unamuno sent to the journal *A Águia*:

PORTUGAL

Del Atlántico mar en las orillas
desgreñada y descalza una matrona
se sienta al pié de sierra que corona
triste pinar. Apoya en las rodillas

los codos y en las manos las mejillas
y clava ansiosos ojos de leona
en la puesta del sol. El mar entona
su trágico cantar de marvillas.

Dice de luengas tierras y de azares
mientras ella sus piés en las espumas
bañando sueña en el fatal imperio

que se le hundió en los tenebrosos mares,
y mira cómo entre agoreras brumas
se alza Don Sebastián, rey del misterio.[11]

Note that that Unamuno has now melded the "mother" of the first
version with her fado-singing issue into a single female figure standing for the Portugal of decadence and Sebastianism. José Rodrigues
Miguéis would go further. He writes:

> Unamuno deu aos hispanos, em *Por tierras de Portugal y España*, e
> num soneto célebre, de inspiração sebástica, o figurino que colheu em
> certa fase da vida portuguesa, penetrada do satanismo junqueiriano,
> do pessimismo de Oliveira Martins e da tristeza de Manuel Laran-
> jeira: e esse figurino ganhou curso livre até na América do Norte, onde
> Don Miguel é muito lido e admirado. Uma *portuguesada* é, no mundo
> hispânico, o mesmo que *une espagnolade* ou *galéjade* para os franceses,
> e para os italianos também. Não temos o exclusivo da farronca![12]

It was not until 1912 that Fernando Pessoa made his first contribution to *A Águia*. He began his collaboration with a pair of related
essays, the first publications of his maturity, in which he assessed the
state of Portuguese poetry before predicting its future and, as he saw
it, noble course. Portugal would become the Quinto Império with
cultural achievements that would rival those of England in the age
of Queen Elizabeth and Shakespeare. Pessoa remained fixed in this
idea to the end of his days. He would perceive an implicit challenge
to it in an interview with Unamuno published in the Lisbon newspaper *Diário de notícias* in 1930. In the course of this interview conducted by António Ferro, Pessoa's friend since the days of *Orpheu*,
Unamuno advocates that all Iberian countries adopt Castilian as the
most expeditious way of working toward common purposes or goals.
Possibly Pessoa intended to take issue with Unamuno publicly, for
he left a sheet on the matter among his papers. But that his intended
audience was not the readership of the newspaper *Diário de notícias*
is clear from the fact that Pessoa had chosen to express himself on
the matter in English.

Since the disintegration of Spain is a definite fact, the case is how to make up for it by a civilizational reaction. The idea is, not to form an Iberian Federation, which would be unacceptable all round, but to split up Iberia into separate nations, which would be wholly separate except in respect of (1) an offensive and defensive alliance, (2) a cultural alliance, (3) the abolition of customs frontiers between all.

Each nation would be wholly independent, with its own army, navy, diplomatic service and the like, Spain to make what it can of the navy and of its colonies, which, fortunately, are few and may either fall to Castile or be somehow administered jointly by the nations now composing what is called Spain.

The problem of language does not matter, for if a Catalan likes to write Castilian, he will do so then as he does now, in the same manner as a Catalan can write in French and get a wider public still. Unamuno put the case: why not write in Castilian? If it comes to that, I prefer to write in English, which will give me a wider public than Castilian; and I am as much Castilian as I am English in blood and much more English than Castilian since my education is English.

Unamuno's argument is really an argument for writing in English, since that is the most widespread language in the world. If I am to abstain from writing in Portuguese, because my public is limited thereby, I may just as well write in the most widespread language of all. Why should I write in Castilian? That U. may understand me? It is asking too much for too little.[13]

Around this time, possibly, Pessoa wrote the emblematic poem that can be read as a rejoinder to Unamuno's "Portugal." Whenever it was written, however, it was not published until 1934, when Pessoa chose it to lead off the collection of historical lyrics he ultimately titled *Mensagem*. It is significant that in 1932 Pessoa reported that the title of his still unpublished book was *Portugal*, describing it as "um livro pequeno de poemas (tem 41 ao todo), de que o *Mar português* (*Contemporânea* 4) é a segunda parte."[14] In fact, Pessoa continued to call the book *Portugal* well into the proof stage, when, at the last moment, it gave way to *Mensagem*.

O DOS CASTELOS

A Europa jaz, posta nos cotovelos:
De Oriente a Occidente jaz, fitando,
E toldam-lhe românticos cabelos
Olhos gregos, lembrando.

O cotovelo esquerdo é recuado;
O direito é em ângulo disposto.
Aquele diz Italia onde é pousado;
Este diz Inglaterra onde, afastado,
A mão sustenta, em que se apoia o rosto.

Fita, com olhar esfíngico e fatal,
O Occidente, futuro do passado.

O rosto com que fita é Portugal.[15]

In place of Unamuno's crone looking pathetically out to sea in search
of the past of her pastness (as well as Higginson's sable-clad widow
and mother), Pessoa offers an alertly staring (ungendered) face looking out for the future of that past.[16] It is actually a profile seen only
on maps (one of Elizabeth Bishop's "profiles investigat[ing] the sea,
where land is") or in our day, perhaps, from the vantage of out-of-
space. Unlike Unamuno's old, barefooted woman, Pessoa's Portugal
is the face and head in profile of "Portugal-Europa," as he called it in
1916 when he vaunted "Sensacionismo" as the first manifestation of
that "Portugal-Europa," not, of course, that "Iberia," an idea to which,
as has been seen, Unamuno attached himself, as he announced as
early as 1910 to Teixeira de Pascoaes.[17] And again, is *Mensagem*, in
Pessoa's mind, the poem of the "supreme poet of Europe," who would
perforce emerge from the Portuguese spirit, as he had foretold in his
essay "A Nova Poesia Portuguesa no Seu Aspecto Psicológico," in
A Águia, the voice of Pascoaes's "Nova Renascença"? There, in 1912,
he had written: "Deve estar para muito breve, portanto, o aparaci-
mento do poeta supremo da nossa raça, e, ousando tirar a verdadeira
conclusão que se nos impõe, pelos argumentos que já o leitor viu, o

poeta supremo da Europa, de todos os tempos. É um arrojo dizer isto? Mas o raciocínio assim o quer."[18] Whether he knew it or not, Pessoa in 1912 had distanced himself from the Unamuno who in 1910 already considered himself more Iberian than European. For if Unamuno's Portugal continued to exist in *saudades* for the past, Pessoa's Portugal points to her future as "Europe-Portugal." Their differences on matters Hispanic and European were not to be effaced. It has not come down to us what Unamuno thought of *Mensagem*, a work that, made famous and notorious by its having been awarded a national prize, could not have escaped the attention of this Spaniard who to the last insisted that "cada día me siento menos europeo y más ibérico."[19]

Unamuno finds in the naturalistic figure of an old woman as grieving, keening crone the symbol for Portugal in the throes of its decadence. Pessoa, on the other hand, finds in the depiction of Portugal in a map of Europe the image of its fate, its past and its present with intimations of its future. Portugal is a metonym; it is the face of Europe, facing west. It is not landscape per se that Pessoa reacts to but the cartographer's barest one-dimensional outline of the outermost reach of the landscape.

Somewhere Jorge de Sena talks about the criticism-poem, by which I take him to mean the poem that offers a literary interpretation or an artistic criticism. *Metamorfoses* (1963) collects criticism-poems, most of them relating to specific works of sculpture or painting. Some of the poems of his *Arte de música* (1968) are criticism-poems relating to works of music and composers. What I would suggest here is that, in "Super flumina Babylonis," published in Sena's second collection of stories, *Novas andanças do demónio* (1966), Sena wrote what he might have called a criticism-story. Focusing on Camões's last days (though the poet's name is never given), it ends with Camões's setting down the first words of his great poem, the title of which Sena has taken for the title of his own story. The story offers a realist depiction of the quotidian days of the sick, infirm, aged Camões. Only at this stage in his life could he compose his famous *redondilha*, drawing on the Psalms. Is Camões producing it for money? Or is it that the artist creates a poem out of his pain?

How Sena's story relates to the subject of this piece—Unamuno's and Pessoa's different figures for Portugal—lies in his depiction of the mother of Camões, his most imaginative creation. Apart from her historical being in the realistic, mimetic mode, she is a harsh figure for "Portugal," a nation that cares for Camões just barely and hardly recognizes the worth of his accomplishment, encouraging him only to work beyond his physical and spiritual means. After Camões's death, the historical mother continued to collect her son's pension. She is, in short, an even harsher version of Higginson's or Unamuno's figure of Portugal as old crone. It was indicative of the times—the story was published in 1966, it will be recalled—that the figure Sena chose for Portugal was not the more optimistic one that Camões created and Pessoa, in 1934, resurrected.

7

The Correspondence

Of the several practical ways of publishing letters, no other way is as immediately satisfactory as the presentation of the complete correspondence exchanged by two individuals. Such collections of the two ways of a correspondence, meeting the requirements that they be of an appreciable duration, that they reflect a more or less mutual engagement (though not necessarily one of intimacy), and that they be presented in total or at least nearly complete, provide their interested readers with an experience quite unlike that offered by any other text or grouping of texts in any genre.

One of the bright spots of contemporary (or is it recent?) Portuguese literature is the continuing if intermittent appearance of Jorge de Sena's letters, mostly under the imprint of the Imprensa Nacional. In a series that now runs to more than ten volumes and promises to continue with at least ten more, we have available to date the two sides of Sena's correspondence with Guilherme de Castilho, Mécia de Sena, José Régio, Vergílio Ferreira, Sophia de Mello Breyner Andresen, Dante Moreira Leite, Eduardo Lourenço, José Augusto França, Delfim Santos and Manuela de Sousa Marques, João Gaspar Simões, Carlo Vittorio Cattaneo, and Eugénio de Andrade. Still awaiting publication is Sena's correspondence with Raul Leal, Luiz Francisco Rebello, Rui Knopfli, José Rodrigues Miguéis, António Ramos Rosa, Vasco Miranda, José Blanc de Portugal, Luís Amaro, Ruy Cinatti, José Saramago, and João Sarmento Pimentel. There is no reason to expect that the correspondence pertaining to these latter eleven will not live up to the high standard set by the volumes of correspondence already in print.

1.

The title of Mécia de Sena's selection of the love letters she exchanged with Jorge de Sena—*Isto tudo que nos rodeia*—comes from one of his letters: "I write to you in sadness, irritated at life, at all this that surrounds me, tired, beaten, in short, all that you already know or that you might even exaggeratedly imagine."[1] The quotation turned title suffers a sea change. Whereas Jorge wrote "me," Mécia's title reads "us," a change that points to the collaborative life that culminated in their marriage and that, as his widow, she continued in her dedication to the editing, publication, and dissemination of his work.

In the aggregate these letters finally do tell how Jorge moved away from the "me" of his own letters to the "us" of his life with Mécia. In most of the letters, however, it is the things that characterize Jorge's life, whether to plague him or, less often, to enhance his self-esteem, that predominate. Mécia has her moments, of course, but once her lover has acknowledged them, he gets down to the business of what is on his mind: military misadventures, money troubles (with mother and publisher), poetry concerns (with two volumes out, he has, in 1945, still another 4,000 poems ready to go), plays in the works that will revitalize the Lisbon theater, and, in a noteworthy instance, plans for a novel. It is not that the poet is not affectionate or considerate, for he is. But feelings he will display only when he so desires.

Jorge de Sena appears here in many guises: serious poet, harassed son, disillusioned recruit, compleat lover. It is accurate, moreover, to describe these letters as histrionic: the productions of a personage conscious of the ways of presenting the self within situations that, mutatis mutandis, presage those fictionalized later in *Os grão-capitães* and, stunningly, in *Sinais de fogo*. One is tempted to say further that the poet, in these letters of courtship, forged the selves—including a hypochondriac Jorge de Sena, even a mad Jorge de Sena—that made him the peculiar beau ideal of his lady. Small wonder it is, then, that there is so much in these letters about the poet's intensive wooing of the theater.

Mécia opens her introduction with an epigraph from Emily Dickinson, a Sena favorite: "'Twas my one Glory— / Let it be / Remembered / I was owned of Thee." She would have it apply, a key to the love story of Jorge and Mécia de Sena. It was recognized as such by Luciana Stegagno Picchio, who used the same lines as an epigraph to her article on Mécia de Sena's *Flashes*, a work-in-progress on the life she shared with Jorge.[2]

2.

The first three collections of Sena's correspondence vary greatly in interest and literary significance. The complete extant correspondence with Guilherme de Castilho came first, its appearance offering encouragement and example to those others of Sena's correspondents (and their families, in the case of the deceased) who might be reluctant to see their letters in print, at least at an early date.[3] The Sena/Castilho volume, it can be readily admitted, is of limited interest to all camps, whether literary, cultural, or historical. The second volume, of Sena's love letters, was a highly selective compendium that does not pretend to completeness. Doubtless there were necessities, more or less compelling, behind Mécia de Sena's decision in the volumes of Sena's letters prepared under her direction to depart, in this volume of love and courtship letters, from what is her otherwise obvious policy of inclusiveness, including inscriptions in books exchanged by the principals; but it is good to report that completeness was the goal in the José Régio correspondence as well as in the more moderately sized Vergílio Ferreira letters.[4] The difference in size of these two volumes—287 pages in the former but only 185 in the latter—reflects the nature of the relationship involved. Sena was personally closer to Régio than he ever was to Ferreira. Hence there were simply more letters exchanged over a shorter period, as well as more business conducted since for several years Sena was trying to gather information for "The Man and His Work" volume on Régio that he had agreed to write. Oddly, only after considerable stalling did Régio reluctantly answer Sena's questions, and then not all of them. The book was never written. With Vergílio Ferreira, on the other hand, things were different. Their meeting was almost by chance, and they saw each other rarely, perhaps only three or four times over a period of more than a quarter of a century, one of those times in late 1949, when they first met in Évora, and the last in 1977, when they were the featured speakers at national ceremonies held in Guarda. They knew each other's work, of course, exchanged inscribed copies of their publications as they appeared, and carried on, sporadically, a correspondence marked by long periods when it lay fallow. In all, there were thirty-three letters, eighteen by Sena and fifteen by Vergílio Ferreira.

The relatively small number of extant letters (and there is no sign that there were any others) offers further indication of what is abundantly clear from the contents of the letters themselves. Theirs was fundamentally a professional relationship between two writers whose good feelings toward one another were inspired not by deep personal affection or social intimacy but by the high respect in which each held the other and his writings. This mutually held, respectfully formal, almost formulaic high regard, it should be noted, did not distort or diminish the honesty of these letters. In sum, they conduct their correspondence on such a highly professional level that even the most passionate confessions of reader neglect, complaints about administrative and bureaucratic interference, and professions of existential depression never drop into the no-holds-barred exchanges of intimate friends whose bond is not merely amicable but deeply loyal. In short, it is doubtful, had they not been writers, that Sena and Ferreira would have had, temperamentally or otherwise, enough in common to promote much more than an acquaintanceship, let alone a friendship.

Only once in these letters is there an exchange of passionate complaint directly involving their relationship (as distinguished from impassioned accounts of emotions tried and expended on matters apart from their shared concerns). Ferreira writes Sena a letter of complaint, does not send it, and writes a second letter voicing (now in a more orderly, quiet way, we are to infer) his puzzlement at the fact that Sena would continue to have anything to do with someone whose writing he considers to be "mediocre." Sena answers succinctly with a rhetorical question: "But frankly—is what I tell you worth less to you than what others say?" Enough said.

Characteristically, Jorge de Sena reveals more about his day-to-day life than does Vergílio Ferreira. But each of them says a good deal about literature and the writer's life. It is in their contributions to the realms of philosophy, literary criticism, and—in Sena's case— early Portuguese history that these letters achieve their greatest value. Inevitably, there is some good gossip (much of it tamed, however, through an editorial decision to obscure identities by turning personal names into innocuous letters that do not even correspond to true initials), but the gossip, one hastens to say, is not what is important here. It is on the subject of what pertains to the intellectual life of the writer that these giants of modern Portuguese letters met, with ease and great intelligence.

Sena wrote long, impassioned, detailed, informed, sometimes angry letters. He simply did not deal in trivialities, suffer fools gladly, pay perfunctory compliments, or indulge in small talk of any kind. His hopes and disappointments, fears and complaints, all find a place in his headlong if controlled accounts of his works and days. His correspondents, sometimes touchingly in awe of this person who had at his command cataracts of informed opinions and precise

and minute analyses of feelings and situations, whether personal
and parochial, political, literary, or spiritual, seem invariably to have
taken their hint from Sena's letters. Their letters too are devoid of
standard small talk and innocuous verbiage—what the American
novelist Henry James called "the mere twaddle of graciousness."

3.

The Eduardo Lourenço/Jorge de Sena exchange, no less pleasurable
to read than the volumes of Sena's letters that preceded it, presents
the surviving correspondence—a bit out of balance, for several of
Sena's letters appear to be missing—between two Portuguese intellectuals in self-chosen exile: Lourenço spending much of his adult
professional life teaching first in Brazil and then in France; Sena
spending the last two decades of his life between Brazil and the
United States.[5] As such, their letters are fraught with confidences
exchanged in the knowing tones of the exile, exquisitely attuned to
the nuances of neglect and absence. They write about each other's
work and about their own. Sena reacts to Lourenço's interpretations
of his stories in *Os grão-capitães*, admitting to the strong autobiographical presence in his story about the aging Camões but denying
any identification with his obscenely unrepentant SS officer. They
exchange opinions on Portuguese literature, contemporary writers,
the true nature of the editors of *presença* (Sena says in 1967: "But
sincerely or conscientiously modernist, with the exception [with res-
ervations] of Casais [Monteiro], who was such?"). They wax hopeful
over the potential dissemination of Fernando Pessoa's poetry in
English when it is announced that Penguin Books will publish Jonathan Griffin's translations of Pessoa and his heteronyms (Lourenço
writes from Nice: "I have hopes that in *English*, finally, our man will
be much more widely read than he has been in French").

These are among the many salient moments in the letters, and I
shall point to only two others. There is Sena's long letter from Santa
Barbara, dated March 13, 1976, in which he talks about his upcoming

plans to visit Europe, his books just out and long in press, his great fatigue marked by loss of appetite and weight, and his "great disillusionment over everything." The letter concludes with the words, "Everybody has won all their battles against me . . . all I want is peace and quiet . . . as I said in a poem . . . to end up peacefully drinking coffee, in Crete, with the Minotaur, under the eyes of gods with no shame." Twelve days later—it now seems almost inevitable—Sena suffered a severe heart attack. The second instance is Lourenço's farewell letter, in which he writes eloquently of the Sena's achievement and of the failure of his contemporaries to recognize the magnitude of his work: "In Portugal what is at bottom unforgivable is not the distraction, not even the tripping-up in the dark, the secret and murderous demolition of the next person . . . but the failure to be contested, to be confronted head-on, to know directly the cultural passion that is involved in all such things, and which your work, like that of so many others, has not received. Yet, in his lifetime, did Camões see his work so favored? Did Eça? Pessoa?" Unfortunately, this expression of sentiments that Sena so much needed to hear did not arrive in Santa Barbara until June 5, 1978, the day after the poet's death.

The letters of Jorge de Sena are not ancillary to the writings that Lourenço praises but are themselves an integral part of his life's work.

8

The Sitwell Papers

If poetry really needs something extra and special, some flash of
color, some dramatic heightening, then, better than all the prizes
and gold medals and fancy dinners and White House flourishes,
would it be to persuade Dame Edith Sitwell to return from the
realm of shades. To see her once again regally or ecclesiastically
robed and seated in a great chair made to simulate a throne, looking like Elizabeth the First or Lady Macbeth or Robert Graves'
portrait of the White Goddess.

And should she find her audience annoying, to hear again her
voice lifted in denunciation. To hear again perchance what she is
reported once to have told an Edinburgh audience:

"No one has ever been more alive than I am. I am an electric eel
in a pond full of flatfish."

—Robert Francis, "Dame Edith" (1968)[1]

A report in the Brazilian *Jornal de Letras* that the famous English
poet Dame Edith Sitwell was going to translate thirty-seven of the
Brazilian poet's poems into English provided Manuel Bandeira
with an opportunity to write a chronicle in full disclaimer. The

distinguished English poet would not be translating thirty-seven poems of his, he corrected; indeed, she would not be translating any of his poems, though even a single translation, he admitted, would have pleased him inordinately. What he had said, rather, was that it was he who would like to do the translating—that is, translating Sitwell's poetry into Portuguese. Yet, as things turned out, he never did so. Perhaps he found the task too difficult. Perhaps there was some other reason. In any case, though he did admire Sitwell's poetry and its creator greatly, Bandeira seems never to have got around to the task.[2]

Bandeira had met Edith Sitwell in London in 1957, through the offices of a young Portuguese poet, Alberto de Lacerda, then working for the BBC. He documented meeting the two of them almost immediately in a poem, "Elegia de Londres," which he dated September 3, 1957.[3] Lacerda had also played a minor role in Jorge de Sena's first meeting with Edith Sitwell. In 1952, at the English poet's request—Sitwell knew about Sena's 1951 review of her work even before she met Lacerda—the Portuguese poet arranged the details of a meeting between Sena and the poet of Façade.[4] Lacerda, who himself had been introduced to her by the South African poet Roy Campbell, became a Sitwell favorite. One need only peruse her letters for this period to see that she was fond of this "very fine poet," calling him one of her "greatest friends."[5] Such a favorite was Lacerda and so much was he in the grande dame's good graces that he was permitted to joke about her. Not only did he tell his jokes with impunity, but Sitwell actually sanctioned them by repeating them to others. To the question of how he got along with the formidable and forbidding poet, Lacerda reportedly answered, "Well, you see, I was born in Portuguese East Africa, and so, as a baby, was lulled to sleep each night by the roar of lions outside the garden gate." Sitwell found the story amusing, she confessed to Jean Cocteau, though she admitted, "I have never been sure how to take that. Sometimes I think it a compliment, at other moments I am not so sure."[6] But Lacerda was safe. He was always safe with Sitwell. Elizabeth Salter, in her memoir of Sitwell, recalls that on the occasion of her own first meeting of the regal poet at one of her evenings at the Sesame Club, where she held court almost daily, she also met Lacerda and the pianist Gordon Watson. "Alberto de Lacerda was small, impeccably dressed, his dark eyes luminous with emotion, and poised like a dart-thrower to insert a compliment into the stream of conversation. His aim was unerring. He belonged to the history of such courts and his flattery was deft and informed," recalled the young Elizabeth Salter. "Edith returned compliment for compliment, as lavish in her praise as she was content to receive it. Gordon was a 'magnificent' pianist, a 'genius'; Alberto a 'superb' translator, an 'excellent' poet."[7] Lacerda served many purposes for Sitwell, including scouting out those poetic luminaries who might well promote her work in Portugal and Brazil. In this capacity, he not only brought Bandeira to meet her, but he translated into English at least one of Sena's reviews of her work.[8]

During Bandeira's visit to London, besides visiting with Lacerda, he met not only Sitwell but also Sena for the first time, though they had previously corresponded. In another of his sprightly chronicles, Bandeira wrote about Sena, who served him as a London cicerone in visits to the National Gallery and Westminster Abbey.[9] Sena promptly wrote up his recent impressions of Bandeira (as well as Sitwell) in "Londres e dois grandes poetas," a piece for the *Diário popular*.[10] At the same time he also wrote "Meditação em King's Road," a poem that he dedicated to both Dame Edith Sitwell and Manuel Bandeira in remembrance of the London afternoon on which, in Sena's presence, these "dois monstros sagrados, o inglês e o brasileiro," met for the first time.[11]

We know that Sitwell could not have read Sena's poem in the original, for like Sena's Minotaur, she, too, knew no Portuguese. But she most likely knew of the poem and Sena's honorific dedication. Bandeira, of course, liked the poem, even seeing in it something (mistakenly, as it turned out, for Sena intended no such meaning) about Bandeira's own decision, despite an official invitation to do so, not to visit Portugal after visiting England.[12]

There is no doubt that Bandeira greatly admired Sitwell's poetry. So did Sena, who, unlike Bandeira, did translate some of her poetry,

sometimes in the context of reviewing her work.[13] From the beginning of his reading of her poetry, several years before he met her,
Sena recognized her primacy as a modernist. To him she was the
equal of the very best poets who had written in English in the twentieth century. When in 1953 an English critic ventured the opinion
that the greatest poet then writing in English was Dylan Thomas,
Sena demurred:

> Sem dúvida que Dylan Thomas é um grande poeta e que a importân-
> cia da sua linguagem e da sua imagística fulgurante é manifesta na
> evolução da mais contemporânea poesia. Mas parece-me que a coisa
> foi dita para fazer pirraça a T. S. Eliot e a Edith Sitwell, já que nunca
> tem grande sentido—a não ser este—dizer que alguém é o maior,
> quando há outros muito grandes em exercício. E sem dúvida que
> os *Four Quartets*, de Eliot, como a majestosa *Song of the Cold* ou *The
> Shadow of Cain*, de Edith Sitwell, dão a medida actualíssima de dois
> poetas, para os quais a magnificência verbal, no caso de Edith, ou a
> contenção oblíqua—qualidades que, paradoxalmente, se encontram
> fundidas em Dylan Thomas—não se limitam a transmitir apenas uma
> transfigurada visão poética, mas apelam para aquela concreta visão do
> mundo, marginal à pura inspiração ou trabalho poético, e sem a qual
> nos custa sempre a reconhecer como transcendentalmente grande
> uma poesia.[14]

Several years later, to Portuguese readers, Sena summed up his sense
of Sitwell's career and importance, views he had been working out
in several pieces published in Portugal in the six years from 1951 to
1957.[15] In 1960 he wrote:

> Edith Sitwell nasceu em Scarborough (num ambiente que Osbert
> [Sitwell] retrataria nas memórias e satirizaria num dos seus melhores
> livros—*Before the Bombardment*, 1926) e fez estudos particulares. A
> sua poesia, desde *The Mother* (1915), *Façade* (1922) e *Bucolic Comedies*
> (1923), passando por *Gold Coast Customs* (1929), até *Green Song and
> Other Poems* (1944), aos monumentais *The Song of the Cold* (1945) e *The
> Shadow of Cain* (1947) e . . . majestade compacta dos *Collected Poems*
> de 1957 que seleccionam e coligem quarenta anos de ininterrupta

actividade poética, é de uma riqueza, de uma complexidade, de um brilho fascinante, e nela vai, com o tempo e as circunstâncias do mundo, desabrochando progressivamente, e adquirindo, senão maestria, estatura, um dos maiores poetas do nosso tempo. O excesso de imagística, de alusões culturais e religiosas abstrusas, a fantasia imaginosa, o vasto sopro rítmico de poemas amplos como odes pindáricas, a insistência em certos tópicos formais pessoalmente absorvidos, o cruzamento periclitante entre uma segurança elegante à Pope (que ela estudou magistralmente—*Alexander Pope*, 1930) e um profetismo neo-platonizante e paralelístico à Whitman, tudo isso tem feito que a grandeza do poeta pareça limitada, um pouco fabricada como a sua conversão ao catolicismo no ano (1954) em que a sua carreira se coroou com o título de Dama do Império Britânico. Nada mais enganoso. O crítico penetrante e sagaz que ela é (o Pope; *The English Eccentrics*, 1933; *A Poet's Notebook*, 1943; e tantos outros escritos e antologias organizadas o provam) nunca se enganou acerca de si próprio como artista, e pode dizer-se que, à vigilância peculiar que ele exerceu sobre a interioridade do poeta, deveram a Segunda Grande Guerra Mundial e a Bomba Atómica que a autora graciosa e perfeita de *Bucolic Comedies* e do *Colonel Fantock* (poemas em que uma refinada atmosfera de ironia bucólica é atravessada por um lancinante dramatismo contido), a divertida autora dos poemas que o compositor William Walton pôs em bailado (*Façade* são experiências rítmicas, cujo recitativo o bailado sublinha, e reciprocamente), tenha escrito os mais poderosos poemas, na força de uma eloquência que não recua perante coisa alguma, que esses trágicos acontecimentos suscitaram. Já Yeats dissera, ao saudar *Gold Coast Customs*, que, com Edith Sitwell, regressava "à literatura algo ausente dela: [. . .] paixão enobrecida pela intensidade, o sofrimento, a sabedoria . . ." E foi isso mesmo, que a actividade seguinte confirmou, o que entrou na poesia inglesa com Edith Sitwell. A par do próprio Yeats, que é outro poeta crescendo sempre com a idade, e de T. S. Eliot, tão dolorosamente restrito ao que fora, Edith Sitwell representa uma das forças mais importantes da poesia inglesa deste século, por muito que lhe prefiram hoje a agressividade restrita de um Robert Graves. A sua poesia—tão sibilina como a de Yeats, tão culta como a de Eliot—vibra de uma paixão cósmica, de uma humanidade solitária, de uma dolorida mas altiva consciência da missão do poeta: dizer, como afirma em *The Song of the Cold*, do "derradeiro frio no coração do Homem."[16]

I have quoted at length, partly because this work, published in fascicles, is hard to come by, and because it presents Sena's early but unchanging assessment of Edith Sitwell's work and towering stature, onc he repeated in *A literatura inglesa*, the history of English literature Sena published in São Paulo in 1963.[17] After Sitwell died, in 1964, just months before the death of T. S. Eliot in 1965, Jorge de Sena noted: "Com as mortes de Edith Sitwell e de T. S. Eliot, ocorridas a pouco tempo de diferença, é uma época da poesia britânica, e pode dizer-se que anglo-saxónica, o que se encerra definitivamente."[18]

Another member of Sitwell's group was Roy Campbell, who, as we have already noted, was the poet who introduced Alberto de Lacerda to Sitwell.[19] Sena knew and admired Campbell's poetry, publishing translations of three poems in the 1950s.[20] Although it is not known when they first met, exactly, it is known that Sena consulted the South African poet on at least one professional matter. When Sena and Adolfo Casais Monteiro first thought of translating Fernando Pessoa's English sonnets into Portuguese, they had difficulty understanding some parts of the poems. They directed their appeal for help to Campbell, who by that time was already living in Portugal, where he would die in an automobile accident in Setúbal in 1957. Years later, in answer to a question put to him by Luciana Stegagno Picchio, Sena recalled:

> Campbell, que detestava muito do modernismo, favorecia uma simplicidade directa da expressão poética, e fazia questão de ser "homem de acção" (era um reaccionário pavoroso, combatente franquista da Guerra Civil Espanhola, admirador do Salazar, e venerador fervoroso da Nossa Senhora de Fátima) que odiava "literatices," não gostou dos sonetos [ingleses de Fernando Pessoa], e muito menos do mais. E confessou que *não entendia* vários dos passos que nós não entendíamos. Isto podia ser mera hostilidade a uma linguagem levada à mais incrível complicação literário-sintáctica, mas não era inteiramente ódio à

complexa ambiguidade. Era realmente uma reacção a uma expressão em que o esforço se sente por de mais e nem sempre funciona.[21]

Sena then goes on to say that it was at about the same time that he presented Edith Sitwell with a copy of Pessoa's English sonnets. Her reaction, he recalled, was highly favorable:

Esta mulher extraordinária (cuja grandeza muita crítica anglo-saxónica insiste em diminuir) admirou profundamente muito dos sonetos, reconhecendo indubitavelmente a riqueza contida neles, e que é, quanto a mim, muitas vezes, a visão do poeta que, em tantos outros lugares, veremos realizada e expressa.[22]

Until now—with the publication below of Sitwell's letter of June 20, 1953—Sena has remained the authority for her favorable reaction to Pessoa's sonnets, since she seems never to have made public her views on the poems.[23] Yet, in presenting her with a pristine copy of Pessoa's *35 Sonnets*, published in Lisbon in 1918, Sena must have hoped in his heart of hearts that the redoubtable Sitwell would take it upon herself to put in a good word in the right English places for the great Portuguese modernist poet. He inscribed the copy to "Doctor" Edith Sitwell, who on June 20, 1951, had been awarded the honorary LittD by Oxford University. The inscription reads:

To Doctor Edith Sitwell,

with gratitude, remembering the
kindness of her genius, this
little and precious side of one
of the greatest portuguese poets.
Lisbon, March 1953

Jorge de Sena[24]

The pages are uncut. Sena's gift of Pessoa's little book, however, prompted Sitwell to write him a letter. Their sporadic correspondence, covering a seven-year span, has never been published. It appears here through the good offices and the kind permission of Mécia de Sena, who generously supplied me with photocopies of Sitwell's letters and typewritten transcriptions of Sitwell's inscriptions in books presented to Jorge de Sena, as well as photocopies of Sena's letters to Sitwell in draft, with one exception—the last letter, dated December 25, 1960, which was forwarded to me in a typewritten transcription.[25] The Edith Sitwell materials are quoted here with the permission of Francis Sitwell, the copyright holder.

In editing the letters I have standardized the placing of the inside return address and date, the salutation, and the complimentary close, and I have italicized or placed within quotation marks, as appropriate, the titles of books, journals, and poems. I have generally followed the originals in spelling, grammar, punctuation, and capitalization, but I have made uniform the beginnings of all paragraphs by indentation.

English was an acquired language for Sena. One admires his insistence on writing to Sitwell in her own tongue, obviously not choosing to write in Portuguese and having someone translate his words. Certainly, in the early years at least, Lacerda could have turned the trick of translation for his two friends. It was characteristic of Sena to have persisted in writing in English. It seems fitting to present Sena's English as he wrote it—warts and all—in preliminary drafts of letters destined for Dame Edith Sitwell, a fellow poet.

The Correspondence

1.

Renishaw Hall, Renishaw, NR Sheffield. Tel. Eckington (Derbyshire) 42. Telegrams, Eckington, Derbyshire. 20 June: 1953

Dear Mr. de Sena,

I am grieved not to have written to thank you for your most kind present of Fernando Pessoa's *35 Sonnets*, long before this. Please do not think me lacking either in courtesy or in gratitude.

The book arrived at a moment when I had a time-limit for finishing the "treatment" of a film in which I have been engaged in Hollywood, and I was, at the same time, suffering from sciatica and fibrositis, both in their most acute form, and I did not want to write to thank you until I could do so with some coherency.

I am most grateful to you for your great kindness in sending me the book, the Sonnets are flawlessly formed. Who translated them? Or were they, actually, written in English? I imagine they were *not*, but they are so flawless as Sonnets, that one can hardly believe they are translations.

They are lucid and lucent, —carved from some transparent stone that is a trap for the light.

I am delighted to hear from Alberto de Lacerda that you have not, after all, gone to Africa, —for, amongst other reasons, I hope this means that we shall soon have the pleasure of seeing you in England again. When—and I hope this will be very soon—you come, please do let me know.

My friendship with Alberto is a great happiness to me. It is one of the very many things I owe to my dear Roy and Mary Campbell.

I hope, in the next few months, to send you another book of poems. It will be called *Gardeners and Astronomers*.

With very many thanks, and all of best wishes

Yours very sincerely
Edith Sitwell[26]

2.

19 July 1953

Dear Doctor Sitwell

How can I think you lacking "either in courtesy or in gratitude," if you had the kindness of writing about the *35 Sonnets*? Any letters from you are to me such a pleasure, and what can I say about the expectancy you put me in promising me your *Gardeners and Astronomers?* I hope I will be able of reviewing "them" somewhere as soon as possible.

About the *35 Sonnets*. They were *not* translated, they were written in English. Fernando Pessoa (1888–1935) has been educated in Durban, where his stepfather was there the Portuguese consul. He "thought" in English as well as in Portuguese—his papers are full of little notes, taken quite in hazard, the English ones being more numerous than the Portuguese ones. He has published, besides the *Sonnets*, two long English poems—*Antinous* and *Epithalamium*—I think magnificent both in imagery and in disregard of all moral literary conventions, and a collection of little *Inscriptions*, in the Greek-Latin manner, that I think graceful but slightly irrelevant. Writing in Portuguese, he was *four* poets entirely different in thought and form (he called them his "heteronims" and treated himself as one of them under his own name): Fernando Pessoa, Alvaro de Campos, Alberto Caeiro, Ricardo Reis. The importance of the English language and of the English-speaking literature in his writing and culture was a great one: he is, sometimes, in my opinion, an English poet, quite aware of his time, writing in Portuguese; and, notwithstanding, a leading Portuguese poet, responsible for all the "revolutions" either in Portuguese or in Brazilian poetry, as soon as his enormous posthumous work has been published (and not the whole of it). During his lifetime, he had published very few Portuguese poems known only by the Portuguese "modernists" who, acknowledged him with his friend Sá-Carneiro (who very young has committed suicide in 1916, in Paris, and is a great and strange poet I think you would love much more than Pessoa) as the renewers of Portuguese poetry. The greater public only knew him then as much as the English people knew you and your brothers for years. To add to the confusion, Pessoa was always mixed, through the most violent manifestoes, with all the literary attitudes or political revolutions he thought would serve what he called the "Portuguese renaissance." His literary criticism and his essays on poetry I have collected and am revising for a new and larger edition are among the brightest, ironic and paradoxical I know from any language.[27]

He was personally a timid, kind and very lonely man, torn between his esoteric culture and an only love . . . drinking. You must remember a French translation of one poem by Alvaro de Campos (the Whitmanian heteronim, as Pessoa-himself is the traditional one, Reis the Horatian one, and Caeiro the most "simple-minded" of all) you have read—"The Tobacconist."[28] Perhaps you would enjoy better, from this pen-name, the extraordinary "Marine Ode." Ask Alberto de Lacerda about some fragments he was rendering in English with a friend and I have heard when I was there and think sometimes more exact than the Portuguese text (perhaps Pessoa has "thought" in English the Campos poems . . .).

Herewith you will find one page torn from a newspaper where I have committed upon your brother Sacheverell the same crimes not long ago committed upon your poetry.[29]

The other day, I met, quite by accident, Roy Campbell. We have spoken a little about you, about London, about Alberto too. He is preparing two books (to America, I think) one of translations from Pessoa and the other a general anthology of Portuguese poetry from the most ancient poems (the "cancioneiros" in galaic language, that have originated somewhat all the Hispanic poetry) to the modern times.[30] Because myself and my wife are great friends of one little boy and very grown-up poet you may know under his pen-name (short-rendering of his long real one)—Alberto de Lacerda—I think that, if his friendship is to you what with your great heart you tell me it is, your friendship is to him an happiness too.[31] Sometimes I find, when I read you or when I hear from you, that you are too modest about your kindness. Isn't that true?

I don't know when I can return to England: I only dream of that. I would enjoy very heartily to see you again.

Sincerely and always yours
Jorge de Sena

P.S. Can you excuse me so horrible an English writing? And give my best wishes to Sir Osbert?

3.

Flat 1, 11 Netherton Grove, London, S.W.10.

24th November 1953.

Dear Senhor de Sena,

Dr. Edith Sitwell has asked me to send you this new book of hers on her behalf, as she is away in America.

Yours sincerely,
H. Mary Fraser.
Secretary to Dr. Edith Sitwell.

4.

Lisbon

February 14, 1954

Dear Doctor Sitwell

At your request, your secretary has sent me, now nearly three months ago, your *Gardeners and Astronomers*. You must forgive me so long a silence in acknowledging and expressing you my gratitude. Indeed, I read you thoroughly at the time—and what a time I had since then! In the meanwhile, you may have already returned to England, perhaps you are now in Italy or in America again.

You must believe me telling you that my life was very hard till now and I wanted constantly to write you at leisure, because if there is now anyone in the world with whom I will do the utmost to lose not the contacts I have, that one is you. I hope you will excuse me, if I may seem another youngster plaguing you—what I am not and don't want to be taken for. It is not an affair of pride, but just of honour, on my side. Not every day we meet with a truly great poet; and, even when you have no time or no sufficient reason for writing to me, yet have I the joy of being able to tell you, "personally," something about your poetry and what this poetry is to me (the scholars may very well do all the rest, which is indeed their duty).

As this letter of mine is one of excuses, I need to let you know another fault, which one perhaps did not reach you. In the same newspaper where I wrote about your brother Sacheverell (and am intending to write about your last book and about Sir Osbert, who is entirely ignored in this country), I had published an essay about "Fernando Pessoa and the English literature" and annotated translations from some of his English sonnets you know.[32] I had no time to ask you the necessary permission and quoted a phrase from your letter on them. I said only that Dr. Edith Sitwell had found them "translucent." I would not quoted you, if to admire Pessoa was not another proof to the public of your poetic mind and Pessoa one of the greatest poets in the world, really worthy your admiration. Am I forgiven?[33]

And now about your book. Its greatness lies not only, as we might think, in the magnificent achievement your poetry *is*, but, curiously enough, also in what you *promise*. You are one of those rarest poets whose poetry is not discovery of oneself or of *their* own poetry. Your poetry is "like the heart of forgetful spring," always "a new-beginning, primal motion, a self-moving game that changes," as "the elements are but as qualities that change for ever, like things that have known generation." Even your profound knowledge and experience are like those of things that have known generation—always bringing a-new what is more truly themselves. And that is why you, who spoke and speak with such overwhelming beauty about a transcended old age, are always *promising*, as prophets know how to promise.

I can not write about your poetry, at this moment, without remembering *The Shadow of Cain* and the voice of Dylan Thomas mingling with yours.[34] His death was for me very surprising and sad news I received when opening one of the issues of *Encounter*. Some day I will write about a poet I prize so much—indeed I had not yet written, because his poetry is nearly untranslatable, and I have been, at times, fighting with some of his poems. I know his death must have been a blow to you; I pray you accept my deepest regret.[35]

Always truly and sincerely yours

JS

P.S. I ask you to notice I have changed my address to:

Rua 18—Restelo—18Lisbon[36]

5.

Castello di Montegufoni Montagnanadi Pesaprov: Firenze

20 September: 1954

Dear Mr. de Sena,

Nothing has ever given me greater pleasure than your most kind review of my *Gardeners and Astronomers*.[37] Indeed, I do not know how to thank you.

Alberto very kindly translated it for me.

It shows such a wonderful comprehension of every thing that I was endeavoring to express. Nobody has ever understood every implication in my poetry more fully than you, and with more complete insight.

I am very deeply grateful to you.

I hope so much that you will be in England again soon—but not, I trust, whilst I am in America, for which I sail in November. I imagine I must be there for some months, as I have to finish the script of my film about Anne Boleyn.

I have just finished writing an "Elegy for Dylan Thomas," for the American magazine *Poetry*. I will send it to you when it appears.[38]

I arrived in New York two days after his death there. It was a terrible shock and great grief, I believe him to have been a very great poet. I hope you do, too.

I have seen a great deal of dear Alberto, to whom I become more and more attached.

With my very deep gratitude and most deep appreciation, and all best wishes.

Yours very sincerely
Edith Sitwell

6.

Lisbon

July 10th, 1955

My dear Poet

Can you understand and forgive me my silence? I did not answer your most kind letter about my review of *Gardeners and Astronomers* and till now I had not acknowledged receipt of your imposing *Collected Poems*, published by Vanguard Press, and which you kindly gave me. I was lately waiting for a moment in my difficult life to write leisurely about them and for the opportunity of doing so in a more widely read newspaper, as it is this one I enclose here.[39] As you may know from our Alberto, this newspaper is not the best, but it is really the most widely read here and overseas. I should like to make you known and respected in Portugal as the great poet you are; and your good words about my understanding fully your poetry, although written out of your kindness, were to me a great warrant to the purpose I am following as best as I can.

You may not remember you have spoken, in your letter, about the grief you felt on the death of Dylan Thomas and the "Elegy" you wrote to his memory. I had met him, in London, at Humphrey Searle's, the same night I had the honour to meet you. Has the "Elegy" appeared in the meanwhile? Also I find him a great poet, a very difficult but a rewarding one; and for long I have hesitated in translating him, as he is, I think, untranslatable. His fullness of tone and imagery is not of the same kind as yours. His imagery is not the display of a concentrated feeling as yours is, but the concentration of language to the utmost limits of transposed meaning. And to render this in another language is to assemble meaningless images. (etc, etc . . .)[40]

7.

Castello di Montegufoni Montagnana Val di Pesaprov: Firenze Italy

15 October: 1955

Dear Senhor de Sena,

It would be quite impossible for me to express that great pleasure your wonderful review of my *Collected Poems* gave, and gives, me, nor how great is my gratitude.

I am so late in writing to thank you because of a most stupid accident. The review, and your letter, reached me the very day I was leaving Renishaw for London. In the general turmoil of finishing my packing I left it behind, and, as I could not ask the housemaid to look over my papers (if I had, all would have been lost for ever!) I had to wait till my return to retrieve it and to ask Alberto to translate it for me.

Nobody has ever understood every intention, every flash, every nuance, of my poetry more profoundly than you.

Nobody has ever done more for my poetry than you.

I am everlastingly grateful to you. And that gratitude goes very deep.

I do not know how to show this sufficiently. But if I ever write another poem that I like enough, that I think good enough, I hope you will allow me to dedicate it to you.

Meanwhile, I am going to send you, tomorrow, under separate cover, my unpublished "Elegy for Dylan Thomas," that I shall copy for you.

I am most grieved to hear that you and Sacheverell did not meet while he was in Portugal.

You know, neither he nor I have seen the essay you were so very good as to write about him. It is very sad. Because he is often in a tragic mood, and it would have meant so much to him![41]

I am very angry with Robert Graves. In a book just published, called *The Crowning Privilege* (—his lectures at Cambridge) he has attacked, in a really monstrous manner, Pope, Blake, Yeats, Tom Eliot, Ezra Pound, Wystan Auden, and Dylan Thomas. The book contains one beautiful, if rather thin, poem. He ought to know better than to do this.[42]

I do hope we shall see you in England again, soon—at a time when we are there.

Do you ever see my dear Roy and Mary Campbell?

With my deepest and most true gratitude, and with best wishes

Yours very sincerely
Edith Sitwell

8.

Lx. 27/8/957

My most dear Poet and good friend

After several years, I can return to England. I will be in London from the 4th September to the 15th. From then on till the 27th I will be at Slough, near Windsor (————) for a specialized course in reinforced concrete. After that, I will stay in London till the first days of October. Would you be so kind as to tell me when and how may I see you? My address at London may be Alberto's.

With anticipated gratitude and my best wishes, I am

Truly and sincerely your
JS

9.

Durrants Hotel
George Street
Manchester Square
W I

4 September: 1957

Dear Mr. de Sena,

It is such an immense pleasure to me that you are now in England,
and that I shall see you before I start for Italy next Monday.

Can you come here for a drink on Friday, at a quarter to 6, with
Alberto?

I do hope so.

I will ask Father D'Arcy also, and Father Caraman.[43]

And I shall have my *Collected Poems* waiting for you. It contains
the "Elegy to Dylan Thomas," the manuscript of which never
reached you. The Italian post, I fear, must have lost it.

All best wishes. I look forward to seeing you.

Yours very sincerely
Edith Sitwell

10.

Wexham Springs

September 26th, 1957

My most dear Poet and Friend

In a few days I'll be back to Portugal. But I wish to thank you, before
I go, from that lovely countryside (I am very close to the churchyard
of Gray's elegy—I don't remember if you have that piece in a very
high esteem) and from England yet, for the great pleasure of having

met you again, spoken with you and received from you the signs of your kindness. It was most delicate you had not forgotten, as you might, celebrating your 70th birthday, having been so dangerously ill and preparing to go abroad, the copy of your *Collected Poems*. And the few minutes of our talk before the visitors started to come, and the pleasure of hearing you after, are things that I will not forget too.

I began my little piece of writing on your book and on having seen you. As soon as it shall be issued, I will send it to you.[44]

Dear Dame, I hope that, with the grace of God, we meet again in a short time. In the meanwhile, you have always the gratitude and the friendship of your admirer

Jorge de Sena

11.

Assis

December the 25th, 1960

Dear Dame Edith Sitwell[45]

You have not for a long time heard from me, which does not matter very much, nor have I heard from you, what matters very much to me, as I am and always have been, an admirer of your poetry and a friend of yours. And now you hear not only from me but from Brazil, where I am living for an year and an half, having been invited to a Congress, and accepted then a chair at this University. My wife and my seven children are here with me. Thus, I have changed the terrible oppression which overcomes all life in my country for the free air of Brazil, where the Portuguese democrats are very well received.

I have just read that you signed a protest against the censorship in Spain, giving with your great name a weight to it, which otherwise it would have not.[46] As you may know, anyone who protests against Franco or the Portuguese Salazar is a "communist." I think it rather difficult to label you or Mr. E. M. Forster so. In my personal name and in the name of the "Portuguese Commission for Freedom of Expression," which I am a member of, and is going to write to you, I warmly congratulate you for an act of Christian Charity. And here I ask you a further act. Why do you, English people, always forget that for now near thirty-five years Portugal lives under a dictatorship as ruthless as the Spanish one, if it is not more, given the situation of being less than the other before the eyes of the world? Do you know that, if you have some character, and not being an aesthete living in the clouds (and willingly forgetting who pays those clouds . . .), your intellectual life is impossible in my country? If such names as yours, which I have made known in Portugal, and Mr. Greene's (whom I have translated and prefaced twice), appeared denouncing a situation which has, some time ago, denied a visa to the late Mr. Bevan on the grounds that he was a "crypto-communist," the Portuguese government would think that he is not so "ignored" in England as he wishes to be.[47]

And coming now to less sad things: as an appendix to a translation I directed of an History of the English Literature, I have written, as a result of two thirds of my life dedicated to England, an History of Modern English Literature. That work is going to be published separately here. As soon as I have a copy (I think in four or five months), it will be sent to you.

Now I am more distant of England than I was; but, who knows, I shall be able to go there next year, and to see you once more.

This is to-day Christmas Day. May I wish you and your family all the happiness which you are worthy of after so much beauty given to the English language?

Truly and sincerely yours
Jorge de Sena

P.S. Soon I expect to ask your permission for an anthology of your poems, translated by me and preceded by a long essay, which a publisher here is interested in.[48] Do you know that English Literature does not exist here, while American Literature has three years in the Universities?

Appendix

There are in Jorge de Sena's library five Edith Sitwell books, gifts of the author. Four of them are signed presentation copies. My source for this information is a list kindly supplied by Mécia de Sena.

1. *A Poet's Notebook* (London: Macmillan, 1950).
"For / Señor Don Jorge de Sena / with gratitude / from / Edith Sitwell" [annotated: "Receb. 16/6/952"]

2. *The Canticle of the Rose: Selected Poems 1920–1947* (London: Macmillan, 1950)
"For / Señor Don Jorge de Sena / with great gratitude / from / Edith Sitwell" [annotated: "Receb. 16/6/952"]

3. *Gardeners and Astronomers* (London: Macmillan, 1953) [annotated: "rec. 27/11/53"]

4. *Collected Poems* (New York: Vanguard, 1954)
"For / Senhor Jorge de Sena / with great gratitude / and best wishes / from / Edith Sitwell"

5. *Collected Poems* (London: Macmillan, 1957)
"For / Señor Jorge de Sena / with great gratitude / and best wishes / from / Edith Sitwell"

9

On American Writing

Jorge de Sena's interest in English-language writing in the United States long preceded his arrival in Madison, Wisconsin, in 1965. He had translated novels and stories by Ernest Hemingway and Erskine Caldwell, plays by Arthur Miller and Eugene O'Neill, and poems by Walt Whitman, Stephen Crane, and, preeminently, Emily Dickinson.

1.

It was as poet and as student of world poetry that Jorge de Sena turned to the task of translating Emily Dickinson. *80 Poemas de Emily Dickinson*, a book based on a text Sena prepared in Araraquara, São Paulo, Brazil, in 1962, and subsequently revised, first in 1967 and then in 1968, appeared posthumously in 1979 under the imprint of Edições 70 in Lisbon.

In agreement with those readers who have seen Dickinson as Walt Whitman's only nineteenth-century competitor as the United States' greatest poet, Sena insists nonetheless upon the modernism of her work, attributing her great success to her conception of herself as a poet "above the concepts of both the professional (writing for professors of poetry) and the amateur (writing for her family)," a conception that enabled, fostered, and nurtured her commitment to poetic and personal privacy. Because of its tone and temper, as well as its peculiar and startling emphases, Dickinson's poetry presents a translator with large challenges and considerable difficulties. Her translator needs to be true to the details of individual poems, of course, but he or she must also respond faithfully to the thrusts and curves of Dickinson's work taken as a whole. With this in mind, it is instructive to attend to Sena's own view of his practice as Dickinson's translator.

> In the Portuguese text, I have sought to reproduce, as closely as possible, the metrics and rhythms of the originals, while still translating each poem line by line. If occasionally I have had to suppress a detail, sacrificing it to the analytical nature of our language, thereisn't a single instance in which the inherent ambiguity of the English text has been compromised by an explanatory interpretation. Translation is not the act of remaking another's poetry into one's own but the making out of one's own language what an Emily Dickinson would have done and said had she attempted, in Portuguese, the same poem.[1]

Fidelity to Dickinson's technique as well as to her thought and emotion is Sena's promised intention. Above all, he does not want to follow the lead of Manuel Bandeira, the Brazilian poet who, as Sena notes, published Portuguese versions ("translations, very free" translations) of four Dickinson poems: "I Died for Beauty," "I Never Lost as Much but Twice," "I Never Saw a Moor," and "My Life Closed Twice." As it so happens, not at all surprisingly, Sena also translates these poems among his selection of eighty. A comparison of the versions of given poems by these two great poets does not always bear out, at least not in every way, Sena's sweeping judgment that Bandeira's versions are very free, perhaps too free. Take the opening lines of their versions of "I Never Lost as Much but Twice," for example. The "content" of the poem emerges faithfully in both versions, but it is notable that Sena is more faithful to the metrics and rhythms of

Dickinson's poem. Dickinson writes, for example, of "Angels—twice descending / Reimbursed My store—." Ignoring Dickinson's meter, Bandeira renders these lines:

> Duas vezes os anjos, descendo dos céus
> Reembolsaram-me de minhas provisões[.]

Sena does better:

> Por duas vezes os Anjos—
> Descem a encher-me os bornais—

A more complicated case is offered by the way in which Bandeira and Sena chose to tackle Dickinson's forceful poem "I Died for Beauty."

> I died for Beauty—but was scarce
> Adjusted in the Tomb
> When One who died for Truth, was lain
> In an adjoining Room—
>
> He questioned softly "why I failed"?
> "For Beauty," I replied—
> "And I—for Truth—Themself are One—
> We Brethren, are," He said—
>
> And so, as Kinsmen, met a Night—
> We talked between the Rooms—
> Until the Moss had reached our lips—
> And covered up our—names—

Bandeira, who was always moved by the poem, translated it:

> Morri pela beleza, mas apenas estava
> Acomodada em meu túmulo,
> Alguém que morrera pela verdade
> Era depositado no carneiro contíguo.
>
> Perguntou-me baixinho o que me matara:

—A beleza, respondi.
—A mim, a verdade—é a mesma coisa.
Somos irmãos.
E assim, como parentes que uma noite se encontram.
Conversamos de jazigo a jazigo,
Até que o musgo alcançou os nossos lábios
E cobriu os nossos nomes.

Again paying close attention to metrics and rhythm, Sena translates Dickinson's poem:

Morri pela Beleza—mas mal eu
Na tumba me acomodara,
Um que pela Verdade entanto morrera
A meu lado se deitara.

De manso perguntou-me por quem tombara . . .
—Pela Beleza—disse eu.
—A mim foi a Verdade—é a mesma Coisa.
Somos irmãos—respondeu.

E quais na Noite os que se encontram falam—
De Quarto a Quarto a gente conversou—
Até que o Musgo veio aos nossos lábios—
E os nossos nomes—tapou.

Apart from noting that the metrics of Sena's version are closer to Dickinson's than are Bandeira's (compare his "Somos irmãos" and Sena's "Somos irmãos—respondeu," for example, with Dickinson's "'We Brethren, are', he said"), the first observation one makes about the two translations is that the translators have found different solutions to certain of Dickinson's more or less problematic words and phrases. Sena takes the line "In an adjoining Room" and converts it into "a meu lado" ("at my side"), while Bandeira, inspired by Dickinson's choice of the word "Tomb," extends the overall notion by rendering the line as "carneiro contíguo" ("the next charnel-house [or sepulchre]"). Much the same thing happens in their rendering of "We talked between the Rooms," which Sena translates as "De Quarto a Quarto a gente conversou" ("from room to room we spoke") and Bandeira as "Conversamos de jazigo a jazigo" ("we talked from vault to vault [or sepulchre to sepulchre]").

As one can readily see, the difference between Sena's typical choices in translating given words and phrases and Bandeira's options results in different poetic effects. If Sena's more neutral word choice "quarto" for "room," for example, contributes to the aura of human domesticity with which Dickinson imbues the tomb, Bandeira's poet's license leads him, in choosing "carneiro" and "jazigo," to build on "tomb," to use the notion of "tomb" as a source of, and control for, the poem's subsequent diction and imagery. The fact is, however, that either principle—(1) that fidelity to the spirit of a poem depends upon fidelity to the letter of the poem, to its literal sense, line by line, word for word, or (2) that it depends upon a higher fidelity to the greater overall poetic sense of the poem—entails choices that inevitably shape one's interpretation of poems. That much is revealed in the difference between Sena's understanding that the "Brethren" died, respectively, for "Love" and "Truth," and Bandeira's decision that they were killed by "Love" and "Truth." It should also be noted that the desire to approximate the poem's rhythm encourages Sena to drop the reference to "Kinsman" in the ninth line. Inhibited by no such concern, Bandeira relaxes the line sufficiently to include the reference, choosing the term "parentes."

Yet things are not always perfect in a Sena translation even when it is an accurate, literal rendition of a single poem, for it does not always strike the right Dickinson note. To render "I never saw a Moor" as "Eu nunca vi Charnecas," as Sena does, for example, is more economical than to render it, as Bandeira does, "Nunca vi um campo de urzes." It is faultless, moreover, if one attends only to the letter of the line. But "Charnecas" does not ring a Dickinson note; the term, hard and harsh, is far more appropriate to one of Sena's more brusque poems than would be the noun "Matos," which though perhaps less precise literally, would come closer to the spirit of Dickinson's "Moor." Indeed, from time to time, as in this case, one detects the too forceful accents of Sena's own poetic voice in these translations. Less defensible are the instances in which Sena makes changes in the poems, the virtue of which eludes the reader. In "I Lost a World—the Other Day!," for example, he translates the last line, "Oh find it—Sir—for me!" as "Procurai-mo, por favor!" Grant it that Dickinson slant-rhymes "me" with "Eye," and that Sena honors the original pairing by rhyming "favor" with "Valor." He does so, however, by introducing the notion of "por favor" ("please") and dropping the reference, in direct address, to "Sir." Something similar happens with "I'm Nobody! Who are you?" in which the seasonably specific phrase, "the livelong June," becomes the quite different "o dia todo" ("the whole day"). Another kind of change results from Sena's penchant for introducing questions unauthorized in the original. In "I've Seen a Dying Eye," Dickinson's line "In search of Something—as it seemed" becomes "Como a procura—de que?" while elsewhere "To make Routine a Stimulus" becomes "A Rotina ser Estímulo?"

On rare occasions Sena misses something essential about a poem. A case in point is Dickinson's

> Surgeons must be very careful
> When they take the knife!
> Underneath their fine incision
> Stirs the Culprit—*Life*!

Dickinson's poem presents itself more as an observation about surgery than as a warning. The poem is directed at no one in particular. Sena's version presents itself explicitly as a warning addressed to surgeons:

> Cirurgiões, tende cuidado
> Com essa faca tão fina!
> Sob o golpe tão subtil
> Treme o culpado—é a Vida!

A fair translation of Sena's version, I think, would read something like this:

> Surgeons, take care
> With that knife that sharp!
> Beneath the incision so fine
> Trembles the culprit—it is Life!

Sena's is still a good poem, but one more in his direct-attack manner than in Dickinson's oblique truth-telling style.

Something can and should be said about the choice Sena makes among the 1775 Dickinson poems he had available to him, as well as about the texts themselves. In the matter of texts for *80 Poemas de Emily Dickinson*, Sena selected, although nowhere does he so indicate, those of the single-volume *The Complete Poems of Emily Dickinson*, edited by Thomas H. Johnson, for the Boston publisher Little, Brown and Company, in 1960. In Sena's bilingual edition the poems and the translations are reproduced on facing pages, their appearance marred only by a handful of typographical errors sprinkled, mainly, over twenty-two of the poems. That in at least one instance Sena did not base his translation on a Johnson text, however, is clear from his version of "I Never Saw a Moor," the last line of which—"As if the Checks were given"—he renders as "Qual se Mapa fora meu." It is most doubtful that Sena would have hit upon "Mapa" ("map") as the equivalent for "Checks" had he not been working from the version first produced in *Poems* (1890), the first volume of Dickinson's poems to achieve print, in which the poet's first editors, Mabel Loomis Todd and T. W. Higginson, substitute, without a shred of authority, their own term "Chart" for Dickinson's "Checks."

On Sena's rationale for the selection he makes for this edition, we can again turn to his own introduction. He notes that the eighty poems he has chosen, although they constitute no more than about four percent of the total available, are in sum far more representative of Dickinson's lasting work than the number and percentage would at first seem to indicate. This is especially so, he argues, when we take into account the many poems that survive as unfinished fragments or as examples of her penchant for occasional verse designed merely to accompany a friendly gift of flowers or cookies. He claims, moreover, that among the eighty poems he has included those, anthologized over and over again, that have become part of the standard canon of universal poetry. Among those in this group, he would name "I Died for Beauty—but Was Scarce," "I Never Saw a Moor," "My Life Closed Twice before Its Close," "The Only News I Know," and "This Is My Letter to the World." But he does not name poems, all of which he does translate, such as "To See the Summer Sky," "To Whom the Mornings Stand for Nights," "The Devil—Had He Fidelity," "A Letter is a Joy of Earth," and "Afraid! Of Whom Am I Afraid." Of course, it may be that in such instances Sena hopes to call attention to poems that have been neglected by Dickinson's critics. But what can one say about his omissions of canonical poems such as, to mention only a few, "After Great Pain, a Formal Feeling Comes," "Because I Could Not Stop for Death," "I Felt a Funeral, in My Brain," "The Soul Selects Her Own Society," "Success Is Counted Sweetest," "A Narrow Fellow in the Grass," "The Brain—Is Wider Than the Sky," "'Hope' Is the Thing with Feathers," "I Cannot Live with You," "There's a Certain Slant of Light," and "The Heart Asks Pleasure-First"? Yet while Sena's selection for *80 Poemas* will not satisfactorily represent the established Dickinson canon to everyone, it does have considerable value in that it has been made by a fellow poet of great distinction. It is useful to have Sena's endorsement of almost universally neglected poems such as "By a Departing Light," "Experiment to Me," "Fame of Myself, to Justify," "Fate Slew Him, but He Did Not Drop," "His Cheek Is His Biographer," "I Cannot Be Ashamed," "I Have No Life but This," "Silence Is All We Dread," "The Beggar at the Door for Fame," "The Pungent Atom in the Air," "To Die—without the Dying," "To Make Routine a Stimulus," "'Twas My One Glory," "We Do Not Play on Graves," and "Where Roses Would Not Dare to Go." Not only have such poems eluded the anthologist, they are virtually absent to Dickinson scholarship.

In the main, Sena's translations are successfully rendered in the spirit of Dickinson's poetry. One might quarrel with individual choices in diction, for example, his employing, in "Wild Nights— Wild Nights!" the term "aconchego" ("comfort" or "warmth") for the much more suggestive "luxury" or, in "Where Roses Would Not Dare to Go," employing "Vanguardas" for "Crimson Scouts," thereby losing the extended metaphor of wartime reconnaissance. If it cannot be said that in either of these cases Sena has made mistakes, there is a case or two in which the charge can be levied. In "Is Immortality a Bane," for instance, the word "bane" is given erroneously as "exílio" ("exile"), the result, probably, of his having misread the original as "ban"; in "A Sepal, Petal, and a Thorn," the phrase "A Flask of Dew" becomes "Brilho de Orvalho," based, again likely, on a mistake, this time his reading "flask" as "flash"; and in "Much Madness Is Divinest Sense," the poem's final word, "Chain," becomes "Cadeia" ("prison"). In the last case, it can be argued that the choice was not made totally in error, for "cadeia" can also mean "chain," though not in the context established by Sena's translation. This decision does not mar the entire translation, however, for Sena's version of Dickinson's poem is one of his many triumphs in *80 Poemas*. For a poet living in Ishmaelite exile, first in Brazil and then in the United States, "Much Madness Is Divinest Sense" might well have had a special meaning. It deserves quotation, in conclusion, as an example of Jorge de Sena's genuine credentials as a translator of Emily Dickinson's poetry:

> Muita Loucura é o mais divino Senso—
> Para o Olhar que distingue—
> Muito Senso—rematada Loucura—
> Só porém a Maioria
>
> Como em Tudo prevalece—
> Concordas—e tens juízo—
> Discordas—e és um perigo—
> Para meter na Cadeia.

2.

As evidências (1955), Sena's fourth book of poems, was a pivotal work, he insisted, coming after *Perseguição* (1942), *Coroa da terra* (1946), and *Pedra filosofal* (1950). In his 1977 preface to *Poesia—III* (the third volume of his collected poems), Sena points to the stages of his poet's journey as indicated in the titles he assigned to each volume: "Man runs in *pursuit* of himself and the other as far as the *earth's crown*, where he shall encounter, in humility, the *philosopher's stone* that will enable him to recognize that which is *evidence*."[2]

Sena could also have claimed that, in an odd way, *As evidências* was, as well, his first American book. Let me explain. In the best modernist fashion, Sena consistently incorporated epigraphs into his work. His discrete volumes of poetry employ quotations ranging from an anonymous "camponês" to the Marquis de Sade. In *As evidências* he drew his epigraphs, for the first and only time, from the poetry of the United States, choosing lines from poems by Daniel G. Hoffman and by Ralph Waldo Emerson.

From Hoffman Sena quotes the title and first two lines of the second poem in *An Armada of Thirty Whales*, the poet's first book of poems, published in 1954 (the year in which the whole of *As evidências* was composed) as volume 51 of the Yale Series of Younger Poets, edited then by the Anglo-American poet W. H. Auden, who provided a foreword to the volume:

> *The seals of Penobscot Bay*
> hadn't heard of the atom bomb
> so I shouted a warning to them.

Sena's second epigraph in *As evidências* derives from Emerson's "Give All to Love." He quotes the poem's first line and its last two lines:

> Give all to love
> . . . .
> When half-gods go,
> The gods arrive.

Sena's ellipsis runs to 46 lines.

Fernando J. B. Martinho has written briefly about these two epigraphs.[3] The lines from Emerson he sees as announcing the theme of love in this book that had been almost entirely missing in "Genesis," the sonnet sequence Sena had included earlier in *Coroa da terra* (1946), a sequence—the poet explained—to which *As evidências* was linked as its "reverse."

Emerson's theme—the gods' vexed response to human love—is crossed in *As evidências*, suggests Martinho, with images of "grace." The essential evident truth reveals itself as grace flickering across real darkness. The epigraph from Hoffman, on the other hand, works as a warning that the advent and constant presence of the atom bomb makes imminent the apocalypse so fearful to most of mankind. This reference to the bomb further links Sena's 1955 collection to the troubled world of the "Genesis" sonnets just after the end of the Second World War that, in its last days, saw the birth of the bomb and its application in Hiroshima and Nagasaki. Martinho acknowledges that there seems to be something of a contradiction in import in the two epigraphs, but he sees the discrepancy between the arrival of Emersonian gods and the clear and present danger of the atom bomb as further evidence of the dialectical nature of Sena's poetry.

The usefulness of Martinho's characterization of Sena's typical practice is apparent in *As evidências* even if the reader goes no further than the few lines baldly quoted from Hoffman's and Emerson's poems; if he or she sees that each of the epigraphs is an allusion intended to promote fruitful intertextuality between Sena's twenty-one-sonnet poem and the poems from which the epigraphs are taken, Sena's poetic practice emerges as richer and deeper than the more conventional notion of the dialectical might imply. First of all, Emerson's poem does not stop with advocating an unalloyed, direct and entire giving over of one's self to love. Yes, the poet urges, "Give all to love; / Obey thy heart . . . Leave all for love," but there is a caveat. "Yet, hear me, yet, / One word more," he cautions:

> Keep thee today,
> Tomorrow, forever,
> Free as an Arab
> Of thy beloved.

For give what you may to love, your loved one will eventually experience "a joy apart from thee," and "free be she, fancy-free; / Nor thou detain her vesture's hem." Yet that there is compensation in this loss, and a great one, too, is the burden of the poem's concluding lines:

> Though thou loved her as thyself,
> As a self of purer clay,
> Though her parting dims the day,
> Stealing grace from all alive;
> Heartily know,
> When half-gods go,
> The gods arrive.

It is to be inferred that the love that was earlier called a "god" was in the service of a "half-god" but is now, after its departure, followed by the arrival of (true?) gods. Perhaps, earthly love (self-love transformed even beyond the self-love that loved "her" as "a self of purer clay") now gives way to a still higher, though unspecified, love.

Sena is also playing off Emerson's poem against Hoffman's, for the latter is also about love but of a different sort, perhaps:

> *The seals in Penobscot Bay*
> hadn't heard of the atom bomb,
> so I shouted a warning to them.
> Our destroyer (on trial run) slid by
> the rocks where they gamboled and played;
>
> they must have misunderstood,
> or perhaps not one of them heard
>
> me over the engines and tides.
> As I watched them over our wake

I saw their sleek skins in the sun
ripple, light—flecked on the rock,

plunge, bubbling, into the brine,
and couple & laugh in the troughs

between the waves' whitecaps and froth.
Then the males clambered clumsily up

and lustily crowed like seacocks,
sure that their prowess held thrall

all the sharks, other seals, and seagulls.
And daintily flipped the females,

Sea-wenches with musical tails,
each looked at the Atlantic as

though it were her looking-glass . . .[4]

It is against no twenty-one-gun salute fired off by this destroyer (on
trial run) into the sky that the seals gambol away in their naturally
sexual play. The seals do not hear the poet's warning (nor would they
heed if they did hear it). The poem is big with a question: what does
it matter to Nature that the bomb exists? Is it only the poet's human
self-love that makes him envy "the sweet agony / of him who was
tied to the mast," a rather self-serving longing that exposes itself as
such before the easeful sexuality of the seals? Or does that longing
expose the lusty human cock-crowing signified by guns that punch
"dark holes in the sky" and the possession of atom bombs that is aped
in Nature by seals who are "seacocks" sure "that their prowess held
thrall / all the sharks, other seals, and seagulls" and "sea-wenches"
who look at the Atlantic as if the ocean were their looking-glass?

Such natural lust is lustily celebrated in Sena's *As evidências*. Especially salient in this regard is the tenth sonnet, which is explicitly
detailed in its naming of human parts and their sexual employment:

Rígidos seios de redondas, brancas,
frágeis e frescas inserções macias,

cinturas, coxas rodeando as ancas
em que se esconde o corredor dos dias;

torsos de finas, penugentas, frias,
enxutas linhas que nos rins se prendem,
sexos, testículos, que inertes pendem
de hirsutas liras, longas e vazias

da crepitante música tangida,
húmida e tersa, na sangrenta lida
que a inflada ponta penetrante trila;

dedos e nádegas, e pernas, dentes.
Assim, no jeito infiel de adolescentes
a carne espera, incerta, mas tranquila.

Breasts rigid from cool, fragile, whitely plump
insertions soft in unaccustomed ways,
waistlines, thighs skirting the hips and rump
in which is hid the corridor of days;

torsos slender, of goose-bumped fledgling hair,
cold, dry lines that at kidneys catch and cling,
genitals, testicles, that inertly hand
from hirsute lyres, long and empty, bare

of the crackling music played, its beat robust
humid and polished, in the bleeding thrust
that the swollen point, penetrant, will trill;

fingers, buttocks, legs, teeth—a full array.
Thus, in the faithless adolescent's way
the flesh awaits, unsure, but calmly still.[5]

These lines seem much less abruptly carnal, of course, when read within the context created by the entire poem comprised of the twenty-one sonnets. And it was the overall singular effect of a single work (following the example most congenial to him, *35 Sonnets*, Fernando Pessoa's luxurious English work) that Sena wanted from the beginning when he insisted that these sonnets be published separately as a whole, not as a part of a larger collection of poems. At first there were no takers for *As evidências*. When Sena did publish it discretely, moreover, he did not do so, as it turned out, discreetly. Without other options, he accepted an offer to publish in the politically suspect series "Cancioneiro Geral" of the Centro Bibliográfico. Immediately after the book achieved print, in early January 1955, the entire edition was apprehended by the PIDE (secret police) in a raid on the Center. Sena found himself trying to defend his book against the charges that it was both subversive and pornographic. It took a month of daily visits to the censor, he tells us, but finally he managed to free up the book for circulation. Only much later, in his preface to the second edition of his *Poesia—I*, a volume that reprints his first five volumes of poetry (including *As evidências*), does he tell how the book had come a cropper with the authorities, along with admitting that the censor had been right in thinking the book subversive and, if not exactly pornographic, certainly respectably obscene.

When Sena levied on Emerson's and Hoffman's poems in 1955, he had no firsthand knowledge of life in the United States. But he was familiar with the nation's culture, especially by way of its literature. Ultimately he would number among the American authors he had translated, novelists such as Ernest Hemingway, Erskine Caldwell, and William Faulkner, poets such as Robert Frost, Theodore Roethke, and Emily Dickinson, and the dramatist Eugene O'Neill. He even produced a sheaf of unmistakably anti-American poems. Gathered under the satirical title of "America, America, I Love You" (*Sequências*, 1980), these judgmental poems are not, of course, the "American" poems one might have anticipated in the 1950s when Sena was most receptive to American culture. The 1960s, marked by the war in Vietnam, exposed the nation to renewed worldwide scrutiny of its moral assumptions and its spiritual pretensions. But these poems are not Sena's great American poems. That distinction belongs to the sequence of deeply moving meditations he composed in 1972 and published as *Sobre esta praia: oito meditações à beira do Pacífico*. Like the sonnets of *As evidências*, these eight poems can also be seen as comprising a single poem. In these subversive, respectfully pornographic meditations set on the shores of the Pacific, the poet looks inward by looking outward. His epigram this time comes, appropriately enough, from Ovid. But just as appropriate, in another way, would have been the lines from Hoffman's poem in which each of the "sea-wenches" finds in the Atlantic her own "looking-glass."

3.

The theater was Jorge de Sena's grand passion. His widow, Mécia de Sena, calls it nothing less than her husband's "dramatic universe." To Portuguese drama he contributed a full-length play, *O Indesejado* (*The Unwanted One*), written in 1944–45 and first published in 1951, and six short plays, collected in 1974 as *Amparo de mãe e mais cinco peças em 1 acto* (*A Mother's Shelter and Five Other Plays in One Act*). To these plays he added theater reviews and essays, which were collected in 1988, a decade after his death, as *Do teatro em Portugal*, a volume that includes two pieces on the production of Eugene O'Neill's *Long Day's Journey into Night* (1958) and another on a production of the American playwright's *Anna Christie* (1947).

Sena concurred with those who consider O'Neill to be one of the greatest of modern playwrights. "O'Neill's plays pose problems, present desperate interrogations," he wrote in 1947, "they are achievements . . . of the highest order."[6] In the same year, he began his contribution to the study and production of O'Neill's work in Portugal with a well-informed critique of an adaptation of *Anna Christie* then playing in Lisbon. The adaptation was the work of Henrique Galvão, later famous for his politics (he opposed the Salazar regime), but who, in the 1940s, could legitimately claim to be O'Neill's official Portuguese translator. In "*Anna Cristina*, de Eugene O'Neill, Teatro Avenida," published in *Seara nova* 26 (March 8,

1947), Sena demonstrates his own mastery of O'Neill's English by juxtaposing passages from O'Neill's original, his own Portuguese translations, and Galvão's rather free adaptations and distortions.[7]

In late November 1957 Sena was asked to translate O'Neill's *Long Day's Journey into Night*.[8] Remarkably, he received this invitation not quite two years after Carlotta Monterey O'Neill, the playwright's widow, released the play for publication and for production—first to the Royal Dramatic Theater of Stockholm, which produced it on February 2, 1956, and then to José Quintero, who staged it in New York on November 7, 1956. Sena began work on his translation immediately, sending off from Lisbon to Porto each day's pages to António Pedro, the director of the Teatro Experimental, who was committed to a January 4, 1958, opening in Porto. Against all odds, Sena finished his translation in less than a month—it was finished on Christmas Day 1957—and Pedro's production opened on schedule. It is unlikely that anyone else in Portugal at that time, especially working within the imposed deadline, could have matched Sena's singular achievement.

Pedro's production of *Long Day's Journey* opened, as planned, in Porto on January 4, 1958. On January 12, Sena contributed a piece, "O testamento de Eugene O'Neill," to the Porto newspaper *Jornal de notícias*.[9] Circumstances prevented Sena from traveling to Porto in January, but he caught the production when in mid-April it was moved to Lisbon for a three-day run (April 11–13, 1958). He reviewed the production—a "*Jornada para a Noite*, de Eugene O'Neill, pelo Teatro Experimental do Porto"—for the Lisbon journal *Gazeta musical e de todas as artes* (May 1958).[10]

Sena had every reason to expect an early publication for his translation, even announcing in print that he was reserving further commentary on the play for the preface that would accompany the publication of the text. But it was not to be. Publication was postponed indefinitely, and the preface was never written. Unpublished for thirty-five years, Sena's translation finally appeared, in a print run of one thousand copies, as the seventeenth title in Livros Cotovia's

"Theater" series under the joint aegis of Cotovia and the Teatro Nacional D. Maria II. In lieu of the preface Sena had not had the occasion or the necessity to write, moreover, Mécia de Sena chose to reprint "O Testamento de Eugene O'Neill," the piece he had written for *Jornal de notícias* in January 1958, while the play was running in Porto.

In this essay, which insists on the primacy of *Long Day's Journey into Night* in the O'Neill canon, we encounter none of the details of the translator's engagements with O'Neill's text, something that a typical Sena preface would undoubtedly have covered. "I do not know who it was that said that the great dramatists end up always by writing the essential play of their own lives," writes Sena, "the one that represents more than any other that examination of conscience, that confession, the Final Judgment. That play which, if not the final one written, stands as if it were, constituting a spiritual testament in dramatic form, a critical exposition of human life dedicated to the theater and—one and the same—theater identified with Life." In O'Neill's case *Long Day's Journey* was this final play—a tragedy. "Along the length of a frightening day in four acts and five scenes, with everything happening to those people, nothing happens," concludes Sena, "save perhaps the tragedy of grace denied and lost."

10

Views of Sena's Work

Jorge de Sena was a man of many talents. He was an engineer, a teacher, a scholar, and a writer. His varied and various writings constitute invaluable contributions to knowledge in several fields and many areas of general and specialized interest. Above all, however, he will be remembered for his poetry and his fiction. Of the studies devoted to his contributions to Portuguese imaginative literature, two are singled out here: Jorge Fazenda Lourenço's *A poesia de Jorge de Sena: testemunho, metamorfose, peregrinação* and Francisco Cota Fagundes's *In the Beginning There Was Jorge de Sena's Genesis: The Birth of a Writer*.[1]

The implications of Fernando Pessoa's prediction that modern poetry would be the poetry of dream were not lost on Jorge de Sena. Indeed, it can almost be said that Pessoa's conviction, taken with his own not inconsiderable efforts toward making his prediction come true, turned Sena's great twentieth-century predecessor and gray eminence into the force and example that he had to exorcise in order to be free to write his own poetry of autobiographical testimony to the reality of the world as it exists and as it is experienced.

If Pessoa insisted on poetry's artificiality and insincerity, Sena would insist on its link to a reality that does not evaporate in the constructions of dream and the weaving of illusions. In fact, if for Sena it was the realism of the entirely misunderstood (he thought) sixteenth-century poet Luis de Camões that had to be unearthed, explained, and established once and for all five centuries after the great poet's death, it was also the ever insoluble world created by Pessoa that had to be mapped, measured, contained, and finally dismissed (he insisted) for vital reasons that were both aesthetic and moral. Of course, none of this, the reinterpretation of Camões or the repudiation of Pessoa, was done casually, high-handedly, or overnight. Sena's entire corpus works simultaneously to clear space for itself in the traditions established by his two strong predecessors and to define his own monumental contribution to Portuguese, Iberian, and world literature. In this regard, his ambition knew no bounds. And if his reach exceeded his grasp, to measure that grasp is the job of critics and literary historians. Jorge Fazenda Lourenço's *A poesia de Jorge de Sena* contributes substantively and originally to our understanding of this poet's stupendous achievements.

In Fazenda Lourenço, Jorge de Sena has found what he seldom found during, as he called them, his "forty years of servitude" to poetry: a sympathetic and well-prepared critic, one he himself might have admired. For in his cogently argued book, Fazenda Lourenço shows to excellent advantage his own mastery of recent Portuguese criticism and European theory, his considerable knowledge of English-language poetry, his passionate, almost religious, dedication to Poetry (an essence that many others might find it difficult to accept), and his thorough immersion in Sena's work. He ranges freely over all the many genres the poet worked without that familiarity's breeding either coziness or appropriation.

Fazenda Lourenço's study began as a dissertation defended at the University of California, Santa Barbara, in 1993, and still shows marks of its origins. It quotes much European criticism and theory, ostensibly for the purpose of placing Sena's thinking and writing within the larger context of his times and as part of a more generously and broadly defined literary tradition, and sometimes in order to contribute to a larger explanation or a more specific clarification. When such quotations stem from the latter impulse they more often than not serve merely to buttress a critic's understanding of Sena's own invariably more precise and clearer explanations of the same notions. Another way of putting this caveat is that there is still no gainsaying the truth of the familiar commonplace among Sena's more dedicated readers that he, who so thoroughly explained himself, his work, and the relation that work had to the literary world and the greater world containing that literature, remains his own best and most precise critic.

Notwithstanding Jorge de Sena's daunting example as a critic of the writings of Jorge de Sena, there is still much to do, especially along the lines of filling out schemes and tracing links and connections. To this necessary if not sufficient end, Fazenda Lourenço's study works both efficiently and responsibly. A case in point is his decision to start out with an analysis of Sena's poem "A máscara do poeta," from the collection entitled *Metamorfoses*, as his point of entry into the nature of Sena's conscious and deliberate decision away from the near-solipsistic world-making poetry of surrealism, dream, and subjectivity to a poetry grounded in the realities of subject-object interdependence. In this poem Sena meditates upon the death mask taken of John Keats in life. The mask stands for poet qua poet (to distinguish him from the man who lived the quotidian life of showing up for meals and whose love for Fanny Brawn bordered on abasement) vis-à-vis the reality that exists beyond himself, what Emerson called the not-me. The mask serves at least the dual purpose of getting the man Keats out of himself into a second self that makes poetry out of his experience of the world and the mirroring point of entry of that world into poems. It is in this way that Sena's work is, paradoxically, both autobiographical and not in the least biographical. It is this notion of the poet as mask of Keats, joined to the English poet's notion of negative capability (to rest in one's world before the antinomian prospect of not knowing any certainties) that enables Sena to escape the traps of subjectivity, a point established convincingly in Fazenda Lourenço's detailed and closely nuanced argument.

Fazenda Lourenço's richly elaborated study interprets Sena's unequivocal insistence that his work is entirely autobiographical and that stories, poems, plays, essays, etc. come together to form a single, complexly textured, intricately interconnected, and rationally conceived and executed whole. If, moreover, the scientifically trained Sena was one of the last of the twentieth-century humanists, as Fazenda Lourenço correctly points out, it should be added that this science-trained engineer knew full well that his faith in his own intellect and reason allied him with the best minds of the Enlightenment.

Sena often explained that he was compelled to provide the explanatory criticism of his own work because, for many and varied reasons, there had emerged no body of published criticism around his work as it appeared. He complained that his books were ignored, went unreviewed, and even when sympathetic, and otherwise understanding, readers commented intelligently on his work they were wont to do so only in private, usually in letters to the author. If he exaggerated the extent to which this was so, it was not by much, and that exaggeration, if it was such, enabled him to write, particularly in his famous (or, as some saw them, infamous) prefaces to his work, that body of criticism. Those prefaces provide not only keys to the meanings he found in his own work but information regarding the principles by which he composed, selected, arranged, and structured individual volumes as well as his work in its entirety. (Incidentally, these prefaces form a remarkably informative unit and should be collected and published in a single small volume.) It is in those prefaces, for instance, that Fazenda Lourenço discovers the essential ideas for understanding Sena's poet's ethos, one of constant attentiveness to the complexities of existence in the world, to his second-nature consciousness of himself as a confluence of thoughts and impressions, and to his insistence that poetry intervene in the metamorphoses of reality. One can only marvel at Sena's fidelity to a dialectics of realism, at his willing, willful, and almost involuntary testimonies, at his acceptance of change and adherence to transformation, at his travel and self-exile. Not the least of Fazenda Lourenço's many contributions in his now absolutely necessary book is his careful discussion of Sena's working through some of the major literary currents, surrealism in Portugal in the later 1940s and the neorealism it countered. Sena was too rational, of course, to embrace surrealism uncritically and too aesthetically and morally intelligent to knuckle under to any political, social, or psychological ideology. While Pessoa recognizes that the reaper sings on, sings on, for no other reason ("canta, canta sem razão"), he laments that the something in him that feels things is always thinking ("o que em mim sente 'sta pensando"). But Sena, recognizing the same thing in himself, welcomes that antinomial association of feeling and thought as essential to his life of poetry, which is to say, simply, his life. The unexamined life is not worth living, for it is in the examination of that life that the humanist is born. Sena is man thinking (not the stereotyped man of thought deplored by Ralph Waldo Emerson), at attention, ever on alert to himself, to his world, to himself as a free-thinking citizen of a world that he would believe into being, if he could. Portugal's pantheon of writers may include other poets, but they cluster around Luís de Camões, Fernando Pessoa, and Jorge de Sena.

Not the least because they were written by the eighteen-year-old Sena for a projected collection that was never finished, the two stories first published in 1983 under the title *Genesis* continue to astonish. First there is the young man's precocity, temerity, audacity, arrogance, and (in anyone else) naïveté in taking on the daunting task of rewriting the stories of Genesis; and then there is the sure-fisted, clear-minded way in which in these modern retellings he shadows forth on a grand scale those literary and spiritual concerns that would metastasize throughout the whole of his life's work.

Francisco Cota Fagundes was among the first and the few to recognize that the very first fictional texts Jorge de Sena produced were a golden key to all that would ensue in the next four decades:

poems, plays, essays, criticism, short stories, translations, letters, a novella, and a novel that constitute one of the most extensively and intensively satisfying bodies of work brought forth by a twentieth-century writer. His study of "the birth of a writer" is divided into six chapters and an appendix. The latter usefully provides the author's translations of both stories in *Genesis*—"Paraíso perdido" (Paradise lost), which tells the story of the temptation and fall of man, and "Caim" (Cain), which recounts Cain's unhappiness over the favoritism shown to his brother Abel—and of the six-sonnet sequence also entitled "Genesis," included in *Coroa da terra* (1946). The first chapter locates the Genesis stories within the context of Sena's other adolescent work, including some five hundred poems written between 1936 and 1941. Chapter 2 presents both an overall view of Sena's attitudes toward religion and a reading of possible precursors for and influences on Sena's Genesis stories: Antero de Quental (some sonnets and the story "Adão e Eva no Paraíso") and Teixeira de Pascoaes (*Regresso ao Paraíso*). Chapters 3 and 4 offer readings of Sena's "Paraíso perdido" and "Caim" respectively.

Chapter 5 delivers the goods implied in the book's title by convincingly demonstrating how the early fiction of Genesis relates to "Homenagem ao Papagaio Verde," Sena's later story of initiation. By a kind of legitimate back-formation it can be seen that the heavily autobiographical story leading off the collection *Os grão-capitães* in 1976 not only illuminates the two stories of *Genesis* but helps establish the manifestly personal allegory that shapes Sena's retelling of Genesis. In chapter 6 Fagundes forges links between Sena's earliest stories and both "Geneses," the sonnet sequence from *Coroa da terra* and the uniquely rationalized story "Razão de o pai Natal ter barbas brancas" (Why Father Christmas's beard is white).

Fagundes has labored long and well in the widespread and fertile vineyards that are Sena's literary domain. In *A Poet's Way with Music: Humanism in Jorge de Sena's Poetry* (1988) he studied in rich detail Sena's *Arte de Música* (1968), that finely executed volume of poems focusing on works of art. He has published translations of

Sena's poetry (done with James Houlihan)—*Art of Music* (1988) and *Metamorphoses* (1991), which reproduces the twenty illustrations of the original—and he has written penetrating essays on Sena's other fiction. Fagundes can always be trusted to guide us surely not only over the main pathways of Sena's work but onto barely perceived, if not entirely unsuspected, pathways into Sena's Daedalian labyrinth. One looks forward to his continued mapping of this near and far territory in full humanistic dimension.

II

The First International
Symposium on Fernando Pessoa

Actas do I Congresso Internacional de Estudos Pessoanos, published in September 1979, presents the papers delivered in Porto, Portugal, on April 3–5, 1978. Its title is misleading, for the fact is that the very first international Pessoa conference had taken place more than six months earlier and on a different continent. The "actas" for that first international were published by Gávea-Brown, Providence, Rhode Island, in 1982, under the title *The Man Who Never Was: Essays on Fernando Pessoa*. What follows herewith is an account of the Brown University symposium on October 7–8, 1977, drawn from the introduction to the published proceedings, followed by seven letters from Jorge de Sena pertaining to the symposium.

I. The Symposium

On October 7–8, 1977, Brown University was privileged to serve as the host to what turned out to be the first international symposium on Fernando Pessoa held anywhere in the world. When in 1976 it first occurred to the faculty at the university's Center for Portuguese and Brazilian Studies to sponsor and organize such a meeting, it did not strike us that, when held, ours would be the first. It could not then have been foreseen that our symposium would anticipate by almost six months to the day the congress held by the Centro de Estudos Pessoanos in Porto, Portugal, in the spring of 1978.

Those who planned and organized the symposium were motivated by the desire to call attention, particularly in the United States and other English-language countries, to the major poetic achievements of one of the world's great modernist poets. Of the stature of the work of Valery, Rilke, Ezra Pound, and T. S. Eliot, Pessoa's work remained, we felt then, terra incognita in the United States. Matters were a bit better in England, perhaps since Pessoa's first significant publications, *Antinous*, *35 Sonnets*, and *Inscriptions* (all originally in English) had reached London (the first two came out in 1918 and the last in 1920), and since the Englishman Roy Campbell, who knew of Pessoa's early years in South Africa, had translated some of his poems. But even in England Pessoa's reputation was slight indeed; and although the translations by Jonathan Griffin, F. E. G. Quintanilha, and Peter Rickard—all in 1971—were giant steps in redress, there was still a long way to go. In the same year, it should be pointed out, the American publisher Alan Swallow brought out its bilingual edition of Edwin Honig's selected translations of Pessoa's poetry. Still, apart from an occasional essay in the *Luso-Brazilian Review*, in the United States Pessoa was relegated entirely to the classroom and to national and regional meetings of the various modern language associations. Yet it cannot be said that even in academia Pessoa had fully arrived. There was then no Prentice Hall Twentieth-Century Views volume on Pessoa, no Twayne World Authors series study, no G. K. Hall bibliographical guide—some of the telltale signs of academic acceptance. These simply did not exist.

But soon the weather in Pessoa studies began to turn around. In *The Poet's Work: 29 Masters of 20th Century Poetry on the Origins and Practice of Their Art*,[1] several excerpts from Pessoa's prose, collected under the title "Toward Explaining Heteronymy," were given a featured place early in the volume, second only to a short poem, "Ars Poetica?" by Czeslaw Milosz. As more and more of Pessoa's work—prose as well as poetry—was translated into English, the clearer it became that his contribution to modern literature and thought was enormous.

At any rate, since Pessoa was not well enough known to English speakers in 1977, it was decided that the program at our symposium would be conducted mainly, if not entirely, in English. Those invited, with one exception, were asked to present papers and lectures in English, and they agreed to do so. As a result we were able to present, over a two-day period, the following program:

Poetry Reading by Jean Longland (Hispanic Society of America) and Nelson H. Vieira (Brown University)

Opening Lecture by João Gaspar Simões (Lisbon, Portugal), "As relações de Fernando Pessoa com a revista *Presença*"

Lecture by Hellmut Wohl (Boston University), "The Short Happy Life of Amadeo de Souza Cardoso"

Lecture by Alexandrino Severino (Vanderbilt University) and Hubert D. Jennings (Republic of South Africa), "In Praise of Ophelia: An Interpretation of Pessoa's Only Love"

Colloquium Presentations:

Catarina Feldmann (Universidade de São Paulo), "The Sun vs. Ice Cream and Chocolate: The Works of Wallace Stevens and Fernando Pessoa"

Gilbert Cavaco (Providence College), "Pessoa and Portuguese Politics"

Ronald W. Sousa (University of Minnesota), "Ascendant Romanticism in Fernando Pessoa"

Closing Lecture by Jorge de Sena (University of California, Santa Barbara), "Fernando Pessoa: The Man Who Never Was"

Poetry Reading by Edwin Honig (Brown University) and Lisa Godinho (Harvard University)

It was a great privilege and, as it turned out, a unique opportunity to include among the participants in the symposium two of the indisputable giants of Pessoa scholarship, João Gaspar Simões and Jorge de Sena, with Simões giving the first lecture (the only one delivered in Portuguese) and Sena the last and culminating one. The program of lectures and colloquium was framed by poetry readings of Pessoa's Portuguese originals and their English translations by the translators themselves, Jean Longland on the first day and Edwin Honig on the second. For the rest of the lectures and papers, with the exception of Hellmut Wohl's (he lectured on Pessoa's contemporary, the artist Amadeo de Souza Cardoso), we chose to invite then-younger scholars—American and Brazilian—who could offer a new generation's perspectives and interests on the subject of Pessoa: Gilbert Cavaco on Pessoa within the context of Portuguese politics, Alexandrino Severino (working in collaboration with Hubert D. Jennings) on Pessoa's one known romantic relationship, Ronald Sousa on the question of Pessoa's romanticism, and Catarina Feldman's comparison of Pessoa to the American poet Wallace Stevens.

The symposium was attended by three hundred people, including the Ambassador of Portugal to the United States, João Hall Themido, and José Stichini Vilela, the Consul of Portugal in Providence, Rhode Island.

From the beginning the symposium's sponsors intended to publish the papers presented on the occasion, and, happily, all but one of those appeared in *The Man Who Never Was*. We were unable to include the Severino and Jennings paper, which could not be published at the time because Ofélia Queirós's permission to quote from her letters to Pessoa was withheld. (I am not aware that this paper was ever published.) To the book, it was later decided to add interviews with Jean Longland and Edwin Honig, Pessoa's earliest American translators, as well as papers by two other young students of Pessoa: Francisco Cota Fagundes (on Álvaro de Campos's "Ode Marítima") and Joanna Courteau (on Pessoa's orthonymic poetry), and a biobibliographical essay prepared by the noted Portuguese novelist and critic José Martins Garcia.

II. The Jorge de Sena Letters

Planned originally for the spring of 1977, the Pessoa symposium was put off until later in the year to accommodate Jorge de Sena, who had prior commitments. During that period Sena was kept apprised of our evolving plans and the necessary changes in their specifics. This resulted, over the months, in an exchange of letters. Sena's side of the correspondence amounted to seven letters. They are reproduced here with the kind permission of Mécia de Sena.

1.

University of California, Santa Barbara, Department of Spanish and Portuguese, Santa Barbara, California 93106

January 7, 1977

Professor George Monteiro, Director, Center for Portuguese and Brazilian Studies, Brown University, Providence, Rhode Island 02912

Dear Professor Monteiro,

Excuse me for only now answering your most kind letter of December 2, which I received by the middle of that month, when already being overwhelmed not only with the usual bureaucratic work of two big departments but also with scores of applications for a vacancy in Spanish that we have advertised. To screen eighty candidates, and brace myself to interview some thirty of them at the New York MLA convention, as I did, kept me busy until the end of the month. Here I am now, thanking you very much for your letter and your invitation which highly honors me, and congratulating you and your Center for the initiative of a Fernando Pessoa Symposium. If I answer in English to your Portuguese letter it is because I suppose that, for administrative purposes, it will be more convenient to you.

To be invited to deliver the closing lecture of the symposium, after the distinguished names who precede me in the tentative program, is a great honor that I cannot refuse. And so, I accept formally your invitation. But there is a problem that may be solved, if you accept me in just word and spirit (and not in "carne y hueso," like our old Garcilaso translating Petrarch would say). In April–June I will have my sabbatical leave, which I was supposed to enjoy last year when struck by a serious illness from which I am recovering very well. My research plans and other contacts require me in Europe by then, since the middle of April to the middle of June. I can send you my speech—and I would like to know if we are supposed to talk in English, as it seems better to me, or in Portuguese. That speech would be read there by someone, or distributed among the attendance. As soon as I have your answer I will concentrate on some theme and inform you of it.

You ask me about suggestions concerning other scholars who, either in Portugal or in the United States could be invited. In the United States Dr. Jean Longland, librarian of the Hispanic Society of America, has been a distinguished pioneer in translating Pessoa. In Germany Georg Rudolf Lind, who has published also in Portugal, has contributed widely to the study of some aspects of Pessoa. As a matter of fact, for instance, Anne Terlinden, a doctoral candidate, who came from Belgium to study here under me, wrote there a splendid master's thesis on Pessoa's English poems (having worked with many of the unpublished ones, which Lind was kind enough to lend her).

As to Portugal, I must say—even if for decades I have not had any personal contact with him—that it seems to me extremely unjust not to invite, as no. 1, Dr. João Gaspar Simões, who is in fact in this world of ours, the dean of Pessoa studies whether we like it or not, and moreover, the critic who first, nearly fifty years ago, proclaimed Pessoa the great poet that even Pessoa himself by then was not quite sure of being. As far as I know, Dr. Gaspar Simões is in good health and spirits, and can perfectly well fly to the United States.

I have no doubt that the Gulbenkian Foundation (whose administrator, my good friend Dr. José Blanco is, being at the same time a great bibliographer on Pessoa, and whose director of the review *Colóquio-Letras*, Professor Prado Coelho is, besides being another outstanding "fernandista"), will give the best support to such an idea of mine. Other names of the highest category in Pessoa studies among Portuguese critics are Professor Eduardo Lourenço, of the University of Nice, and Professor José Augusto Seabra, I believe of the University of Porto now.

Expecting to hear from you, and sending to you and all the members of your Center my best,

I remain, sincerely yours,
Jorge de Sena, Professor of Portuguese & Comparative Literature
Chairman, Spanish and Portuguese Department
Chairman, Comparative Literature Program
JS/ps

2.

University of California, Santa Barbara, Department of Spanish and Portuguese, Santa Barbara, California 93106

January 14, 1977

Professor George Monteiro, Director, Center for Portuguese and Brazilian Studies, Brown University, Providence, Rhode Island 02912

Dear Professor Monteiro,

You must have received in the meanwhile my previous letter, thanking you for your kind invitation and accepting it (as I say, in word and Spirit, as it cannot be otherwise). This one is just a continuation, to redress a forgetfulness of mine. When I was giving you names in the US—and I may be forgetting some really worthy ones—I should have mentioned Professor Joaquim Francisco Coelho, Stanford University, who can very well and in the most distinguished way represent Brazil and the good criticism of Pessoa produced there and here (in his case, also with articles printed in Portugal). Excuse me for bothering you again, but I felt that it was my duty to add this excellent name of a Brazilian critic who lives and teaches in the US.

Sincerely yours,
Jorge de Sena

3.

University of California, Santa Barbara, Department of Spanish and Portuguese, Santa Barbara, California 93106

March 5, 1977

Professor George Monteiro, Director, Center for Portuguese and Brazilian Studies, Brown University, Providence, Rhode Island 02912

Dear Professor Monteiro,

Please forgive me for only now more than three weeks after receiving your kind letter of February 9, answering it. But my life as double chairman in a crucial moment of several changes which must be enacted before I start my leave of absence, has been a perfect hell, with the collapse of my entire personal work and correspondence.

Thank you very much for having accepted my suggestions about a meeting which I hope it will be the great success which Pessoa deserves and as not yet found in this country so deaf to what does not come with the blessings of France or Mittel-Europa. So, I will send you, to be read as the closing speech of your symposium, a paper written in English—you can read it yourself, doing me such favor, being so willing. Before I leave, my paper will reach you.

What an excellent idea to have the papers published! I believe that, in good time, a biobibliographical note about each of the contributors will give to the book some "pessoana" authority. Of course you have already my authorization for such an enterprise. And I expect that the Gulbenkian Foundation will help you as I think that they should, and that the invited people may come (one or another may not, either because one never knows how things are worked out in Portugal, or just because they may feel that to come to the US may tarnish their socialist paint—for many, you know, quite fresh).

Keep me posted on any developments, call for my poor help if you think that I may be useful, and count on my remaining

Sincerely yours,
Jorge de Sena

P.S.—I would appreciate very much your announcing or advertising our prosperous (but in need of even more students) Summer Session, with Gulbenkian grants, at the Symposium, and around you. Here follow some leaflets. The brochure can go, if you wish.

4.

University of California, Santa Barbara, Department of Spanish and Portuguese, Santa Barbara, California 93106

September 3, 1977

Personal Address: 939 Randolph Road, Santa Barbara, California

Professor George Monteiro, Director, Center for Portuguese and Brazilian Studies, Brown University, Providence, Rhode Island 02912

Dear Professor Monteiro,

I was going—asking your forgiveness—to answer your letter of July 29, which had the Program of the Symposium attached, when I received your phone call. Here I am now, answering the letter, confirming what I told you in our conversation, and providing you with the information that you have asked for. My silence was the result of, overwhelmed with work, having to write in good time and acceptable Spanish, the opening speech of the convention of the Asociación Internacional de Hispanistas, which I had been invited to deliver. Then, from the 21st to the 29th I was travelling or being in Toronto.

Round-trip—price and schedules

It seems that it is not quite easy from LA to reach Providence, and that there are more than one combination of routes. Anyhow, my travel agency came to the following conclusion:

We will fly (my wife goes with me) from Santa Barbara to LA, from LA to Cleveland, from Cleveland to Providence (always United Airlines), Thursday October 6, arriving there at 8:34 p.m. And I will fly back. The 9th, by the 8:40 a.m. flight to New York (?). The price of one round-trip is 431.00.

Allow me to tell you (and it is up to you and your budget to come to a decision on such question) that if the Calouste Gulben-kian Foundation is, as I believe it is, sponsoring your symposium, they know that I do not travel alone because I cannot, and not just because I like to be with my wife; and so, the Foundation, in inviting me to go to Europe, giving me any grant, etc., accepts the provision of my wife's round-trip being paid by them or included in the fore-seen expenses covered by the grant.

Almeida Faria—I was going to mention this point in my letter, but I took the opportunity of talking to you on the phone. He is one of the most admired and respected among the younger Portuguese writers (b. 1943), having published two novels of outstanding quality, and being a cultivated and intelligent mind. The proposed essay on Pessoa (Pessoa thinks Campos feels) is scheduled to be published as the opening text of the 2nd issue, also dedicated to Pessoa, of *Quaderni Portoghesi*, published by the Universities of Rome and Pisa. If you could extend to him an invitation, he will come on his own or with some kind of support which he may obtain having received the invitation, and he could then tour a few universities around the country. I know for sure that Stanford University will have him, like mine here. Looking at your schedule, quite crowded to be true, I feel that—even if you have to find a place for Octavio Paz, if he really will be there—it could be done, and I would be extremely pleased. Mr. Almeida Faria has been in the USA before (as a special guest and resident at Iowa writers' gathering, held some years ago for several months); and his address is Travessa Nova de S. Francisco de Borja—5—1º—Lisbon.

It was most kind of you, in sending me the flier for your recent series, "Roads etc.," to tell me that my person and my works were mentioned by *several* of your lecturers. Apart from the fact of some subjects not allowing such mentions to be made, I know perfectly well who would and who would not mention me in such a list of names. In general, scoundrels and mediocre people have always been my sworn enemies, not because I have hindered them (on the contrary, many of them even owe me the money that I do not have), but just because I exist as a kind of shadow of decency falling upon them all the time (and the shadow will remain, they know, even if I die, becoming even darker).

I was extremely pleased with the possibility of Octavio Paz being present—and I do not think that he will prepare a lecture for the occasion, and perhaps you could have some special "round-table" with him and a couple of us, the others—, since I never had any occasion of meeting a poet and an essayist whom I respect, and who has been among the rare high ranking persons for whom Pessoa has been a discovery—to be made. Our globe-trotters' paths never crossed—will they now? Certainly for people who have written on Pessoa for around half-a-century like Gaspar Simões or 35 years like me it will be a special pleasure to meet with an illustrious "convert," whose fame can do for Pessoa more than millions writing in Portuguese, a language that Spanish-speaking people or hispanists are not supposed to know; for fear of losing their status in a world ignoring them altogether, since a big part of that world believes that God himself speaks also only English (a language which Pessoa could write too well for not being too literary in writing English poems).

Above, I forgot to reiterate the title of my lecture, as I told it to you over the phone: *Pessoa, the man who never was.*

Sincerely yours,
Jorge de Sena

P.S.—For sure, we will be in contact before my arrival. Anyhow, a tall, lean (not too much) man, with glasses and a dark beret on, and a wife at his side—it will be me.

5.

University of California, Santa Barbara, Department of Spanish and Portuguese, Santa Barbara, California 93106

September 22, 1977

Professor George Monteiro, Director, Center for Portuguese and Brazilian Studies, Brown University, Providence, Rhode Island 02912

Dear Professor Monteiro,

Thank you very much for your letter of the 15th, which reached me yesterday (mail is using again stagecoaches, and the old country roads, I believe), and for all the copies of other letters that you were kind enough to write on behalf of my wife going with me, and about Almeida Faria's possible visit to this country and your symposium. I expect that the Gulbenkian Foundation will say yes, what will be quite a relief for me. As to AF I think that the letters of yours, the two, will help him to solve the problem. I am glad to hear that you liked my idea of a "round-table" with Octavio Paz, and that your efforts to get him there are going ahead. It came to me (and the idea of the "table" to make things easier) the awful news—are they true?—that he had just undergone some cancer surgery. But it is possible that his condition may be by then already normal, as far as it can be. Sad thing, my God.

We are looking forward at being there and meeting with you. I would appreciate, just in case, to know the name of the motel where everybody will stay. If there is any misunderstanding, delay in flights, wrong flights, etc., I will know where to go from the airport, if, in spite of your and my efforts, we do not find each other. By the way: a tall and rather lean white man, with glasses and a béret on, and a wife at his side, that's me.

Most truly yours
Jorge de Sena
Chairman

P.S.—From now on, use my private address to speed matters (univ. means a delay of a couple of days): 939 Randolph Road, Santa Barbara, CA, 93111.

6.

University of California, Santa Barbara, Department of Spanish and Portuguese, Santa Barbara, California 93106

September 28, 1977

Professor George Monteiro, Director, Center for Portuguese and Brazilian Studies, Brown University, Providence, Rhode Island 02912

Dear Professor Monteiro,

I have just received your letter of the 26th, giving me, just in case, the name and address of the motel where we will be staying, and asking for my social security number. Thank you very much for that information which I had asked for and here is that number:

XXX-XX-XXXX

Looking forward to be there, and expecting our symposium to be a success, with all good wishes,

Jorge de Sena

7.

University of California, Santa Barbara, Department of Spanish and Portuguese, Santa Barbara, California 93106

November 10, 1977

Professor George Monteiro, Director, Center for Portuguese and Brazilian Studies, Brown University, Providence, Rhode Island 02912

Dear George Monteiro,

Thank you very much for your letter of October 31, sending me the checks. You have not to apologize for the delay, since delays are becoming our daily bread in this era of supersonic speeds, in which the mail service, it seems as I usually say, has returned to or revived stage-coaches: in fact, this letter of yours arrived only a couple of days ago. Be sure that in good time I will claim back the money that unduly was taken from my check by your bureaucracies, even if, nowadays, returned money is always money coming too late for such poor people, heading for the workhouse like we, scholars and teachers.

As to the Symposium, which was such an excellent event, I received from Dr. José Blanco a letter, just yesterday, in which he tells me how happy they were about the success reported to them (it seems that Gaspar Simões has talked—*urbi et orbi* about our

meetings etc.), and how they—meaning the Foundation are prepared to help with the publication of some *actas* perpetuating the
event.

It was for me and my wife a great pleasure to visit your University,
to have (unfortunately the time did not allow very much) the opportunity of visiting a most interesting area for me, which I had never
seen before, and, the last but not the least, to make your acquaintance
and to meet with your most kind and dynamic staff (please, extend
to them all our best "saudades")—so you have nothing to thank me
for. My pleasure and a great honor for me. I hope that one of these
days we may have the occasion of getting together again.

Cordially
Jorge de Sena, Chairman

P.S.—Have you seen in the Fall River newspaper the attack to my
wife, incredibly stupid, launched by that crazy doctor whom you
have had in those parts, I suppose, since the time of the Corte-Reais,
and as uncertain in his mind as they have been in their historical
physicality around there?[2]

12

Mécia de Sena

He who would do good to another must do it in Minute
Particulars.

—William Blake, *Jerusalem*.

This piece is a tribute to someone who has practiced to the letter
what the great English poet so wisely preached.

To this day the return address label on an envelope carrying a
letter from Mécia de Sena reads as follows—

Mrs. Jorge de Sena, 939 Randolph Road,
Santa Barbara, CA 93111-1031

This return address speaks volumes to me. Four decades after the
death of Jorge de Sena, his widow still lives in the same house the
Sena family lived in over four decades ago, and, more strikingly, it
keeps the world informed that Mécia de Sena continues to affirm
that she is "Mrs. Jorge de Sena." This creative spirit, who, judging
from the marvelous letters she writes (in my case, invariably and
astonishingly always by return mail), has taken on willingly as one

of her life's tasks the maintenance and enhancement of Jorge de Sena's literary, historical, and cultural importance. She has edited (and found publishers for) his unpublished work, prepared and prefaced previously published work in new editions, and published his correspondence with his contemporaries, close friends, and other notables. This modest but always convivial house on Randolph Road could justly be called the Editorial Center for the Publication of the Works of Jorge de Sena. Moreover, as the late Luciana Stegagno Picchio, herself a great student of Portuguese-language literature, once put it on a public occasion (and I paraphrase from memory), "While teams of editors have been assembled to publish the works of other major writers, this woman, working alone, has single-handedly taken on the task of editing and publishing the vast corpus of Jorge de Sena's work, and she has done the job (and continues to do it) both expertly, and with dispatch." I am reminded of a counterexample, that of Lady Isobel Burton, the widow of the adventurer-scholar Sir Richard Burton, who published translations of Camões's poetry and a book-length introduction to the great Portuguese poet and part of what was intended to be a ten-volume work. When Burton died she set about bringing to fruition the collecting of all his work and did manage to write a two-volume life of Burton, but made sure, all the while, that she should enjoy the near-status of Burton's collaborator. Fact or fiction, she even claimed to have been the author of the famous sonnet about Camões that earlier she had permitted to be credited to her husband. No one can ever accuse Mécia de Sena of mindless impartiality on the subject of Jorge de Sena, but neither can she be accused of being purposely unfair.

One could talk at some length about Mécia de Sena's own skillful and accomplished writing, only hinted at in her spare but utterly efficient prefaces and notes to the various Sena works in so many genres, but so clearly manifested (almost ingenuously) in the natural, no-nonsense style of her letters. (One hopes that someday someone will have the confidence and taste to put together at least a selective volume of Mécia de Sena's own letters.) As for the publication of

Jorge de Sena's letters, that additional task she assumed very early on in the midst of preparing his books for publication with, over time, a number of different publishers. She made the crucial decision of bypassing the chance to do a "selected" letters edition, in one or more volumes—an edition, which, onerous enough, would call for its own set of difficult choices: which letters by which recipients to include, when and where to add explanatory or contextualizing texts. If such a selective edition had the advantage of reaching its readers within a few short years, it would almost certainly exhaust the public appetite for additional Sena letters, putting off to a distant future the work of some team on what would undoubtedly be a multivolume edition of his correspondence—a possibility, to be sure, that might never come to pass. Rather, she hit on the idea of publishing seriatim individual volumes of his letters by including both sides of a given correspondence chronologically, and beginning right away with discrete volumes of letters Sena exchanged with notable contemporaries. Of course, these contemporaries, in the main, were alive and functioning, and therefore available to answer an editor's questions, also providing letters and cards from Sena for which there were no copies in his extensive letter files, as well as copies of inscriptions appearing on the pages of Sena's books offered as gifts to the recipient, which inscriptions were to be accompanied by the recipient's inscriptions in the books in Sena's personal library.

The first of these volumes, the complete correspondence of Sena with Guilherme de Castilho, appeared in 1981, published by the Imprensa Nacional–Casa da Moeda. Interestingly (and understandably so), the volume that followed it a year later, also under the imprint of the Imprensa Nacional, *Isto tudo que nos rodeia (cartas de amor)*, offered a well-culled selection of the love letters exchanged by Jorge and Mécia herself. "Serão para cima de 3000 cartas," which she deposited with the Calouste Gulbenkian Foundation, "evidentemente porque estaria fora de causa esperar poder publicá-las," she explained to me. Thus the selection in *Isto tudo que nos rodeia*, limited to "cartas de amor," opens with a letter dated November 22, 1944, and closes with one dated March 10, 1949, less than five years later. In her "Introdução a umas cartas de amor," the editor permits herself a small literary flourish right at the start by opening with an epigraph, in two parts. First she quotes lines from a poem by the nineteenth-century American poet Emily Dickinson, a Jorge de Sena favorite:

'Twas my one Glory—
Let it be
Remembered
I was owned of Thee

These lines are followed by their translation:

Foi minha única Glória—
Que seja
Recordado:
Fui possuída por Ti.

No surprise, the translation is credited to Jorge de Sena. Besides its poetic indication of the genuine feeling inherent in Mécia and Jorge's regard for one another, the epigraph has the correlative benefit (even if not so purposed, at least not consciously) of calling attention to *80 poemas de Emily Dickinson*, a volume of Sena's translations of the nineteenth-century American poet's work that was published by Edições 70, just over a year after Jorge de Sena's death on June 4, 1978.

Now let me turn to an instance in which Mécia de Sena and I corresponded over the matter of Jorge de Sena's correspondence with Edith Sitwell, the twentieth-century grande dame of English poetry. Dame Edith and Sena met just once, a meeting arranged by a mutual friend pleased to serve as an intermediary. Following the meeting there was an exchange of a handful of letters written over a seven-year period (1953–60). I did not know about any of this when, in 1990, while ferreting around in the University of Texas at Austin library catalogue, I came upon an entry for a copy of Fernando *Pessoa's 35 Sonnets*. The chapbook, now part of the Sitwell collection of papers

and books housed in the Harry Ransom Humanities Research
Center at UT Austin, was, of course, Sitwell's copy, given to her in
1953 by someone whose name had proven to be indecipherable to the
librarian who had catalogued the book for the University of Texas
library. Although I was not at that moment researching anything in
particular, certainly not Dame Edith Sitwell or, at the time, Fernando
Pessoa, I filled out a call slip and presented it to the librarian at the
desk. My request presented no problem for this clerk, even though I
had not asked for approval to conduct research on either poet. Imagine my delight when I opened the chapbook and came upon this
inscription, written in what was to me a most familiar hand:

To Doctor Edith Sitwell,

> with gratitude, remembering the
> kindness of her genius, this
> little and precious side of one
> of the greatest portuguese poets.

Lisbon, March 1953 Jorge de Sena

I could hardly wait to report my serendipitous find to Mécia de
Sena. Characteristically like clockwork, she answered my letter by
return mail. She wrote that I was not bringing her news, however,
for both she and her husband had known that the copy of Pessoa's *35
Sonnets* that Sena had so generously inscribed for Sitwell was at the
University of Texas. She explained:

> Voltando à Sitwell—eu sabia dessa existência no Texas porque o
> David Jackson, salvo erro, quando foi para lá, ou na altura em que foi
> comprado, disse ao meu marido. Fez fotocópia da dedicatória do meu
> marido? Creio que a não tenho. De facto, meu marido achou sempre,
> e jamais mudou de opinião, que ela era um grande poeta.

At this point our epistolary conversation about Jorge de Sena's
acquaintance with Edith Sitwell might well have come to an end.

But Mécia de Sena took it up again by telling me that there existed a modest but engaging exchange of letters between the two poets, that she had both sides of that correspondence (Sena customarily kept copies of his own letters), and that she would send the small batch of them to me if I had any interest in seeing them and perhaps doing something with them of a scholarly nature. I jumped at the offer, and subsequently when I had a draft of the piece presenting the letters I sent it on. She promptly wrote back encouragingly with some very useful recommendations, including the pointed suggestion that I would do well to omit Evelyn Waugh's anti-Semitic description of Alberto Lacerda who had brought Sena and Sitwell together for their one and only meeting. (Curiously, she was the very one who had alerted me to this bit of Evelyn Waugh malice in the first place—"um pequeno judeu português que exercia uma espécie de serviço de câmara," she had translated from Waugh's published memoirs.) She had provided me with copies of Sena's writings on Sitwell and of translations of her poems published in Portuguese newspapers, items difficult, sometimes, to track down in Lisbon, let alone in the United States. Later, when I sent her a draft of my piece, she wrote back encouragingly: "Quanto à Sitwell—acho o seu encadeado excelente e realmente de um tamanho que não *abafa* a pequena mas muito bonita correspondência."

When the time came, it was agreed that an additional set of proofs for "Jorge de Sena/Edith Sitwell: Correspondence" would be sent for her consideration. She attended to them immediately, meticulously correcting misprints in the Portuguese, returned them to the editor of the journal that was publishing the letters, and wrote to me with an account of what she had done, along with the explanation that she had not corrected the English part of the piece, leaving that part of the proofreading to me. Obviously, she liked the piece—well enough to request extra reprints beyond those that were originally set aside for her (and they were supplied), which she wished to distribute herself. Finally, she found a place for the piece on the list of such collections of correspondence, along with the published volumes of Sena's correspondence in the "Bibliografia de Jorge de Sena" that is appended to all first and subsequent editions of his work, joining the volumes dedicated to Sena's correspondence with Guilherme Castilho, José Régio, Vergilio Ferreira, Eduardo Lourenço, Dante Moreira Leite, Sophia de Mello Breyner Andresen, José-Augusto França, António Ramos Rosa, and José Saramago, among others. Creating and maintaining this "Correspondence" category in the Sena bibliographies at the back of his books has been still another way that Mécia de Sena has implemented her overall plan to keep Jorge de Sena's work before the reading public. How many such volumes have already been prepared but have not yet found a publisher I do not know, though I am aware of the existence of one such volume, the correspondence of Sena and José Rodrigues Miguéis, which was finally published in 2013.

Thus letters, which could have been treated as merely an adjunct to this writer's creative and critical works, have become an integral part of his living literary legacy. In fact, there is already published evidence to indicate that this part of Mécia de Sena's project has worked. For besides providing material for the historian and the biographer, some of Sena's letters have already been studied for their own sake as part of his literary legacy. In this regard, a first such study has already been done—José Costa's *A correspondência de Jorge de Sena: um outro espaço da sua escrita*, a doctoral dissertation published by Salamandra in 2003. The book's thesis is stated in the subtitle. Perhaps it was Mécia de Sena's desire to make Jorge de Sena's correspondence acceptable in this way that led her to drop silently those names and references in the letters that may have been hurtful, in her opinion, to living persons or their survivors, as well as deciding against providing what I would consider to be useful and in some cases necessary explanatory or contextualizing notes. But these are minor caveats in what is by all other measurements a grand achievement.

Yet, on balance, can anyone today even suggest that professional editors could have done more for Jorge de Sena in this area than

Mécia de Sena has? It is no mean feat that she has accomplished, and she has accomplished it without any of the fanfare we are accustomed to expect surrounding the efforts of the usual professional editors of texts. Nor have readers had to wait patiently until all the letters known to have survived have been located and collected so that the job of transcribing and editing them could take place.

To the best of my knowledge, Mécia de Sena's work on behalf of Jorge de Sena's well-deserved reputation, maintaining it and nurturing it, continues to this day. But what she has already done, one must say, has been done astonishingly well. Moreover, it can be safely ventured that, all things considered, no one else (individual or team) could have done it nearly as well as she has. Not even close. Mrs. Jorge de Sena has succeeded in her efforts to keep her husband's work in print and his memory alive and green, down to the last crucial detail. When she affixes to envelopes printed labels that read, erroneously, "Mrs. Jorge *De* Sena" (my emphasis), she finds it necessary (and, perhaps, satisfying) to correct them, so as to read: "Mrs. Jorge de Sena."

WORKS CITED

Adamson, John. *Memoirs of the Life and Writings of Luís de Camoens*. 2 vols. London: Longman, Hurst, Rees, Orme, and Brown, 1820.

Anonymous. Abstract for Jorge de Sena, "Camões: Novas observações acerca da sua epopeia e do seu pensamento." *Ocidente*, n.s., 35 (November 15, 1972): 24.

———. "Camoens, the Portuguese Shakespeare." *Motion Picture Herald* 10 (December 2, 1911): 744.

———. "Columbia University Lists $56,125 in Gifts." *New York Times*, November 7, 1931, 5.

———. "Lectures on Portuguese Poetry." *New York Times*, March 31, 1901, 3.

Arendt, Hannah. *Eichmann in Jerusalem*. New York: Viking, 1963.

Bandeira, Manuel. "Aviso aos Navegantes." In *Andorinha, andorinha*, 2nd ed., edited by Carlos Drummond de Andrade, 12–13. Rio de Janeiro: José Olympio, 1986.

———. "Edith Sitwell." In *Prosa*, edited by Antonio Carlos Villaça, 137–38. São Paulo: Agir, 1983.

———. "Elegia de Londres." In *Poesia completa e prosa*, 2nd ed., 379–80. Rio de Janeiro: Aguilar, 1967.

———. "Vi a Rainha." In *Inglaterra revisitada*, by Jorge de Sena, 73–74. Lisboa: Edições 70, 1986.

Barnes, Julian. *Flaubert's Parrot*. London: Jonathan Cape, 1984.

Batchelor, C. Malcolm. "Joaquim Nabuco e Camões." *Hispania* 57 (May 1974): 246.

Belchior, Maria de Lourdes, and Enrique Martínez-López, eds. *Camoniana Californiana: Commemorating the Quadricentennial of the Death of Luís de Camões*. Santa Barbara: Jorge de Sena Center for Portuguese Studies, University of California, Santa Barbara, ICALP, and Bandanna Books, 1985.

Blanco, José. *Fernando Pessoa: esboço de uma bibliografia*. Lisboa: Imprensa Nacional–Casa da Moeda, 1983.

Butler, Samuel. *The Way of All Flesh*. New York: Modern Library/Random House, 1998. First published 1903.

Campbell, Roy. *Collected Works IV: Prose*. Craighall, South Africa: Ad. Donker, 1988.

———. "A South African Poet in Portugal." Broadcast, National English Programme (SABC), April 19, 1954.

Conrad, Joseph. *Nostromo*. Edited by F. R. Leavis. New York: New American Library, 1960.

Daghlian, Carlos. *Os discursos americanos de Joaquim Nabuco*. Translated by João Carlos Gonçalves. Recife: Fundação Joaquim Nabuco/Massangana, 1988.

Delgado, Antonio Sáez. *Órficos y ultraístas: Portugal y España en el diálogo de las primeras vanguardias literarias (1915–1925)*. Mérida: Editora Regional de Extremadura, 1999.

Dickinson, Emily. *The Poems of Emily Dickinson*. 3 vols. Edited by Thomas H. Johnson. Cambridge, MA: Harvard University Press, 1955.

Dios, Angel Marcos de, ed. *Epistolario portugués de Unamuno*. Paris: Fundação Calouste Gulbenkian/Centro Cultural Português, 1978.

Dissertações de doutoramento sobre temas portugueses em universidades norte-americanas. Compiled by José F. Salgado. Lisboa: Fundação Luso-Americana para o Desenvolvimento/Center for Portuguese Studies, University of California, Santa Barbara, 1995.

Elbron, Geoffrey. *Edith Sitwell: A Biography*. Garden City, NY: Doubleday, 1981.

Fagundes, Francisco Cota. "The Transmutation of Autobiographical Experiences in Jorge de Sena's *Os grão-capitães*." *Kentucky Romance Quarterly* 30 (1983): 203–16.

————. "A transmutação das experiências autobiográficas em 'Os grão-capitães' de Jorge de Sena." Translated by Mécia de Sena. In *Estudos Sobre Jorge de Sena*, edited by Eugénio Lisboa, 344–67. Lisboa: Imprensa Nacional–Casa da Moeda, 1984.

————. *In the Beginning There Was Jorge de Sena's GENESIS: The Birth of a Writer*. Santa Barbara: Jorge de Sena Center for Portuguese Studies, University of California, Santa Barbara/Bandanna Books, 1991), 124–30.

Francis, Robert. "Dame Edith." In *The Satirical Rogue on Poetry*, 52. Amherst: University of Massachusetts Press, 1968.

Frost, Robert. *Prose Jottings of Robert Frost: Selections from His Notebooks and Miscellaneous Manuscripts*. Edited by Edward Connery Lathem and Hyde Cox. Lunenburg, VT: Northeast Kingdom, 1982.

Graves, Robert. *Between Moon and Moon: Selected Letters of Robert Graves 1946–1972*. Edited by Paul O'Prey. London: Hutchinson, 1984.

————. *The Crowning Privilege*. London: Cassell, 1955.

Guerber, H. A. *The Book of the Epic*. Philadelphia and London: Lippincott, 1913.

Higginson, Thomas Wentworth. "Portugal's Glory and Decay." *North American Review* 173 (October 1856): 456–76.

Hoffman, Daniel G. *An Armada of Thirty Whales*. New Haven, CT: Yale University Press, 1954.

Hower, Alfred, and Richard A. Preto-Rodas, ed. *Empire in Transition: The Portuguese World in the Time of Camões*. Gainesville: University of Florida Press, 1985.

Hughes, Merritt Y. "Camoens, 1524–1924." *New York Evening Post Literary Review*, September 20, 1924, section 5, 1–2.

Jones, Roger Stephens. "The Epic Similes of *Os Lusíadas*." *Hispania* 57 (May 1974): 239–45.

Laughter for the Devil: The Trials of Gilles de Rais, Companion-in-Arms of Joan of Arc. Translated and introduction by Reginald Hyatte. Rutherford, NJ: Fairleigh Dickinson University Press, 1984.

Lewis, Wyndham. *Hitler*. London: Chatto & Windus, 1931.

Lisboa, Eugénio, ed. *Estudos sobre Jorge de Sena*. Lisboa: Imprensa Nacional–Casa da Moeda, 1984.

————. "Breve perfil de Jorge de Sena." In *Estudos sobre Jorge de Sena*, 29–42.

Locke, John. *An Essay concerning Human Understanding*. Edited by John Yolton. London: Dent.

Lopes, Óscar. "Camões e Jorge de Sena." *Literatura comparada: os novos paradigmas*. Edited by Margarida L. Losa, Isménia de Sousa, and Gonçalo Vilas-Boas. Porto: Associação de Literatura Comparada, 1996.

Lourenço, Jorge Fazenda. *A poesia de Jorge de Sena: testemunho, metamorfose, peregrinação*. Paris: Centre Culturel Calouste Gulbenkian, 1998.

Lourenço, Jorge Fazenda, and Frederick G. Williams. *Uma bibliografia cronológica de Jorge de Sena (1939–1994)*. Lisboa: Imprensa Nacional–Casa da Moeda, 1994.

Madden, Eva. "Portugal's Poetical One-Eyed Devil." *New York Times*, July 13, 1924, SM9.

Martín, José Luís García. "Fernando Pessoa y Miguel de Unamuno: las razones de un desencuentro." *Actas IV Congresso Internacional de Estudos Pessoanos (Secção Brasileira)*. Porto: Fundação Eng. António de Almeida, 1990.

Martinho, Fernando J. B. "Uma leitura dos sonetos de Jorge de Sena." In *Estudos sobre Jorge de Sena*, edited by Eugénio Lisboa, 170–87. Lisboa: Imprensa Nacional–Casa da Moeda, 1984.

Martins, Luis. "O Assassino de Milhões." *O Estado de São Paulo*, April 11, 1961, 10.

Miguéis, José Rodrigues. "Há sempre um bei em Tunes." *É proibido apontar: reflexões de um burguês*, 2nd ed. Lisboa: Estampa, 1984.

Monteiro, Adolfo Casais, and Pierre Hourcade. *Fernando Pessoa: Bureau de Tabac*. Lisboa: Inquérito, 1952.

Monteiro, George. "Shades and Intimations of the Prison-House: Observations on Some Portuguese Films of the 1940s." *Luso-Brazilian Review* 22 (Summer 1985): 51–61.

Moser, Gerald M. "Camões' Shipwreck." *Hispania* 57 (May 1974): 218–19.

O'Neill, Eugene. *Jornada para a noite*. Translated by Jorge de Sena. Introduction by Mécia de Sena, Lisboa: Cotovia/Teatro Nacional D. Maria II, 1992.

Oram, Mary C. "Camões Visits Uncle Sam." *Américas* 2 (December 1950): 10–12, 29–30.

Pascoaes, Teixeira de. *A Águia* 1 (March 19, 1911): 14–16

Pepperberg, Irene Maxine. *The Alex Studies: Cognitive and Communicative Abilities of Grey Parrots*. Cambridge, MA: Harvard University Press, 1999.

Pessoa, Fernando. *Cartas de Fernando Pessoa a João Gaspar Simões*. Edited by João Gaspar Simões. Lisboa: Europa-América, 1957.

———. *Correspondência 1905–1922*. Edited by Manuela Parreira da Silva. Lisboa: Assírio & Alvim, 1999.

———. *Mensagem: poemas esotéricos*. Edited by José Augusto Seabra. Madrid: Archivos, SCIC, 1993.

———. "Movimento sensacionista." *Exílio* 1 (April 1916).

———. *Páginas de doutrina estética*. Lisboa: Inquérito, 1946–47.

———. *Páginas de estética e de teoria e crítica literárias*. Edited by Georg Rudolf Lind and Jacinto do Prado Coelho. Lisboa: Ática, 1966.

———. *Pessoa inédito*. Edited by Teresa Rita Lopes. Lisboa: Livros Horizonte, 1993.

———. *Textos de crítica e de intervenção*. Lisboa: Ática, 1980.

———. *Ultimatum e páginas de sociologia política*. Edited by Maria Isabel Rocheta and Maria Paula Morão. Introduction by Joel Serrão. Lisboa: Ática, 1980.

Pessoa, Fernando (Bernardo Soares). *Livro do desassossego*. Edited by Jacinto do Prado Coelho. Lisboa: Ática, 1982.

Picchio, Luciana Stegagno. "Esercizi su di una vita: I 'Flashes' di Mécia de Sena," *Quaderni portoghesi* 13/14 (Autumn 1983): 313–22.

Pierce, Frank. "Ancient History in *Os Lusíadas*." *Hispania* 57 (May 1974): 220–30

Piper, Anson C. "The Feminine Presence in *Os Lusíadas*." *Hispania* 57 (May 1974): 231–38.

Plath, Karl, and Malcolm Davis. *This Is the Parrot*. Neptune City, NJ: TFH Publications, 1971.

Portugal, José Blanc de. "Provocação do tradutor." In *O louco rabequista*, 8. Lisboa: Presença, 1988.

Régio, José. *Páginas do diário íntimo*. 2nd ed. Introduction by Eugénio Lisboa. Notes by José Alberto Reis Pereira. Lisboa: Imprensa Nacional–Casa da Moeda, 2000.

Ribeiro, Thomaz. "To Portugal." Translated by Aubrey F. G. Bell. *Portugal: A Monthly Review* 1 (February 1915).

Rothberg, Irving P. ["Camões"]. *Hispania* 57 (May 1974): 213.

Salter, Elizabeth. *The Last Years of a Rebel: A Memoir of Edith Sitwell*. Boston: Houghton Mifflin, 1967.

Sena, Jorge de. *Antigas e novas andanças do demónio*. Lisboa: Edições 70, 1978.

———. "Camões: The Lyrical Poet." In *Camões: Some Poems*, translated by Jonathan Griffin. London: Menard Press, 1976.

———. "Camões—verbete para uma enciclopédia." In *Trinta anos de Camões*, 1:295–96.

———. *Diários*. Porto: Caixotim, 2004.

———. *Do teatro em Portugal*. Lisboa: Edições 70, 1988.

———. "Edith Sitwell." *O Primeiro de Janeiro* (November 7, 1951).

———. "Edith Sitwell." *Diário de notícias* (June 23, 1955): 6–7.

———. "Edith Sitwell e T. S. Eliot." *O tempo e o modo* 23 (January 1965): 5.

———. *A estrutura de "Os Lusíadas" e outros estudos camonianos e de poesia peninsular do século XVI*. Lisboa: Portugália, 1970.

———. *Estudos de cultura e literatura brasileira*. Lisboa: Edições 70, 1988.

———. *The Evidences*. Translated by Phyllis Sterling Smith. Santa Barbara: Center for Portuguese Studies, University of California, Santa Barbara, 1994.

———. "Fernando Pessoa: o homem que nunca foi." *Persona* 2 (July 1978): 27–41.

———. *Fernando Pessoa & Ca. Heterónima*. Lisboa: Edições 70, 1984.

———. "Fernando Pessoa e a Literatura Inglesa." *O comércio do Porto* (August 11, 1953): 6.

———. *40 anos de servidão*. 2nd ed. Lisboa: Moraes, 1982.

———. *Genesis*. Lisboa: Edições 70, 1982.

———. *Os grão-capitães*. 2nd ed. Lisboa: Edições 70, 1978.

———. *Inglaterra revisitada*. Lisboa: Edições 70, 1986.

———. "Jardineiros e astrónomos." *Comércio do Porto* (April 27, 1954): 5.

———, ed. *Líricas portuguesas*. Lisboa: Edições 70, 1983.

———. *A literatura inglesa*. Lisboa: Cotovia, 1989.

———. *Literatura inglesa*. Vol. 6 of *História ilustrada das grandes literaturas*. Lisboa: Estúdios Cor, 1959–60.

———. "Londres e dois grandes poetas." *Diário popular* (October 24, 1957).

———. "The Man Who Never Was." In *Man Who Never Was: Essays on Fernando Pessoa*, edited by George Monteiro, 19–31. Providence, RI: Gávea-Brown, 1982.

———. "Maquiavel e o 'Príncipe.'" In *Maquiavel e outros estudos*, 15–51. Porto: Livraria Paisagem, 1974.

———. *Metamorfoses.* Lisboa: Moraes, 1963.

———. "Nota de abertura." In *Poesia de 26 séculos*, 8–9. Coimbra: Fora do Texto, 1993.

———. "Nota introdutória a uma dupla reedição." In *Antigas e novas andanças do demónio.* Lisboa: Edições 70, 1978, 9–12

———. *Peregrinatio ad loca infecta.* Lisboa: Portugália, 1969.

———. "Os poemas completos de Edith Sitwell." *Diário popular* (November 7, 1957): 1–2.

———. "Da poesia maior e menor (a propósito de Manuel Bandeira)." In *O poeta, um fingidor*, 131–50. Lisboa: Ática, 1961.

———. *Poesia—II.* Lisboa: Moraes, 1978.

———. *Poesia—III.* Lisboa: Moraes, 1978.

———, ed. *Poesia do século XX (de Thomas Hardy a C. V. Cattaneo).* Porto: Inova, 1978.

———. *O poeta, um fingidor.* Lisboa: Ática, 1961.

———. *O reino da estupidez.* Lisboa: Moraes, 1961.

———. *O reino da estupidez—II.* Lisboa: Moraes, 1978.

———. "Roy Campbell." *O comércio do Porto* (February 10, 1953): 6.

———. "Sacheverell Sitwell." *O comércio do Porto* (March 10, 1953).

———. "Sobre Roy Campbell." *O comércio do Porto* (May 21, 1957): 6.

———. "Sobre uma estrofe de Jorge de Sena." In *Sequência*, 14. Lisboa: Moraes, 1980.

———. *Os sonetos de Camões e o soneto quinhentista peninsular.* Lisboa: Portugália, 1969.

———. "Uma carta." *O Estado de São Paulo* (April 19, 1961): 8.

Sitwell, Edith. *Fire of the Mind: An Anthology.* Edited by Elizabeth Salter and Allanah Harper. London: Michael Joseph, 1976.

———. "Elegy for Dylan Thomas." *Poetry* 87 (November 1955): 63–67.

————. *Selected Letters, 1919–1964.* Edited by John Lehmann and Derek Parker. New York: Vanguard, 1970.

Sitwell, Sacheverell. "O poeta e o espelho." Translated by Jorge de Sena. In *Poesia do Século XX*, 351–53.

Taylor, Edmond. "Camoëns." *Horizon* 14 (Autumn 1972).

Thomas, Dylan. *The Collected Letters.* Edited by Paul Ferris. New York: Macmillan, 1985.

Unanumo, Miguel de. *Epistolário ibérico: cartas de Pascoaes e Unamuno.* Edited by José Bento. Lisboa: Assírio & Alvim, 1986.

————. "La literatura portuguesa contemporanea." In *Por tierras de Portugal y de España.*

————. "La pesca de Espinho." In *Por tierras de Portugal y de España.*

————. *Por tierras de Portugal y de España.* 2nd ed. Buenos Aires: Espasa-Calpe Argentina, 1944.

Ward, A. C. *História da literatura inglesa.* Lisboa: Estúdios Cor, 1959–60.

Woodberry, George Edward. "Camoens." In *The Inspiration of Poetry*, 56–84. New York: Macmillan, 1910.

NOTES

Chapter 1: In Quest of the Minotaur

1. Sena's lecture was published in *The Man Who Never Was: Essays on Fernando Pessoa*, ed. George Monteiro (Providence: Gávea-Brown, 1982), 19–31. His Portuguese version appeared as "Fernando Pessoa: O homem que nunca foi" in *Persona* 2 (July 1978): 27–41, and was reprinted in Jorge de Sena, *Fernando Pessoa & Ca Heterónima* (Lisboa: Edições 70, 1984), 409–38.

2. Jorge de Sena, *Poesia—III* (Lisboa: Moraes, 1978), 204–5.

3. Jorge de Sena, *Genesis* (Lisboa: Edições 70, 1982), 23. Subsequent pages numbers within the text refer to this edition.

4. Jorge de Sena, "Nota introdutória a uma dupla reedição," in *Antigas e novas andanças do demónio* (Lisboa: Edições 70, 1978), 11.

5. Jorge de Sena, "Maquiavel e o 'Príncipe,'" in *Maquiavel e outros estudos* (Porto: Livraria Paisagem, 1974), 15–51.

6. Jorge de Sena, "(Auto-exame)," in *Versos e alguma prosa de Jorge de Sena*, ed. Eugénio Lisboa (Lisboa: Arcadia e Moraes, 1979), 139.

7. Jorge de Sena, *O reino da estupidez—II* (Lisboa: Moraes, 1978), 51–52.

8. Sena, *Poesia—II*, 78.

9. Jorge de Sena, "Sobre uma estrofe de Jorge de Sena," in *Sequência* (Lisboa: Moraes, 1980), 14.

10. The best of these studies, in my opinion, is Francisco Cota Fagundes's "The Transmutation of Autobiographical Experiences in Jorge de Sena's *Os Grão-Capitães*," *Kentucky Romance Quarterly* 30 (1983): 203–16.

11. Jorge de Sena, *Os Grão-Capitães*, 2nd ed. (Lisboa: Edições 70, 1978), 17. Subsequent pages numbers within the text refer to this edition.

12. Jorge de Sena, *40 anos de servidão*, 2nd ed. (Lisboa: Moraes, 1982), 234.

13. Sena, *40 anos*, 221–22.

Chapter 2: "If This Be Treason"

1. Jorge de Sena, "Aos cinquenta anos," in *40 anos de servidão* (Lisboa: Moraes, 1979), 116.

2. Fernando Pessoa, *Pessoa inédito*, ed. Teresa Rita Lopes (Lisboa: Livros Horizonte, 1993), 298.

3. Jorge de Sena, "Fernando Pessoa: o homem que nunca foi," in *Fernando Pessoa & Ca Heterónima* (Lisboa: Edições 70, 1984), 416.

4. Jorge de Sena, "Nota de abertura," in *Poesia de 26 séculos* (Coimbra: Fora do Texto, 1993), 8–9.

5. Jorge de Sena, "Chopin: um inventário," in *Poesia—II* (Lisboa: Moraes, 1978), 192.

6. Sena, *Poesia—II*, 44–45.

7. Jorge de Sena, *Peregrinatio ad loca infecta* (Lisboa: Portugália, 1969), xiii.

8. Sena, *Peregrinatio*, xiiin.

9. Sena, *Peregrinatio*, xv.

10. Sena, *Peregrinatio*, 29, 35, 47, 53, 79, and 128.

11. Jorge de Sena, "A Portugal," *40 anos de servidão*, 89. In "Fidelidade" (1958) Sena had already broached the theme of betrayal and treachery. In "Mensagem de finados," for example, he writes:

> Não desesperarei da Humanidade. / Por mais que o mundo, o
> acaso, a Providência, tudo, / à minha volta afogue em lágrimas
> e bombas / os sonhos de liberdade e de justiça; / por mais que
> tudo o que a maldade busque / para encobrir-se traia o que ainda
> esperamos; / por mais que a estupidez rica de bens e audácia /
> estrangule a lucidez dos que vêem claro; / por mais que tudo
> caia, acabe, se suspenda; / por mais que a Humanidade volte ao
> bando apavorado / que os cães servis acossam aos redis avaros;
> / por mais que a noite desça, o frio gele / as últimas esperanças,

em luar cendrado / cujo silêncio nem gritos de criança / possam trespassar— / não desesperarei da Humanidade. Em vão / me atudem, me intimidam, me destroem; / em vão se juntam todos imprecando ignaros. Não! / Podem fazer o que quiserem. Podem / tornar-me anónimo, traidor ou prostituta, / que não desesperarei.

Poesia—II, 49

And later in the same poem he writes:

Mas de verdade e de erro nos unimos; / e de má-fé nos repartimos tanto / que nada resta: a própria morte morre / em vossas bocas que se fecham falsas / ou se abrem falsas para mais traição. / E em vossos gestos que, medrosos, tecem / a rede vil da falsa solidão. / Como quando a nós abandonamos / e aos outros entregamos o saber incerto / do que pensamos ser; ou como quando / levados vamos pelo vento odioso / que o mal profunda à nossa volta e em nós; / como quando não somos, além do que nos prende, / a soma derradeira que o fulgor da morte / instantânea fará no estrondo em que chegar: / eis a má-fé, eis a traição, a infâmia, / talhadas com fervor nas cómodas lembranças / de quanto é de família não amar o próximo / senão como um farrapo que se demitiu / qual nós nos demitimos não amando nele / a liberdade irredutível de ser quem / covardemente em nós não procuramos. Que mundanal solicitude a vossa! / Protestai, defendei, gritai palavras / que bocas sujas de ouro já rilharam. / Essas palavras hão de abandonar-vos, / a ver-vos-eis sem elas, nus, despidos, / ante o espelho da vida que, real, / não há-de reflectir-vos essa imagem vã com que iludistes a dignidade humana / na hora em que o silêncio era a verdade / do Amor traído em suas faces todas. *Poesia—II*, 50.

Nor is Sena's obsession with notions of treachery absent in *Metamorfoses* (1963). In "Cabecinha Romana de Milreu" he writes of "povos que foram massacrados e traídos"; in "Pietà de Avignon" he writes that the painting "não traia a esperança ou traia aquele amor / que escorre lívido pelo cadáver"; in "A morte, o espaço, a eternidade," he writes of his fear that "vamos / traindo esta ascensão, esta vitória, isto / que é ser-se humano, passo a passo, mais"; and, later in the same poem, of his further fear: "O estado natural é complacência eterna, / é uma traição ao medo por que somos, / àquilo que nos cabe: ser o espírito/ sempre mais vasto do Universo infindo." *Poesia—II*, 71, 88.

In "Tão complicados," another poem from the same years, but published only in *40 anos de servidão*, Sena attacks the actions of the recently embourgeoised: "a primeira coisa que fazeis, / rapada a casca de miséria pura, / ter gravata e graxa, ir morar / nos bairros chiques, trair o povo / que ainda tendes nas veias. Traí-lo, / mais do que ao povo ao que seria vero / na vossa mesquinhez de hipotecados" (120). On the other hand, in "Boris Godunov," in *Arte de Música*, he writes of the "povo que não sabe nunca / quem trai ou salva." *Poesia—II*, 200.

On translation Sena writes: "Quem traduza consciente do tempo em que eles viveram não poderá nunca traí-los, se se ativer ao que escreveram, embora uma tradução, para ser viva, deva ser um compromisso entre o estilo da época e do autor e a linguagem do nosso tempo." "Introdução à primeira parte," in *Poesia de 26 séculos*, 19.

12. Sena, *Peregrinatio*, 110.

13. It would not be surprising to learn that Sena was aware that in his last years Sir Richard Burton, the English writer-traveler, who not only wrote a book about Camões but also translated both his lyric poetry and *Os Lusíadas*, was studying Volapük.

14. Somewhat confusingly, there is an earlier poem also bearing the title "Noções de linguística" (1962), which appears in *Peregrinatio ad loca infecta*. This first poem can be seen as being less about the betrayal of language than about its failings when confronted with matters such as the smoke "das chaminés dos campos de concentração" and of the "fogo dos fuguetes nucleares" (84).

15. Jorge de Sena, "Noções de linguística," in *Poesia—III*, 147.

16. Bernardo Soares, *Livro do desassossego*, ed. Jacinto do Prado Coelho (Lisboa: Ática, 1982), 1:17.

17. Quoted in Eugénio Lisboa, "Breve perfil de Jorge de Sena," in *Estudos sobre Jorge de Sena*, ed. Eugénio Lisboa (Lisboa: Imprensa Nacional–Casa da Moeda, 1984), 42.

18. Jorge de Sena, "Paráfrase de Melina Mercouri," in *40 anos de servidão*, 128. It is precisely through its irony and ambiguity that this poem evades the danger Sena warns about in the patriotic poem: "Toda a poesia patriótica do mundo, se não atinge o mais alto plano de um esclarecido

amor da pátria, fica ridiculíssima, como merece, em tradução." *Poesia de 26 séculos*, 20.

Chapter 3: The Green Parrot

1. Quoted in John Locke, *An Essay concerning Human Understanding*, ed. John Yolton (London: Dent, 1961), 1:279–80.

2. *Prose Jottings of Robert Frost: Selections from His Notebooks and Miscellaneous Manuscripts*, ed. Edward Connery Lathem and Hyde Cox (Lunenburg, VT: Northeast Kingdom Publishers, 1982), 80.

3. Jorge de Sena, "Prefácio (1971)," in *Os grão-capitães* (Lisboa: Edições 70, 1978), 15–21. In *The Way of All Flesh* (1903) Samuel Butler writes: "Every man's work, whether it be literature or music or pictures or architecture or anything else, is always a portrait of himself, and the more he tries to conceal himself the more clearly will his character appear in spite of him. I may very likely be condemning myself, all the time that I am writing this book, for I know that whether I like it or not I am portraying myself more surely than I am portraying any of the characters whom I set before the reader." *The Way of All Flesh* (New York: Modern Library/Random House, 1998), 67.

4. On the autobiographical content of *Os grão-capitães*, see Fagundes, "The Transmutation of Autobiographical Experiences in Jorge de Sena's *Os Grão-Capitães*," *Kentucky Romance Quarterly* 30 (1983): 203–16; "A transmutação das experiências autobiográficas em 'Os grão-capitães' de Jorge de Sena," trans. Mécia de Sena, in *Estudos sobre Jorge de Sena*, ed. Eugénio Lisboa (Lisboa: Imprensa Nacional–Casa da Moeda, 1984), 344–67; and *In the Beginning There Was Jorge de Sena's GENESIS: The Birth of a Writer* (Santa Barbara: Jorge de Sena Center for Portuguese Studies, University of California, Santa Barbara/Bandanna Books, 1991), 124–30.

5. Jack Tresidder, *Dictionary of Symbols* (San Francisco: Chronicle Books, 1998), 26.

6. Nathaniel Owen Wallace, "The Responsibilities of Madness: John Skelton, 'Speke, Parrot,' and Homeopathic Satire," *Studies in Philology* 82 (Winter 1985): 60–80; Bruce Boehrer, "'Men, Monkeys, Lap-Dogs, Parrots, Perish All!' Psittacine Articulacy in Early Modern Writing," *Modern Language Quarterly* 59 (June 1998): 177.

7. Boehrer, "Men, Monkeys," 191. See also Graham Huggan, "A Tale of Two Parrots: Walcott, Rhys, and the Uses of Colonial Mimicry," *Contemporary Literature* 35 (Winter 1994): 643–60.

8. In several places Sena acknowledges Flaubert's contribution to the novel, singling out *Madame Bovary* for praise. See, e.g., *A literatura inglesa* (São Paulo: Cultrix, 1963), 318–19. "O 'Bom Pastor,'" the fourth story in *Os grão-capitães*, employs the epigraph "Martyrs—Tous les premiers chrétiens l'ont été," which Sena assigns to Flaubert's *Dictionnaire des idées reçues*.

9. Gustave Flaubert, "The Legend of St. Julian the Hospitaller," in *Three Tales*, trans. Arthur McDowall, intro. Harry Levin (Norfolk, CT: New Directions, 1947), 120–21.

10. See, for example, Jefferson Humphries, "Flaubert's Parrot and Huysmans's Cricket: The Decadence of Realism and the Realism of Decadence," *Stanford French Review* 11 (Fall 1987): 323–30.

11. Julian Barnes, *Flaubert's Parrot* (New York: Knopf, 1985), 16–17. Félicité's final vision (or hallucination) is parodied by Flannery O'Connor in "The Enduring Chill," which concludes: "But the Holy Ghost, emblazoned in ice instead of fire, continued, implacable, to descend." *The Complete Stories* (New York: Farrar, Straus and Giroux, 1990), 382.

12. All quotations from "Homenagem ao Papagaio Verde" are taken from the text of *Os grão-capitães* (Lisboa: Edições 70, 1979), 25–50.

13. For an absorbing account of one parrot's ability to know and speak, see Irene Maxine Pepperberg's *The Alex Studies: Cognitive and Communicative Abilities of Grey Parrots* (Cambridge, MA: Harvard University Press, 1999).

14. Fagundes, "Transmutation of Autobiographical Experiences," 206–7.

15. When the tyrannical father is at home, the parental bedroom becomes a prison within the larger prison of the house that houses the constricting and secretive family. It is not merely coincidental, perhaps, that prison-like enclosures abound in films produced throughout Salazar's dictatorship. See my essay, "Shades and Intimations of the Prison-House: Observations on Some Portuguese Films of the 1940s," *Luso-Brazilian Review* 22 (Summer 1985): 51–61.

16. I say "conflicted" because the boy is excitedly curious about what the father brings with him in those crates from Africa but obviously apprehensive about how his father will behave toward him and his mother. In *Flaubert's Parrot* Julian Barnes notes: "In her *Souvenirs intimes* Caroline [Flaubert's

niece] recalls her uncle's return from Egypt when she was a small girl: he arrives home unexpectedly one evening, wakes her, picks her up out of bed, burst out laughing because her nightdress extends far below her feet, and plants great kisses on her cheeks. He has just come from outdoors: his moustache is cold, and damp with dew. She is frightened, and much relieved when he puts her down. *What is this but a textbook account of the absent father's alarming return to the household*—the return from the war, from business, from abroad, from philandering, from danger?" *Flaubert's Parrot* (London: Jonathan Cape, 1984), 103–4; emphasis added. What seems to be especially disturbing to the child in Sena's story is that the father's return is both periodic and ominously punctual, turning the boy's ordeal fearfully Sisyphean.

17. "Samuel Butler," *The Way of All Flesh*, vi.

18. Sena, *A literatura inglesa* (Lisboa: Cotovia, 1989), 316, 318. See also Sena's comments on Edmund Gosse's *Father and Son* (1907), 316.

19. According to Tresidder, the parrot is "a messenger or link between humanity and the spirit world, an obvious symbolism in view of its talkativeness. Parrots were therefore associated with prophecy." *Dictionary of Symbols*, 153. This notion certainly squares with Sena's intentions in "Homenagem ao Papagaio Verde," but so does the following: "Some of the parrots which were sailors' pets on long voyages from distant lands became very famous. The sailors took delight in teaching them objectionable language which, of course, greatly reduced the value of such birds. With their long memory, these birds did not easily forget such talk. One man, however, on hearing such a bird in a pet shop said, 'This is just the bird for me,' and delightedly took her home." Karl Plath and Malcolm Davis, *This Is the Parrot* (Neptune City, NJ: T.F.H. Publications, 1971), 126.

20. Joseph Conrad, *Nostromo*, ed. F. R. Leavis (New York: New American Library, 1960), 69.

21. Jorge de Sena, "À memória de Adolfo Casais Monteiro," in *Conheço o sal e outros poemas* (1974), *Poesia—III* (Lisboa: Moraes, 1978), 207–9.

Chapter 4: An "Eichmann" Story

1. Luís Martins, "O assassino de milhões," *O Estado de São Paulo*, April 11, 1961, 10. Quotations from Martins's columns are given in my English translation, as are all subsequent passages of prose and poetry translated from Portuguese in this essay.

2. "Uma carta," *O Estado de São Paulo*, April 19, 1961, 8. I have translated into English this quotation from Jorge de Sena's letter. I wish to thank Mécia de Sena for her kindness in supplying me with copies of Luís Martins's two columns.

3. Jorge de Sena, *O reino da estupidez* (Lisboa: Moraes, 1961), 126–35.

4. Sena, *Poesia—II* (Lisboa: Moraes, 1978), 99.

5. Sena, "Maquiavel e o 'Príncipe,'" in *Maquiavel e outros estudos* (Porto: Livraria Paisagem, 1974), 50.

6. Sena, *Poesia—II*, 12–28.

7. Jorge de Sena, *Antigas e novas andanças do demónio* (Lisboa: Edições 70, 1978), 171–82.

8. Sena, *Poesia—II*, 15.

9. Quoted in Wyndham Lewis, *Hitler* (London: Chatto & Windus, 1931), 126.

10. Lewis, *Hitler*, 125.

11. Sena, *O reino da estupidez*, 134.

12. Hannah Arendt, *Eichmann in Jerusalem* (New York: Viking, 1963), 23.

13. Arendt, *Eichmann*, 19.

14. Arendt, *Eichmann*, 255–56.

15. Arendt, *Eichmann*, 253.

16. Arendt, *Eichmann*, 27.

17. *Laughter for the Devil: The Trials of Gilles de Rais, Companion-in-Arms of Joan of Arc (1440)*, trans. Reginald Hyatte (Rutherford, NJ: Fairleigh Dickinson University Press, 1984), 62.

18. *Laughter for the Devil*, 84–85.

19. Sena, *O reino da estupidez*, 131–32.

20. Sena, *O reino da estupidez*, the fifth page (unnumbered) after page 183.

21. *The Poems of Emily Dickinson*, ed. Thomas H. Johnson (Cambridge, MA: Harvard University Press, 1955), 1:467.

Chapter 5: The Case for Camões

1. Óscar Lopes, "Camões e Jorge de Sena," in *Literatura comparada: os novos paradigmas*, ed. Margarida L. Losa, Isménia de Sousa, and Gonçalo Vilas-Boas (Porto: Associação de Literatura Comparada, 1996), 23.

2. See Mary C. Oram, "Camões Visits Uncle Sam," *Américas* 2 (December 1950): 10–12, 29–30.

3. José Régio, *Páginas do diário íntimo*, 2nd ed., intro. Eugénio Lisboa, notes José Alberto Reis Pereira (Lisboa: Imprensa Nacional–Casa da Moeda, 2000), 168.

4. *Dissertações de doutoramento sobre temas portugueses em universidades norte-americanas*, compiled by José F. Salgado (Lisboa: Fundação Luso-Americana para o Desenvolvimento; Santa Barbara, CA: Center for Portuguese Studies, University of California, Santa Barbara, 1995).

5. "Lectures on Portuguese Poetry," *New York Times*, March 31, 1901, 3.

6. "Columbia University Lists $56,125 in Gifts," *New York Times*, November 7, 1931, 5.

7. See Carlos Daghlian, *Os discursos americanos de Joaquim Nabuco*, trans. João Carlos Gonçalves (Recife: Fundação Joaquim Nabuco/Editora Massangana, 1988).

8. George Edward Woodberry, "Camoens," in *The Inspiration of Poetry* (New York: Macmillan, 1910), 59.

9. H. A. Guerber, *The Book of the Epic* (Philadelphia and London: Lippincott, 1913).

10. Merritt Y. Hughes, "Camoens, 1524–1924," *New York Evening Post Literary Review*, September 20, 1924.

11. Eva Madden, "Portugal's Poetical One-Eyed Devil," *New York Times*, July 13, 1924, SM9.

12. Sena, "Camões revisitado," in *Trinta anos de Camões* (São Paulo: Edições 70, 1980), 2:241–52.

13. C. R. Boxer to António Cirurgião, December 21, 1971, António Cirurgião papers. Private collection.

14. The second day of the conference concluded with a "workshop on the development of Luso-Brazilian studies in the United States" conducted by Gilbert Cavaco of Providence College, Providence, Rhode Island.

15. António Cirurgião, in conversation with George Monteiro, April 15, 2002.

16. Sena, "Camões em 1972," in *Trinta anos de Camões*, 1:272.

17. Copy of Francis M. Rogers to Irving P. Rothberg, March 9, 1971, George Monteiro papers, private collection.

18. Irving P. Rothberg, ["Camões"], *Hispania* 57 (May 1974): 213.

19. Gerald M. Moser, "Camões' Shipwreck," *Hispania* 57 (May 1974): 218–19.

20. Frank Pierce, "Ancient History in *Os Lusíadas*," *Hispania* 57 (May 1974): 229.

21. Anson C. Piper, "The Feminine Presence in *Os Lusíadas*," *Hispania* 57 (May 1974): 231–32.

22. Roger Stephens Jones, "The Epic Similes of 'Os Lusíadas,'" *Hispania* 57 (May 1974): 239.

23. C. Malcolm Batchelor, "Joaquim Nabuco e Camões," *Hispania* 57 (May 1974): 246.

24. Edmond Taylor, "Camoëns," *Horizon* 14 (Autumn 1972): 56.

25. Taylor, "Camoëns," 57.

26. Taylor, "Camoëns," 61, 64.

27. The film was described as being 610 feet in length, accompanied by a travelogue about Paris, 320 feet in length. The account of its story reveals that the film takes liberties with the then-accepted facts of Camões's biography, notably in the appearance of Barbara during the poet's last days as his slave and only companion. The film was reviewed in the *Motion Picture Herald* 10, December 2, 1911, 744.

28. Abstract for Jorge de Sena, "Camões: New Observations on His Epic and Thought" ["Novas observações acerca da sua epopeia e do seu pensamento"], *Ocidente*, n.s., 35 (November 1972): 24.

29. Jorge de Sena, "Camões—Faria e Sousa," in *Trinta anos de Camões*, 1:171.

30. Jorge de Sena, "Camões na Ilha de Moçambique," in *Poesia—III* (Lisboa: Moraes, 1978), 189–90.

31. Full bibliographical details for Sena's publications on Camões during this period are listed in Jorge Fazenda Lourenço and Frederick G. Williams's *Uma bibliografia cronológica de Jorge de Sena (1939–1994)* (Lisboa: Imprensa Nacional–Casa da Moeda, 1994).

32. This similarity has also been noticed by Jorge Fazenda Lourenço in *A poesia de Jorge de Sena: Testemunho, metamorfose, peregrinação* (Paris: Centre Culturel Calouste Gulbenkian, 1998), 297–98.

33. Jorge de Sena, "Babel e Sião," in *Trinta anos*, 1:127. Sena is anticipated by John Adamson, who quotes Camões's title as "Sobre os rios que vão" in *Memoirs of the Life and Writings of Luís de Camoens* (London: Longman, Hurst, Rees, Orme, and Brown, 1820), 1:157.

34. Mécia de Sena, note, *Trinta anos*, 1:331.

35. Jorge de Sena, "Camões—Verbete para uma enciclopédia," *Trinta anos*, 1:295–96.

36. Jorge de Sena, "Camões: The Lyrical Poet," *Camões: Some Poems*, trans. Jonathan Griffin, with essays by Jorge de Sena and Helder Macedo (London: Menard Press, 1976), 13; reprinted as "Camões: O Poeta Lírico," in *Trinta anos*, 1:287–94.

37. *Camoniana Californiana: Commemorating the Quadricentennial of the Death of Luís de Camões*, ed. Maria de Lourdes Belchior and Enrique Martínez-López (Santa Barbara: Jorge de Sena Center for Portuguese Studies, University of California, Santa Barbara, ICALP, and Bandanna Books, 1985).

38. *Camoniana Californiana*, 10.

39. *Empire in Transition: The Portuguese World in the Time of Camões*, ed. Alfred Hower and Richard A. Preto-Rodas (Gainesville: University of Florida Press, 1985). Chapters focused on Camões are those by A. H. de Oliveira Marques ("A View of Portugal in the Time of Camões"), Peter Fothergill-Payne ("A Prince of Our Disorder: 'Good Kingship' in Camões, Couto, and Manuel de Melo"), José Sebastião da Silva Dias ("Camões perante o Portugal do seu tempo"), Graça Silva Dias ("Cultura e sociedade na infância e adolescência de Camões"), Harold V. Livermore ("On the Title of *The Lusiads*"), Jack E. Tomlins ("Gil Vicente's Vision of India and Ots Ironic Echo in Camões's 'Velho do Restelo'"), René Concepción ("The Theme of Amphitryon in Luís de Camões and Hernán Pérez de Oliva"), William Melczer ("The Place of Camões in the European Cultural Conscience"), Norwood Andrews, Jr. ("Camões and Some of His Readers in American Imprints of Lord Strangford's Translation in the Nineteenth Century"), and Alberto de Lacerda ("*Os Lusíadas* e *Os Maias*: Um binómio português?").

40. The proceedings of the conference appeared in the journal *Portuguese Literary and Cultural Studies* 9 (2003), published by the Center for Portuguese Studies and Culture at the University of Massachusetts Dartmouth. The contributors include Helen Vendler (Harvard University), Miguel Tamen (University of Lisbon), Rita Marnoto (University of Coimbra), Helder Macedo (King's College, University of London), Fernando Gil (New University in Lisbon), Hélio J. S. Alves (University of Évora), Josiah Blackmore (University of Toronto), Eduardo Lourenço, Anna Klobucka (University of Massachusetts Dartmouth), George Monteiro (Brown University), João R. Figueiredo (University of Lisbon), Lawrence Lipking (Northwestern University), Balachandra Rajan (University of Western Ontario), and Michael Murrin (University of Chicago).

41. Jorge de Sena, "Em Creta, com o Minotauro," in *Peregrinatio ad loca infecta* (Lisboa: Portugália, 1969), 112.

42. Sena, *Some Poems*, 13–14.

43. Mécia de Sena assures me that she has no memory of Sena's having any such contract with G. K. Hall.

Chapter 6: Portugal in "Figura"

1. Thomas Wentworth Higginson, "Portugal's Glory and Decay," *North American Review* 173 (October 1856): 476.

2. Teixeira de Pascoaes, *A Águia* (March 19, 1911): 14–16.

3. Jorge de Sena, *Diários* (Porto: Caixotim, 2004), 170.

4. Fernando Pessoa, *Páginas de estética e de teoria e crítica literárias*, ed. Georg Rudolf Lind and Jacinto do Prado Coelho (Lisboa: Ática, 1966), 355.

5. Pessoa's letter is included in *Epistolario Portugués de Unamuno*, ed. Angel Marcos de Dios (Paris: Fundação Calouste Gulbenkian/Centro Cultural Português, 1978), 303; and in Fernando Pessoa, *Correspondência, 1905–1922*, ed. Manuela Parreira da Silva (Lisboa: Assírio & Alvim, 1999), 158–59.

6. Antonio Sáez Delgado, *Órficos y ultraístas: Portugal y España en el diálogo de las primeras vanguardias literarias (1915–1925)* (Mérida: Editora Regional de Extremadura, 1999), 90.

7. Miguel de Unanumo, *Obras completas*, vol. 6, *Poesia* (New York: Las Américas, 1966), 821.

8. Thomaz Ribeiro, "To Portugal," trans. Aubrey F. G. Bell, *Portugal: A Monthly Review* 1 (February 1915): 4.

9. Miguel de Unamuno, "La literatura portuguesa contemporanea," in *Por tierras de Portugal y de España*, 2nd ed. (Buenos Aires: Espasa-Calpe Argentina, 1944), 16.

10. Unamuno, "La pesca de Espinho," in *Por tierras de Portugal*, 56–57.

11. The variants in Unamuno, *Obras Completas*, 6:362–63, are matters, mostly, of punctuation, capitalization, and diacritical marking.

12. José Rodrigues Miguéis, "Há sempre um bei em Tunes," in *É proibido apontar: Reflexões de um burguês*, 2nd ed. (Lisboa: Estampa, 1984), 1:142.

13. Fernando Pessoa, *Ultimatum e páginas de sociologia política*, ed. Maria Isabel Rocheta and Maria Paula Morão, intro. Joel Serrão (Lisboa: Ática, 1980), 193–94. That Pessoa is responding directly to Unamuno's ideas in the interview conducted by Ferro is affirmed by Delgado, *Órficos y ultraístas*, 90–91.

14. *Cartas de Fernando Pessoa a João Gaspar Simões*, ed. João Gaspar Simões (Lisboa: Europe-América, 1957), 117.

15. Fernando Pessoa, *Mensagem* (Lisboa: Parceria António Maria Pereira, 1934; 10th ed., Lisboa: Ática, 1972), 21. http://arquivopessoa.net/textos/1264, accessed February 10, 2020.

16. José Luís García Martín mentions in passing the possibility of a link between Pessoa's and Unamuno's poems; see "Fernando Pessoa y Miguel de Unamuno: Las razones de un desencuentro," in *Actas IV Congresso Internacional de Estudos Pessoanos*, Secção Brasileira (Porto: Fundação Eng. António de Almeida, 1990), 1:436–37.

17. Fernando Pessoa, "Movimento sensacionista," *Exílio* 1 (April 1916): 46.

18. Fernando Pessoa, *Textos de crítica e de intervenção* (Lisboa: Ática, 1980), 72.

19. Teixeira de Pascoaes, *Cartas de Pascoaes e Unamuno*, ed. José Bento (Lisboa: Assírio & Alvim, 1986).

Chapter 7: The Correspondence

1. Translation mine. Mécia de Sena and Jorge de Sena, *Isto tudo que nos rodeia (cartas de amor)* (Lisboa: Imprensa Nacional–Casa da Moeda, 1982).

2. Luciana Stegagno Picchio, "Esercizi su di una vita: I 'Flashes' di Mécia de Sena," *Quaderni portoghesi* 13/14 (Autumn 1983): 313–22.

3. Jorge de Sena and Guilherme de Castilho, *Correspondência* (Lisboa: Imprensa Nacional–Casa da Moeda, 1981).

4. Jorge de Sena and Jose Régio, *Correspondência*, ed. Mécia de Sena (Lisboa: Imprensa Nacional–Casa da Moeda, 1986); Jorge de Sena and Vergílio Ferreira, *Correspondência*, ed. Mécia de Sena (Imprensa Nacional–Casa da Moeda: Lisboa, 1987).

5. Eduardo Lourenço and Jorge de Sena, *Correspondência*, ed. Mécia de Sena (Lisboa: Imprensa Nacional–Casa da Moeda, 1991).

Chapter 8: The Sitwell Papers

1. Robert Francis, "Dame Edith," *The Satirical Rogue on Poetry* (Amherst, MA: University of Massachusetts Press, 1968), 52.

2. Manuel Bandeira, "Aviso aos Navegantes" (January 19, 1958), in *Andorinha, Andorinha*, 2nd ed., ed. Carlos Drummond de Andrade (Rio de Janeiro: José Olympio, 1986), 12–13. See also his "Edith Sitwell," a piece dated

October 6, 1957, reprinted in *Prosa*, ed. Antonio Carlos Villaça (São Paulo: Agir, 1983), 137–38.

3. Manuel Bandeira, "Elegia de Londres," *Poesia completa e prosa*, 2nd ed. (Rio de Janeiro: Aguilar, 1967), 379–80.

4. Letter, Mécia de Sena to George Monteiro, February 6, 1992.

5. Edith Sitwell, *Selected Letters, 1919–1964*, ed. John Lehmann and Derek Parker (New York: Vanguard, 1970), 215.

6. Sitwell, *Selected Letters*, 215.

7. Elizabeth Salter, *The Last Years of a Rebel: A Memoir of Edith Sitwell* (Boston: Houghton Mifflin, 1967), 16.

8. The three-page typescript of Lacerda's translation of Sena's review of *Gardeners and Astronomers*, published in *Comércio do Porto* on April 27, 1954, is at the Harry Ransom Humanities Center, University of Texas at Austin.

9. Manuel Bandeira, "Vi a Rainha" (October 9, 1957), in Jorge de Sena, *Inglaterra Revisitada* (Lisboa: Edições 70, 1986), 73–74.

10. Jorge de Sena, "Londres e dois grandes poetas," *Diário popular* (October 24, 1957): 1, 2. See also Sena's "Da poesia maior e menor (a propósito de Manuel Bandeira)," in *O poeta, um fingidor* (Lisboa: Ática, 1961), 131–50; collected in *Estudos de cultura e literatura brasileira* (Lisboa: Edições 70, 1988), 111–20.

11. "Meditação em King's Road" first appeared in *Fidelidade* (1958) and was reprinted in *Poesia—II* (Lisboa: Moraes, 1978), 46. Sena's description of the two poets occurs in his note on the poem in *Poesia—II*, 228.

12. *Poesia—II*, 228–29.

13. Sena's translations of Sitwell's poems are collected in *Poesia do século XX (de Thomas Hardy a C. V. Cattaneo)*, ed. Jorge de Sena (Porto: Inova, 1978), 276–80. Sena's biographical note on Sitwell appears on pages 533–34.

14. Sena, *Inglaterra revisitada*, 22–23.

15. See Jorge de Sena, "Edith Sitwell," *O Primeiro de Janeiro* (November 7, 1951); "Jardineiros e Astrónomos," *Comércio do Porto* (April 27, 1954); "Edith Sitwell," *Diário de notícias* (June 23, 1955); and "Os poemas completos de Edith Sitwell," *Diário popular* (November 7, 1957).

16. Jorge de Sena, *História Ilustrada das Grandes Literaturas, vol. 6, Literatura Inglesa* (Lisboa: Estúdios Cor, 1959–60), 504–5. To Rogério Fernandes's translation of A. C. Ward's *Illustrated History of English Literature*, Sena contributed a preface, explanatory notes throughout, and nine chapters on modern English literature (1900–1960).

17. *A literatura inglesa* was not reprinted until 1989, when Cotovia brought it out in Lisbon.

18. Jorge de Sena, "Edith Sitwell e T. S. Eliot," *O tempo e o modo* 23 (January 1965): 5.

19. Sitwell, *Selected Letters*, 216.

20. Sena's translations of Campbell poems—"Luís de Camões" (originally published in *Diário de Lisboa* on June 9, 1952, and in *O comércio do Porto* on February 10, 1953, and again on May 21, 1957); "Criação do poeta" (*O comércio do Porto*, February 10, 1953); and "Dobrando o cabo" (*O comércio do Porto*, May 21, 1957)—are collected in his anthology *Poesia do século XX*, 402–4. Sena's biographical note on Campbell appears on page 551.

21. "Jorge de Sena responde a três perguntas de Luciana Stegagno Picchio sobre Fernando Pessoa," in *Fernando Pessoa & Cª*, 407. Sena wrote about Campbell on several occasions: "Roy Campbell," *O comércio do Porto* (February 10, 1953): 6; "Sobre Roy Campbell," *O comércio do Porto* (May 21, 1957): 6; *Literatura inglesa* (1959–60), 6:501–2; and *A literatura inglesa* (1963), 370–71.

22. Sena, *Fernando Pessoa & Cª*, 407–8.

23. Interestingly enough, José Blanc de Portugal seems to imply that he is indirectly quoting Edith Sitwell, in French no less, when he writes: "Indiscretamente, citarei a opinião da tão britânica autora de *Façade*, que achava o inglês de Pessoa *plus beau que nature* . . ." "Provocação do tradutor," in *O louco rabequista* (Lisboa: Presença, 1988), 8. The statement is undocumented.

24. Sena's presentation copy is part of the Dame Edith Sitwell Collection at the Harry Ransom Humanities Research Center, the University of Texas at Austin. The inscription is quoted with the Library's consent and the permission of Mécia de Sena.

25. Edith Sitwell's papers are at the Harry Ransom Humanities Research Center, the University of Texas at Austin. Jorge de Sena's letters to Edith Sitwell appear not to be among them

26. Sitwell's return address on the back of the mailing envelope reads: "from Edith Sitwell. D.Litt. D.Litt. & D.Litt / Renishaw Hall / Renishaw / near Sheffield."

27. Fernando Pessoa, *Páginas de doutrina estética* (Lisboa: Inquérito, 1946–47). The second edition of this collection, in 1964, was unauthorized. Sena's own augmented second edition has not been published.

28. According to José Blanco, at the time of Jorge de Sena's reference to a French translation of "Tabacaria" there were already two of them—Armand

Guibert's, in his "Fernando Pessoa ou l'homme quadruple," *Exils* (Paris, 1952), and Adolfo Casais Monteiro and Pierre Hourcade's, in *Fernando Pessoa: bureau de tabac* (Lisboa: Inquérito, 1952). See Blanco, *Fernando Pessoa: esboço de uma bibliografia* (Lisboa: Imprensa Nacional–Casa da Moeda/Centro de Estudos Pessoanos, 1983), 465, 467.

29. Jorge de Sena, "Sacheverell Sitwell," *O comércio do Porto* (March 10, 1953), and "Edith Sitwell," *O Primeiro de Janeiro* (November 7, 1951).

30. Actually, Roy Campbell was translating poems by Fernando Pessoa to be included in a critical study commissioned by the British publisher Bowes and Bowes, as well as preparing an anthology of Portuguese poetry "from the Troubadours to the present day, to be published simultaneously by the Portuguese government, who commissioned the work, and by the Harvill and Pantheon presses, respectively in London and New York." Roy Campbell, "A South African Poet in Portugal (Broadcast, National English Programme [SABC] [19 April 1954])," in *Collected Works IV: Prose* (Craighall, S. A.: Ad. Donker, 1988), 435. Neither of these works was realized, although Campbell did manage to write three short chapters of a book on Pessoa.

31. Sena gives Lacerda's "long real name" as Carlos Alberto Portugal Correia de Lacerda in the headnote to a selection of his poems in *Líricas portuguesas*, ed. Jorge de Sena (Lisboa: Edições 70, 1983), 2:384.

32. In *Poesia do século XX* Jorge de Sena includes "A próxima guerra," his translation of an Osbert Sitwell poem (320–21), along with a brief biographical note (541). For some other references to Osbert Sitwell, see Sena, *A literatura inglesa* (1963), especially page 387, and *Literatura inglesa* (1959–60), 5:504–7.

33. Jorge de Sena first published "Fernando Pessoa e a Literatura Inglesa" in *O Comércio do Porto* (August 11, 1953), 6. It was later reprinted in *Estrada Larga—1* (Porto, 1968). In a footnote the organizer of the literary supplement wrote, incorporating Sena's translation into Portuguese of Sitwell's words of praise for Pessoa:

> Edith Sitwell, a quem os seus compatriotas ingleses consideram não só grande poeta, como também não menor autoridade em questões de técnica e linguística poéticas, em carta ao nosso colaborador Jorge de Sena, escreveu a propósito do presente assunto:
>
> . . . Os "Sonetos" são impecáveis de forma. Quem os traduziu? Ou foram, de facto, escritos em inglês? Suponho que o não foram,

mas são tão impecáveis como sonetos, que dificilmente cremos que sejam traduções. São lúcidos e luzentes—esculpidos numa pedra transparente que capta a luz . . .

When the essay was collected in *Fernando Pessoa & Cª* (1:91–96), the illustrative Pessoa sonnets, Sena's and Adolfo Casais Monteiro's headnote, and this editorial annotation were omitted.

34. *The Shadow of Cain* in Humphrey Searle's musical setting was performed by the London Symphony Orchestra at the Palace Theatre, London, on November 16, 1952, with Edith Sitwell and Dylan Thomas as readers. It is an odd fact that when Thomas first read *The Shadow of Cain* he called it, in a letter to his wife Caitlin, "Edith's vast, bad poem." *Dylan Thomas: The Collected Letters*, ed. Paul Ferris (New York: Macmillan, 1985), 669n1.

35. In *Poesia do século XX* Sena includes translations of four poems by Dylan Thomas: "The Force That through the Green Fuse Drives the Flower," "Light Breaks Where No Sun Shines," "A Refusal to Mourn the Death, by Fire, of a Child in London," and "Do Not Go Gentle into That Good Night" (450–54). His biographical note appears on pages 555–56. Sena also writes about Thomas in *Literatura inglesa* (1959–60), 6: 518–20, and *A literatura inglesa* (1963), 421–23.

36. Sitwell had been writing to Sena at Rua José Falcão, 55, 1ᵉ, Lisboa.

37. Jorge de Sena, "Jardineiros e Astrónomos," *O comércio do Porto* (April 27, 1954): 5.

38. Edith Sitwell, "Elegy for Dylan Thomas," *Poetry* 87 (November 1955): 63–67.

39. Jorge de Sena, "Edith Sitwell," *Diário de notícias* (June 23, 1955): 7, 6. Of this review, Roy Campbell wrote to Sitwell from Sintra: "There was a magnificent photo of you in the *Diário de notícias* with a long article by Sena. I put it away when I was too ill to post it and now I've mislaid it but will send it when I find it." Ms. letter, no date, Harry Ransom Humanities Research Center, University of Texas at Austin. Quoted with the library's consent.

40. The draft breaks off here, with Sena's own indication: "(etc, etc . . .)."

41. Besides publishing the piece on Sacheverell Sitwell in *O comércio do Porto*, Sena included "O poeta e o espelho," his translation of a Sacheverell Sitwell poem, in *Poesia do século XX* (351–53), along with a biographical note (545). Brief comments on the youngest of the Sitwells appear in Sena's *A literatura inglesa* (1963), especially pages 386 and 387, as well as in his *Literatura inglesa* (1959–60), 5:504–7.

42. Robert Graves's 1954–55 Clark Lectures, sponsored by Trinity College, Cambridge, were published with additional essays on poetry and sixteen new poems as *The Crowning Privilege* (London: Cassell, 1955). Graves's attack on the "moderns"—Yeats, Eliot, Pound, Auden, and Thomas—comes in "Lecture VI: These Be Your Gods, Israel" (112–35). Graves wrote to fellow poet and critic James Reeves on November 8, 1955: "*Crowning Privilege* has made a lot of people cross." *Between Moon and Moon: Selected Letters of Robert Graves 1946–1972*, ed. Paul O'Prey (London: Hutchinson, 1984), 154.

43. The references are to Father Martin D'Arcy, S.J., "whose book *The Nature of Belief*," it is said, "bridged the gap for her [Sitwell] between belief and commitment" (Edith Sitwell, *Fire of the Mind: An Anthology*, ed. Elizabeth Salter and Allanah Harper [London: Michael Joseph, 1976], 276), and Father Philip Caraman, S.J., who, as her confessor, received Sitwell into the Roman Catholic Church on August 4, 1955.

44. Sena, "Os poemas completos de Edith Sitwell."

45. In June 1954, Edith Sitwell was "awarded a DBE (Dame Commander of the British Empire) in Queen Elizabeth II's Birthday Honours list." Geoffrey Elbron, *Edith Sitwell: A Biography* (Garden City, NY: Doubleday, 1981), 215. Her mailing address (as it appears on the back of one of the mailing envelopes that have survived) now read: "from Dame Edith Sitwell D.B.E. / D.Litt. D.Litt. D.Litt. / Castello di Montegufoni / Montagnana / Val di Pesa / prov: Firenze."

46. The London *Times* reported the matter: "To support the protest of 300 Spanish intellectuals against censorship in Spain, members who attended a London meeting of the English Centre of International PEN have signed a manifesto to the Spanish Government. Signatories include Mr. E. M. Forster, Mr. Victor Gallancz, Dame Edith Sitwell, Miss Storm Jameson, and Mr. Graham Greene. They say that the censorship 'is freezing the development' of creative work in Spain and has had a deplorable effect on the education and knowledge of the Spanish reader and student." December 23, 1960, 8.

47. "Mr. Greene" is Graham Greene, two of whose books—*The End of the Affair* (1951) and *Stamboul Train* (1933)—were translated, with prefaces, by Jorge de Sena (respectively as *O fim da aventura* and *Oriente-Expresso*). The "late Mr. Bevan," who died on July 6, 1960, is Aneurin Bevan, a leader of the British Labour Party.

48. Sena's plan for an anthology of Edith Sitwell's poetry in Portuguese translation was not realized.

Chapter 9: On American Writing

1. Jorge de Sena, *80 poemas de Emily Dickinson* (Lisboa: Edições 70, 1979), 34–35, my translation.

2. Sena, *Poesia—III* (Lisboa: Moraes, 1978), 16. The original reads: "O homem corre em *perseguição* de si mesmo e do seu outro até *à coroa da terra*, aonde humildemente encontrará a *pedra filosofal* que lhe permite reconhecer *as evidências*." Sena's emphasis.

3. Fernando J. B. Martinho, "Uma leitura dos sonetos de Jorge de Sena," in *Estudos sobre Jorge de Sena*, ed. Eugénio Lisboa (Lisboa: Imprensa Nacional–Casa da Moeda, 1984), 170–87.

4. Daniel G. Hoffman, *An Armada of Thirty Whales* (New Haven, CT: Yale University Press, 1954), 4–5.

5. Jorge de Sena, *The Evidences*, a bilingual edition, trans. Phyllis Sterling Smith (Santa Barbara: Center for Portuguese Studies, University of California, Santa Barbara, 1994), 36–37.

6. Jorge de Sena, *Do teatro em Portugal* (Lisboa: Edições 70, 1988), 69.

7. Reprinted in Sena, *Do teatro em Portugal*, 43–51.

8. Eugene O'Neill, *Jornada para a noite*, trans. Jorge de Sena, intro. Mécia de Sena (Lisboa: Cotovia/Teatro Nacional D. Maria II, 1992).

9. Reprinted in Sena, *Do teatro em Portugal*, 383–86.

10. Reprinted in Sena, *Do teatro em Portugal*, 191–92.

Chapter 10: Views on Sena's Work

1. Jorge Fazenda Lourenço, *A poesia de Jorge de Sena: testemunho, metamorfose, peregrinação* (Paris: Centre Culturel Calouste Gulbenkian, 1998); Francisco Cota Fagundes, *In the Beginning There Was Jorge de Sena's Genesis: The Birth of a Writer* (Santa Barbara, CA: Jorge de Sena Center for Portuguese Studies, 1991).

Chapter 11: The First International Symposium of Fernando Pessoa

1. Reginald Gibbons, ed., *The Poet's Work: 29 Masters of 20th Century Poetry on the Origins and Practice of Their Art* (Boston: Houghton Mifflin, 1979).

2. Born in Portugal, Manuel Luciano da Silva (1926–2012) practiced med-
    icine in Bristol, Rhode Island. He was also an amateur historian, sup-
    porting famously the notion that the Corte-Reais had survived their final
    voyages to the edge of the New World, the evidence for thinking so being
    the "discovery" of markings on a much-scarred and mysteriously marked
    rock in the Dighton River in Taunton, Massachusetts. The good doctor
    also defended the theory that Christopher Columbus was Portuguese by
    birth.